Praise for Ruth Reichl's *Garlic and Sapphires*

"[A] vivacious, fascinating memoir. . . . Reichl's ability to experience meals in such a dramatic way brings an infectious passion to her memoir . . . reading this work ensures that the next time readers sit down in a restaurant, they'll notice things they've never noticed before."
—*Publishers Weekly* (starred review)

"Sure, she can write; sure, sure she knows about food. But what finally distinguishes her response is the passion she brings to the table . . . beguiling."
—*Newsweek*

"As much as I've enjoyed her work over the past twelve years, it's her new book, *Garlic and Sapphires: The Secret Life of a Critic in Disguise,* that I've really been waiting for. Here, at last, is the behind-the-scenes story of Reichl's years at the *Times.* . . . We get all the mouth-watering food writing that Reichl is famous for, as well as well as a fascinating peek at what it's like to be the most powerful restaurant critic in the country, but we also get Reichl's take on the theater and politics of eating out."
—*Newsday*

"For foodies with a penchant for the inside scoop, Reichl's behind-the-scenes stories of the Gray Lady deliver the goods. . . . Spicy and sweet by turns, with crackle and bite throughout."
—*Kirkus Reviews*

"Reichl is so gifted that she can make any topic interesting . . . the reader remains hungry for more of Reichl." —*USA Today*

"Costume mixed with cuisine—a delicious read any way you slice it."
—*Gotham*

"Ruth Reichl is simultaneously a world-class foodie and an unfailingly approachable writer." —*The Cleveland Plain Dealer*

"Wise and thoroughly satisfying; highly recommended."
—*Libr*

D0189625

PENGUIN BOOKS

GARLIC AND SAPPHIRES

★

RUTH REICHL is the bestselling author of the memoirs *Tender at the Bone*, *Comfort Me with Apples, Garlic and Sapphires, For You, Mom, Finally* and *Save Me the Plums*; the novel *Delicious!*; and the cookbook *My Kitchen Year*. She was editor in chief of *Gourmet* magazine for ten years. Previously she was the restaurant critic for *The New York Times* and served as the food editor and restaurant critic for the *Los Angeles Times*. She has been honored with six James Beard Awards for her journalism, magazine feature writing, and criticism. She lives in upstate New York with her husband and two cats.

Garlic and Sapphires

**THE
SECRET LIFE
OF A
CRITIC IN
DISGUISE**

Ruth Reichl

PENGUIN BOOKS

PENGUIN BOOKS

Published by the Penguin Group

Penguin Group (USA) Inc., 375 Hudson Street, New York, New York 10014, U.S.A.

Penguin Group (Canada), 90 Eglinton Avenue East, Suite 700, Toronto, Ontario,
Canada M4P 2Y3 (a division of Pearson Penguin Canada Inc.)

Penguin Books Ltd, 80 Strand, London WC2R 0RL, England

Penguin Ireland, 25 St Stephen's Green, Dublin 2, Ireland
(a division of Penguin Books Ltd)

Penguin Group (Australia), 250 Camberwell Road, Camberwell, Victoria 3124,
Australia (a division of Pearson Australia Group Pty Ltd)

Penguin Books India Pvt Ltd, 11 Community Centre, Panchsheel Park,
New Delhi – 110 017, India

Penguin Group (NZ), 67 Apollo Drive, Rosedale, North Shore 0632, New Zealand
(a division of Pearson New Zealand Ltd)

Penguin Books (South Africa) (Pty) Ltd, 24 Sturdee Avenue,
Rosebank, Johannesburg 2196, South Africa

Penguin Books Ltd, Registered Offices: 80 Strand, London WC2R 0RL, England

First published in the United States of America by The Penguin Press,
a member of Penguin Group (USA) Inc. 2005
Published in Penguin Books 2006

27 29 30 28 26

The following columns originally appeared in *The New York Times* and they are reprinted here with permissions: Le Cirque review, October 29, 1993; Honmura An, September 10, 1993; Lespinasse, March 11,
1994; Daniel, November 11, 1994; Kurumazushi, October 6, 1995; Tavern on the Green, December 8,
1995; Windows on the World, November 8, 1996; Box Tree, March 11, 1998; Sparks, March 25, 1998;
Union Pacific, August 5, 1998; "Why I Disapprove of What I Do" (*The New York Times Magazine*), March 10,
1996. The New York Times owns the copyright in the columns. Inquiries concerning permission to reprint
any column or portion of it should be directed to The New York Times Company, Rights and Permissions,
Ninth Floor, 229 West 43rd Street, New York, New York 10036.

THE LIBRARY OF CONGRESS HAS CATALOGED THE HARDCOVER EDITION AS FOLLOWS:
Reichl, Ruth.
Garlic and sapphires / Ruth Reichl.
p. cm.
Includes index.
ISBN 1-59420-031-9 (hc.)
ISBN 978-0-14-303661-6 (pbk.)
1. Cookery. 2. Reichl, Ruth—Biography. I. Title
TX649.R45A3 2005
641.5'092—dc22
[B] 2004051362

Printed in the United States of America
Designed by Stephanie Huntwork

For my family, all of you,
with many thanks and much love.

CONTENTS

Garlic and Sapphires

The Daily Special

Y ou gonna eat that?"

The woman is eyeing the tray the flight attendant has just set before me. I can't tell if she wants reassurance that I find it as repellent as she does or if she is simply hungry and hopeful that I will hand my food over. I loosen my seatbelt, swivel in the narrow seat, and see that her face holds a challenge. Is she *daring* me to eat the food?

It steams unappetizingly up at me: a squishy brown square of meat surrounded by a sticky stockade of potatoes that might have been mashed last year. The wrinkled gray peas look as if they were born in a laboratory test tube. The roll glows with such an unearthly lunar yellow that I can feel its chill before my fingers even touch the surface. The lettuce in the salad has gone brown at the edges, and the tomatoes are too tired to even pretend that nature intended them to be red. The dressing in its little cup stares up at me, bright orange. I stare back.

"Nah," says the woman, "you won't eat that. Not our little Ruthie!"

Triumphantly she snatches the neon roll from my plate. "I'd like your butter too, please," she says, reaching for it.

I stop her hand in midair. "Do I know you?" I ask. She grins enigmatically, and I realize that she has a slight gap between her teeth. Her hair is blond and she is blowsily attractive; for a moment I wonder if she's Lauren Hutton. But what would Lauren Hutton be doing here, wedged into steerage, stealing my roll?

"No," she says, retrieving her hand. She snags the butter. "But I know you. I even know why you're on this plane."

"You do?" I say, rather stupidly. She has wolfed down the roll and now has her eye on the dubious meat. "Please," I say, "help yourself." She grabs the plate.

"I didn't think that *you* would be eating this stuff," she says. "Truth be told, I'd be disappointed if you did."

"But who do you think I am?" I ask.

"Oh, sweetie," she says, the *s* hissing snakelike from the gap in her teeth, "I don't think. I know. In fact, if you would be kind enough to tell me where you're going to eat when we land in New York, you'd be doing me a big favor."

"What on earth are you talking about?" I am truly baffled now. She has gobbled up the protein, avoided the peas, and her pale blue eyes are staring longingly at the sad salad. "Be my guest," I say, holding out the plate.

"Your picture is all over New York," she says, her mouth full of lettuce. "You're the restaurant critic of the *Los Angeles Times,* but you're about to become the most important restaurant critic in the world. You start at the *New York Times* on"—she pauses for a moment, calculating—"Friday, September third!" She forks up the last of the salad and adds, "Every restaurant in town has your picture pinned to the bulletin board, next to the specials of the day."

"You can't be serious," I say.

She nods her blond head vigorously, and the lank hair whips across her face. As she shoves it out of her eyes I notice that she is wearing a sparkly little bracelet that spells out "Jackie" in rhinestones, that her nails are covered with chipped purple polish, and that her muscled arms look as if they have carried a lifetime of heavy trays. "I am. The place I work isn't the world's best restaurant, but the boss has a standing offer of five hundred bucks to anyone who spots you. Forget anonymity. A good review from the *New York Times* is worth thousands." She considers for a few seconds. "Could be millions."

"But it's only June! It's three months till I even start the job." I am truly stunned.

"I know," she says, wagging one of those purple fingers in my face, "but if your first review's in September you've got to be eating somewhere now, don't you?" There's a certain triumph in her voice as she adds, "You see, there's not much we don't know about you."

"What do you know?" This comes out a little more nervously than I'd like.

"Oh," she says breezily, "ask me anything. You'll see."

"Am I married?"

"Please," she scoffs, "ask me something harder than that. Your husband's name is Michael Singer, he's a producer at CBS, and he does mostly investigative work. I know he won a Peabody Award last year for something he did on the Mafia and the recording industry."

"How could you know that?" I ask.

"I told you," she says, "we've been studying you. We all have. Didn't I say we were on the lookout for you? No critic eats alone, so that means watching for him too. Not to mention your kid. He's about four—"

"Four and a half," I say, the response so automatic that it is out before I realize that I ought to be feeding her misinformation, not filling her in.

"At least I know you're alone on this trip," she says a little too smugly. "That's useful."

"They could be joining me later," I point out.

"They could . . ." she says, considering. Then she cocks her head to one side and says, "Nah, I'd guess not. Guys don't have any patience, and in my experience it's always the woman who has to travel with the children. If Michael were coming, you'd have the kid."

"What are you," I ask, "Mickey Spillane?"

"In this business," she confides, "it pays to keep your eyes open. You'd be surprised how much you can figure out about people after they've been sitting at your table for a couple of hours. It makes the job more fun. This is how I figure it: You're on your way to New York to do a little restaurant research. And maybe look for an apartment?" Her eyes meet mine as she says this, and they light up.

"Gotcha!" she says. "You are!"

I'm also looking for a nursery school for Nick, but I manage not to blurt this out. When I don't reply, my new friend examines my tray to see if it contains anything else she might desire. She seems to be waging an inner skirmish over the ice cream bar that now sits there, forlorn and alone. But she abandons the struggle to say smugly, "Well, don't think one of those big hats is going to protect you." She studies my face, as if memorizing it, her eyes slowly moving from the long, tangled brown curls, past my thick bushy eyebrows and slightly tilted brown eyes to take in my pale skin and large mouth. At last she produces a bumptious New York smile and adds, "You're going to find that being our critic is very different from being the restaurant critic of the *L.A. Times*. We're not so easy to fool."

"I can see that," I say sincerely. In the fifteen years I've been a restaurant critic in San Francisco and Los Angeles, nobody has ever bothered to study me before. This woman knows a scary lot about me: I wouldn't be surprised if she knows that the *New York Times* is going to pay me $82,000 a year (a cut from what I've been making in Los Angeles), or even that CBS has been very good about letting Michael move to the New York bureau. Knowing that my personal life is now public makes me so nervous that I try to change the subject. "Please," I say, holding out my ice cream, "take this. I need to save my appetite for dinner."

She accepts. "No wonder you're so thin," she says. Peeling off the paper wrapper, she looks at the ice cream before taking a bite. Mouth full, she adds, "This isn't bad. But I'd much rather have the name of the restaurant you're going to tonight. It's worth a lot of money, and I could certainly use it."

"Not a chance," I reply, and turn to stare at the clouds floating outside the window like great billows of Marshmallow Fluff.

"You've finished everything!" says the flight attendant when she picks up the trays. She seems genuinely surprised.

I smile up at her. "This was an educational lunch."

"Oh," she says, looking slightly bewildered, "I'm glad." Piling the trays onto her cart, she adds, "People don't usually say that." Then she pushes off quickly, as if she's afraid that I will attempt to engage in further discussion of the food.

But food is the farthest thing from my mind: I am considering my next plan of action. One of the primary requisites of a good restaurant critic is the ability to be anonymous. Clearly I am going to have to do something. But what?

Flying east, it takes four and a half hours to go from LAX to JFK. It is just long enough. By the time we land I have figured the whole thing out.

Backstory

"T his is Warren Hoge," announced a self-satisfied voice when I picked up the phone, "assistant managing editor of the *New York Times.*" He proclaimed it proudly, as if faint trumpets were sounding off in the background.

"Yes?" I said, hoping my tone conveyed more interest than I was actually feeling. It was two months before that fateful trip to New York, and I was staring across the sad, low landscape of downtown Los Angeles, wondering how to make Easter more exciting. Holidays are a restaurant critic's nightmare, and this one, with its perennially boring brunches featuring ham or lamb, is particularly gruesome. The copy I had just produced was deadly.

"I suppose you've heard that our restaurant critic, Bryan Miller, has decided to leave the job?" the voice continued. This bland assurance that the eyes of the entire world were focused on Times Square was so irritating that I lied. "No," I said, "I hadn't heard that."

The voice ignored this. "I was thinking," it continued smoothly, "that it can't be much fun for you, being a restaurant critic in the middle of a recession . . ." I dropped Easter; he had captured my attention.

The eighties hit Los Angeles like the month of March: they came roaring in, then tiptoed sheepishly out as the money stopped and the good times ended. It all happened so fast: First the aerospace industry shut its doors and the city slumped into depression. Then the cops beat Rodney King on the nightly news, exposing the racism that had been hiding behind the prosperity. The anger simmering just below the surface erupted into a furious boil. Riots were followed by floods and then fires, which spilled out across the city in an almost biblical manner. When the tide of disasters finally receded, the city it left behind was thin, brittle, dangerous, and poor.

The very rich retreated into their golden communities—into Bel Air, the Palisades, and Beverly Hills—locking the gates behind them. The valleys on the far side of the mountains swelled with fleeing people. Those of us left in Los Angeles huddled in our houses, haunted by memories of snipers shooting from freeway overpasses, looters setting fires that came creeping inexorably into our neighborhoods, contorted faces throwing rocks. Staying home seemed the safest option, and the great Los Angeles restaurant boom came screeching to a halt.

"New York is the center of the American restaurant world." The man's sinuous voice wormed its way into my ear and I imagined him holding out an enormous, bright red apple.

I was not about to bite. "I have a job, thank you," I said crisply. "I love working at the *Los Angeles Times*. I'm not looking to move."

But he wouldn't take no for an answer," I told my husband when I got home. "When I told him I was going to be in New York in a couple of weeks for the James Beard Awards, he made me agree to meet him for coffee."

"I'd love to leave L.A.," Michael said wistfully.

"Don't even think about it," I warned him. "It's not an interview. It's just coffee. I'll only be there fifteen minutes. I can't resist the chance to see the *Times* offices, but I have no interest in working there."

"Of course not," said Michael. "Why on earth would you want to work at the best paper in the world?"

For the next two weeks Michael issued nightly bulletins about the *New York Times* and its search for a new critic. He refused to tell me where he was getting his information, but he seemed to know everything. The paper, he said, had offered the job to Molly O'Neill, who did not want it. "Apparently," Michael said, "she has a weight problem." Bryan Miller was pushing one of his friends as a replacement, and the editors were being inundated by calls from critics all over the country. Michael, nevertheless, was convinced that the job was mine.

"They haven't even offered it to me," I kept telling him.

"They will," he said loyally. "You're the best critic in the country." It's comforting when the people you love believe in you, but his confidence also unnerved me. When I was honest with myself, I saw that I was terrified of going to work at the *New York Times*.

"There are lots of good critics out there," I told him.

"Not like you," he said steadfastly. "The job's yours for the taking."

He was still repeating this mantra when I left for the airport. "Be nice when you meet Warren Hoge," he urged.

"Mommy's always nice," said Nicky with the uncritical devotion of a four-year-old.

Michael picked him up and cradled him in his arms. "Wouldn't you like to live in New York?" he asked.

"No," said Nicky.

I gave him a kiss, nuzzling the soft skin of his neck. "I'm just going for coffee," I murmured, breathing in his sweet baby smell.

"Right," said Michael, closing the door.

· · ·

But I landed in New York to find the weather itself conspiring against me. It was one of those magical Manhattan springs; fresh winds were blowing gently across the island so that each time I inhaled, I breathed in the faint salt smell of the ocean. Daffodils and tulips nodded from every corner; lilacs and apple blossoms danced through the parks. On the avenues tables and chairs edged slyly onto sidewalks, promising summer. The sun poured from the sky like honey, and people threw back their heads and drank it in.

At Tiffany's the windows were filled with eggshells, cracked open, spilling diamonds. Customers strolled through fancy food stores collecting wild strawberries imported from France, Japanese beef bred on beer, hand-churned cream from grass-fed cows, and caviar by the pint. The restaurants were packed with handsome people begging for tables, and great crowds jockeyed in the museums, trying to get a better view. Marble buildings once black with soot had been polished to a shine, and the statues all over town were newly gilded. Alone in New York, I wandered the streets and allowed the city to seduce me.

I made my way back to the hotel, thinking that life in New York might not be so bad. Then a sharp female voice jerked me back to reality.

"This is Carol Shaw," said the woman on the phone. "I'm calling to give you your schedule at the *New York Times*."

"Schedule?" I asked. "What schedule? I'm supposed to meet Warren Hoge for coffee at three."

"Oh," she said, her voice softening slightly, "you haven't heard."

"Heard? Heard what?"

"About Warren," she said. And now her voice dropped to a whisper. "He's in the hospital."

"I hope it's not serious?" I said. "I guess we'll have to meet some other time."

"But we were hoping you'd go see him tomorrow!" she cried. "We've planned your whole day!"

"Excuse me?"

"You start by visiting Warren at New York Hospital at nine. Then we have set up appointments for you with—" she started ticking off names. "And finally," she continued, "you'll go to the five o'clock editorial meeting and end the day in private session with the editor, Max Frankel, and the managing editor, Joe Lelyveld."

"I don't have time for all that," I said. "I'm really very busy. I'd only planned to spend fifteen minutes with Warren."

"I understand perfectly," she replied. Her voice was as brittle as ice. Even the secretaries here have attitude, I thought, wondering how I could allow a woman I had never met to guilt-trip me. This Shaw person was somehow able to make her voice convey both empathy and accusation.

"What happened to him?" I asked, relenting a little.

"He was in a restaurant," she said. "He fell down some stairs, broke a rib, and the rib punctured his lung." There was a strangled sound to her voice; was she trying to repress a laugh? In response I found myself biting back an inappropriate giggle.

"Please give him my best wishes," I said, grateful that my voice sounded normal. "Tell him I hope he'll be better soon. And that I look forward to meeting him the next time I come to New York."

"I'll do that," she said.

I immediately dialed Michael. "Can you believe the nerve of these people?" I asked. "They just went ahead and set up a whole day of interviews without even asking me!"

"C'mon, Ruth," he replied, "it's the *New York Times*! You know you won't be able to resist meeting with them at some point. Why not see them now and save yourself another trip?"

"You just want to get out of Los Angeles," I said.

"It's true," he said. "But if you'd spent the last two years covering the riots, the Rodney King trial, the gang wars, and then another Rodney King trial, you'd want to get out too. This job isn't much fun; all the news in L.A. is depressing and it's not going to get better any time soon. There's no political will for change. I look down the road and I see myself reporting on racism, gangs, and poverty, with the occasional earthquake thrown in for variety. I'd like to go somewhere, anywhere, with a different story. But that's only part of it; I really think that this is an important opportunity for you. New York could change your life. I know you're scared, but you can do this. I'll be there for you in every way I can, but don't walk away from this job."

Michael's faith in me was so touching that it forced me to consider the consequences of talking to the editors of the *Times*. I realized that once I had gone for the interview and made a good impression, it would be difficult to refuse the job. By the same token, if I was certain that I had no interest in becoming the restaurant critic of the *New York Times*, all I had to do was make sure they didn't want me. I had to make myself undesirable. Now, I decided, was the perfect time to begin the campaign.

"Fine," said Carol Shaw when I called back. "I'm glad you've changed your mind." She did not sound the least bit surprised. "Do you know how to get to New York Hospital?"

Hey girlie," said the grizzled coot in the second bed. Monitors above his head flashed his pulse and heart rate; bells pinged, lights flashed. "You here to see Warren?" He eyed my legs.

"Yes," I said, smoothing my black suit, wishing my skirt were a little longer. The two other men occupying beds in the room looked on with interest.

"They took him down for X-rays, sort of unexpected. He said for you to wait."

"Here?" I asked.

"That would be fine with me," he said. "But Warren said something about the waiting room. It's down there." He jerked his head to show me.

The waiting room looked like a graveyard for rejected flower arrangements. A couple of potted palms drooped in the corner, and vases filled with dying flowers were everywhere. The scent was funereal. I looked out the window at a sign that read, "New York Hospital is under construction. Please bear with us." I suddenly remembered that this was where I was born.

"You must be Ruth." I looked up. A tall man in a hospital gown was standing by my chair. He was carrying what looked like a plastic suitcase filled with liquid that seemed to be coming from a tube somewhere beneath his gown. I looked away, embarrassed.

"Warren?" I asked. I had not expected him to be so handsome. I indicated the plastic suitcase. "How did that happen?"

"I was coming out of a Russian restaurant in Brighton Beach," he said. "I fell down two flights of stairs."

"Was it one of those places that gives you all the vodka you are foolish enough to drink?" I asked, wasting no time. He winced. I smiled inwardly; I had begun the onslaught of charm.

But I found it hard to continue being rude to this extremely agreeable man. We talked about restaurants. We talked about food. We talked about movies. He was very amusing and the job never came up. After forty-five minutes of delightful conversation, Warren said that he was starting to get tired. I helped him down the hall and into his bed. "You're going to meet all the assistant managing editors today," he said as I turned to go.

"What should I say to them?" I asked.

"Don't worry," he replied. "You'll do fine."

"But I don't want the job," I said.

"Of course you don't," he replied.

I wouldn't fit in here," I assured the first assistant managing editor I was taken to meet. He was a tall, unassumingly elegant man with a courtly manner. He had drooping gray hair and a surprisingly small and dreary office.

"Why is that?" he asked.

"Because," I explained, "I don't review restaurants the way your critics do."

"Oh?" he said. "And how do our critics review restaurants?"

"They hand down judgments from on high," I said. "They seem to think that they are right."

"They're wrong?" he asked.

"There is no right or wrong in matters of taste," I said. "It's just an opinion. And in the case of restaurants, an extremely subjective one, given that no one has the faintest idea if what you taste when you bite into an apple is the same thing that I do."

He looked a little taken aback, and I saw that he had expected me to lobby for the job. "You may be right," he said in a conciliatory tone that clearly indicated I was not. "But of course," he continued, "should you come to the *Times,* you would do things our way."

"No," I said, "I wouldn't. But why would you hire me if you don't want what I do?"

"I think it's time for your next appointment," he replied, ushering me to the door.

Next up was Al Siegal, the much-dreaded arbiter of linguistic style. He turned out to be a thoughtful man of considerable girth. "Mr. Five by Five" played in my head as he said, "You've been very successful at the *Los Angeles Times.* You run your own department. Why would you consider coming to New York at this point?"

I was surprised by my answer. Looking him straight in the eye, I said, "My mother died a year ago. I wouldn't have considered living here while she was alive, but now that she's gone, I guess I can come home."

He looked utterly shocked and a thrill ran through me. "That's done it!" I thought. "They'll never hire me now."

I saw one bigwig after another, surprised that none of them seemed to know what questions they should be asking. But it gave me the opportunity to ask a few of my own. "Who tells your critics what to review?" I queried one man.

His head jerked back as if I had just suggested that the paper was riddled with corruption. "I certainly hope," he said stiffly, "that the *Los Angeles Times* does not attempt to influence its critics."

"Never," I replied. "But I've been told that things are different at the *New York Times*. They say that Bryan Miller doesn't choose his own restaurants and that the editors even decide how many stars a restaurant should receive."

"I can assure you," he said, looking extremely solemn, "that there is no truth in that rumor. Our critics are given the widest possible latitude. It is unthinkable that anyone would ever, ever, interfere with a critic's opinion. That would be"—he cast about, searching for a suitably derogatory word—"unethical." And then, to make his point perfectly clear, "Absolutely unethical. And not at all in the tradition of the *Times*."

As they escorted me from one gray cubicle to the next, I thought how itchy this would be if I actually wanted the job. These men in suits had a pompous gravitas, a kind of sureness we lacked at the *Los Angeles Times*. We were eager to please; they dared you to please them.

The physical differences were also shocking. In Los Angeles we had big airy, open offices. Light poured in through walls of windows, bathing the attractive modern furniture in California sunshine. The great *New York Times*, on the other hand, was a dreary landscape of worn metal desks heaped with stacks of papers, broken chairs abandoned in corners, and windows that had not been washed in years. Around every corner you found some pallid individual engaged in a tug of war with an overstuffed metal filing cabinet, valiantly struggling to get it shut; there just didn't seem to be enough room. The faces we passed were all ashen, as if a wicked witch had cast a spell preventing anyone from leaving the building. I suspected that mice were scampering behind the walls. The natural light was meager and smiles were in very short supply.

They dragged me through the newsroom and then over to the Culture Department, introducing me to so many editors that my hand grew sore from being shaken. Then I was turned over to a short, tidy woman with clipped gray hair. She was wearing a chic dark pantsuit that looked very expensive and her feet were clad in handsome oxfords.

"We've spoken," she said, holding out her hand. "Carol Shaw. I'm here to escort you to the Living section."

Her tone was so dry that I couldn't help asking, "Is it that bad?"

"Oh," she said pressing the elevator button, "pure paradise. You'll see."

Going from the newsroom to the Style Department was like going to visit a stepchild who has been exiled to the attic. The room was even dingier than those I had already seen, and very subdued, as if someone had turned down the lights and lowered the volume.

"I'm going to introduce you to a lot of people, but if I were you I wouldn't bother trying to remember names," said Carol. "It'll be much easier that way."

There was an edge to her voice, a New York wariness that was a clear warning to keep your distance.

"I see Carol has you in tow," said a shaggy man, coming toward us, his hand outstretched. His voice had an odd but appealing cracked quality, as if he couldn't quite control it. With his rumpled clothes, scraggly hair, and pocked face, he seemed more like someone I might have known in Berkeley than an editor at the *New York Times*. "I'm Eric Asimov, the editor of the Living section. Carol may be my secretary, but she's the important person to get to know around here. She'll insist that you march for all her causes, but she knows where the bodies are buried, and she's got the nicest house in the department. She lives in a perfect Chelsea townhouse while I camp out in a miserable apartment on upper Broadway."

"There's a reason for that," said Carol, swatting his arm. I assumed the reason had something to do with his reputation as a ladykiller, but he certainly didn't look the part. He looked more like an R. Crumb character than a suave lover, and I found myself thinking that maybe this *Times* wouldn't be that different from the one out west.

"Home section," said Carol, walking me briskly down the line of desks. "Fashion. Sports is over there." She glanced at her watch. "It's time for your editorial meetings. You'll be happy to know that they are back downstairs, where the grownups sit."

"Thanks for the tour," I said.

"Anytime," she replied. "Are you planning on coming back?"

"That's not up to me," I said.

"That's not what I hear," she replied, turning to walk away.

The editors met in a modest conference room around a table far less imposing than the richly polished wooden rectangle at the *L.A. Times* office. But the air bristled with energy as they laid out the paper, discussing the news with great passion and ferocious intelligence. From the squawk box in the center of the table a caustic and disembodied voice from the Washington Bureau kept up a stream of constant challenges. Were they sure about the number of ground troops Clinton had agreed to send to Bosnia? Shouldn't that story about the slaying of a gay sailor be above the fold?

Los Angeles piped in, offering a story on well-to-do blacks and their response to the King beating trials. The third in a series about Muslims in America was briefly discussed, along with a story about the way the children of the Branch Davidians had been abused in the compound.

It was fascinating, and I suddenly understood what it was that I was so wantonly rejecting. These were the finest news minds of my generation, and I had been offered the chance to work with them. I began to regret my behavior.

But it was too late; there was only one interview to go and I had been burning bridges all afternoon. So I went into my final meeting and shook hands with the editor, Max Frankel, and his deputy, Joe Lelyveld. And when they asked what I thought of the way they covered food, I went back to the campaign. "Not much," I said.

They looked taken aback.

I had charted my course and I sailed bravely on, telling the editors of the world's most powerful paper that they were doing things wrong.

"Your reviews," I said, "are very useful guides for the people who actually eat in the restaurants you review. But how many of your readers will go to Lutèce this year? A thousand? That leaves out more than a million readers. And at a time when people are more interested in food and restaurants than they have ever been in the history of this country, that's a shame. You shouldn't be writing reviews for the people who dine in fancy restaurants, but for all the ones who wish they could."

I remember Joe looking at Max over my head and saying, "This is interesting. And you know, we've heard this argument before. Only it was about books. What she's really saying is that we've been selling restaurants and that isn't our business. We should be selling newspapers."

Max nodded thoughtfully and allowed me to natter on. I can't remember what I said. But I do remember that after a while they had had enough. Max stuck out his hand and thanked me for coming. It was already getting dark when I walked out of the New York Times building.

I was outrageous," I reported to Michael when I got back to the hotel. "They'll never hire me."

I expected him to be annoyed, but all he said was "Good for you."

"What?" I asked. "What do you mean?"

"Do you think I don't know you?" he asked. "I knew you were trying to blow it. That job would make you the most powerful restaurant critic in the world, and the idea scares you to death. You think you don't know enough, but you do. You're ready. You'll be great. And I'll bet they loved you."

"Why would they? I was really snotty."

"Because," said Michael, "powerful people are accustomed to being sucked up to. When you don't, it makes you more desirable. The less you want them, the more they want you. Wait and see."

· · ·

For days I jumped every time the phone rang. I was afraid it would be Warren offering me the job; I was afraid it would be Warren *not* offering me the job. I didn't know what I wanted and I hoped he wouldn't call at all.

In the meantime I fell in love with Los Angeles all over again, and found myself dreading going back to humid summers and chapped winters. I thought about all the friends I would miss, my wonderful kitchen, the ease of life with a car. I looked around my office and thought how depressing it was at the *New York Times,* how brittle all the people there seemed to be. And then I thought about what had happened when I first came to Los Angeles, the avalanche of mail lamenting the loss of the former critic, Lois Dwan. Was I going to have to go through all of that again?

And then the call came, and my heart was pounding and my hands were shaking as I listened to the voice saying, "It's Warren."

"We would like you to be our chief restaurant critic," he said. "Please say yes. We don't have any other candidates. If you don't take the job I don't know what we'll do."

"Of course," said Michael when I told him. "CBS already has a desk waiting for me at the New York bureau. When you told me Bryan Miller was leaving the job, I went to my boss and told him we were moving to New York."

New York Cheesecake

This book is going to have recipes instead of pictures because I want you to be able to taste what I am talking about. And what is the taste of New York? To much of the world, it's cheesecake.

Cheesecake is something every cook should have in his or her repertoire, if only because it's such a cheap trick. It's fast, it's easy, and it can make the most modest meal a celebration.

This one is an absolute classic. I've been modifying the recipe since I first spied it in a magazine when I was in high school. The magazine called it Lindy's New York Cheesecake, but it's nothing like the one they served at the restaurant, which had a cookielike crust and a fairly horrid gooey cherry topping. This one is cleaner, simpler, and a whole lot easier to make.

1½ cups graham cracker crumbs (about 6 ounces)
1 cup sugar
½ cup melted unsalted butter
*1½ pounds cream cheese, preferably without gum, at room
    temperature*
4 eggs
3 teaspoons vanilla
Grated zest of one lemon
2 cups sour cream

Preheat oven to 350 degrees.

Mix the graham crackers with ¼ cup sugar and the melted butter and press into bottom and sides of a 9-inch ungreased springform pan. Chill while preparing filling.

Beat the cream cheese, ½ cup sugar, eggs, 2 teaspoons of the vanilla, and lemon zest until smooth. Pour into chilled crust and bake 50 minutes to an hour, or until the cheese is set and starting to turn golden in spots. Remove from the oven (leave oven on) and cool for about 15 minutes on a wire rack.

Stir together the sour cream, remaining ¼ cup of sugar, remaining teaspoon of vanilla and spread over cooled cake. Return to oven for 12 minutes until glossy and set.

Cool completely, cover, and chill at least 8 hours.

Serves 8

Molly

The *Los Angeles Times* was known as "the velvet coffin" because it was such a cozy place to work. When I went to tell the editor that I was leaving, he didn't let me down. "We'll leave the light on," said Shelby Coffey. "If it doesn't work out, you can always come back."

This only made me feel worse. It also made me wonder, once again, if it was a mistake to take a job at a paper with a reputation as a snake pit, a place where you constantly had to watch your back. My day at the *New York Times* had not given me any reason to think of it as warm and fuzzy. On top of that, the tabloids soon started sniffing around for gossip.

Arriving at the *Los Angeles Times* nine years earlier, I had been welcomed by letters from outraged readers crying "Bring back Lois Dwan!" and accusing me of being an interloper from up north. Now the New York gossips were playing up the California angle; no matter how many times I told reporters I was a native New Yorker, they insisted upon calling me "the critic from California," as if I were fit to judge nothing but salads. They even ran stories about my food preferences: "She likes unadorned food," they reported, and I could feel the city heave a collective groan, as if everyone would now be forced to give up sauce.

Still, until that fateful airplane ride I had not understood how busy the restaurants had been in gathering information, and I was shocked at their intrusiveness. They knew so much! As I sat there watching Jackie surreptitiously study my face as if memorizing the details, I realized that the remedy was simple: if every restaurant in New York knew what I looked like, I had to look like someone else. I even knew the person who could show me how to do it. As soon as the plane landed in New York, I went to a phone booth and called Claudia Banks.

In her prime Claudia had been a famous acting coach. She had been retired for many years, but she instantly agreed to help me create a disguise. "Oh my darling," she said in her smoky British accent, "what a wonderful idea. I shall meet you directly at your hotel."

Of all my mother's friends, Claudia had always been my favorite. Her size alone was endearing: she was so short that by the time I was eight, I towered over her square little body. She wore ridiculously high heels on her tiny feet and tight little snail-like curls on her small round head. She exaggerated everything, smoked like a chimney, and told wonderful stories about the people she had known in what she called, in a long, slow drawl, "the theater."

She was past seventy, but when she exploded into my hotel room I saw that she was eerily unchanged. This was undoubtedly because there had never been anything natural about her to begin with. Claudia's hair was dyed, her teeth were fake, and her body had always been trussed up in corsets. Even her snooty accent was made up. "At one time," my mother used to say, "Claudia was actually born in the Bronx. But that's ancient history, and she'd rather we forgot it."

Now she came swirling dramatically toward me in a cloud of jasmine perfume. "Sit down," she said, pressing a finger into my chest. "Let me have a look at you."

For such a tiny woman she was astonishingly strong, and I tumbled onto the bed. Humming lightly under her breath, she took my jaw in her hands and twisted it into the light. "Tell me, my darling, what were you planning to do about *that*?" Her hand was tugging at my tangled mop of curls.

"A wig? " I suggested timidly.

She grimaced. "I anticipate that it will present a problem," she said. "Have you considered clothing?"

"No," I said apologetically. "I thought you might help me with that."

"I will help you," she said, dropping onto the bed beside me, "but only if you are willing to do this properly. You are about to discover the extraordinary amount of effort that is required to turn one's self into another person. If you are intent on deception, you must go all the way; the restaurant critic of the *New York Times* can *not* afford to look foolish."

I nodded, and Claudia folded her hands. "Let us begin by contemplating who you are going to become." She stared at me for a long time, studying my wild hair and colorful clothes with amused detachment. "One certainly has no difficulty imagining someone quite different from yourself," she said dryly. She scrutinized me for a few more minutes, mentally dressing me in various clothes as if I were a paper doll. "I have it!" she decided at last. "You will be one of those ladies who lunch. A very proper person. What would you like to be called?"

When I remained silent, she glared at me with exasperation and said, "Please bestir yourself a bit, my darling. Surely you can think of a name?"

"Molly Hollis?" I asked. "Would that do?"

She savored the name, chewing on it as if she could actually taste the words. "It is not perfect," she said, repeating it a few times. Her mouth was pursed as if the flavor was not quite right, and I remembered that she had been famous for the rigorous training she imposed upon her actors, and for her attention to detail.

"I just got a credit card in that name," I added.

"How," she asked, raising an eyebrow, "did you contrive that?"

"I got the idea from Mom," I admitted. "After Dad died she had no credit so she asked if I would add her to my charge accounts. It was so easy—they didn't ask for any information—and one day it occurred to me that if I could get supplementary cards in Mom's name, I could probably get them in other names as well. I made one up and that was that; two days later I had my first fake credit card. It makes my life as a critic so much easier: I don't have to carry cash and as soon as the name gets known, I throw it out and make up a new one. Molly's card just came; I haven't even used it yet."

"Fascinating!" said Claudia, looking impressed. "Perhaps you will find acting less stressful than I had thought. May I ask where Molly is from?"

My adventures in deception had not included thinking up personalities for the people I invented, but I didn't want to let Claudia down. "Birmingham, Michigan" was the first town that came into my head.

"And what does Molly do?"

"She was a high school English teacher," I said, making it up as I went along. "She stopped teaching twelve years ago when her husband made a killing in real estate. He's in strip malls. They have two children, both in college." I was getting into it and Claudia looked pleased. "They go to Europe once a year," I continued, "and they come to New York every few months to go to the theater and do some shopping."

"Whoa," said Claudia. "Slow down, my darling. Do not get carried away. You must inhabit the character and allow her to develop naturally." She produced a small notebook. "We have a great deal of work ahead of us. Have you a pen?"

I nodded and flipped the book open. "You will need a wig. Write down this address, tell them I sent you, and be sure to buy something quite straight, short, and nondescript. I would say ash brown, if it looks at all plausible. Clothing: I believe that Molly would look best in a beige Armani suit."

"An Armani suit!" I said, alarmed. "I can't afford an Armani suit."

"Nonsense," said Claudia briskly. "It need not be new. It *should* not be new. Molly would be a woman who takes good care of her clothes. You will go to a resale shop. Write down these addresses. If you are unable to find beige, be sure to purchase something pale. Midwestern women do not wear black. More importantly, it will make you look plumper. Buy yourself some suitably plain pumps, the heels not too high. And a hand-bag." She glanced disdainfully at mine, which was sitting on the bed. "A small, proper handbag, if you please, not one of those birdbaths."

Now she turned her attention to me. "A manicure is imperative. Have them give you some modest fingernails, not too long. Molly, I am quite certain, does not have those stubby, and might I add, grubby, little paws of yours." I quickly put my hands beneath me, but not before Claudia had noticed that they were ringless.

"Jewelry?" she inquired.

"Not much," I replied.

"Miriam left you nothing when she had that unfortunate stroke last year? I mean, other than that frightful costume jewelry she draped around herself? The Mollys of the world wear wedding rings, and I seem to recall that your mother had a minor diamond from her first marriage."

"She hated it," I said, "and I do too. But I'll see if I can find it."

"Do," said Claudia, plunging onward. "I am convinced that Molly is the sort of woman who would feel naked without her ring. If Miriam's does not turn up, you will have to buy a fake one."

This was going to be more work than I had anticipated. And Claudia was far from finished.

"Meanwhile," she continued, "we will require the services of an excellent makeup artist. It must be someone who is not overly theatrical." She shook her head. "It will not be easy, not easy at all. But a few people do come to mind. I shall look into it and we will meet again on your next trip to New York. Happily we are not pressed for time. This is going to demand a great deal of preparation. I do hope you are up to it . . ."

I spent the summer shuttling between Los Angeles and New York, and on each trip east Claudia and I conferred. She refused to even think about my physical transformation until Molly's costume was complete. And that took a while: she was such a stickler for detail that she made me change the color of Molly's stockings three times before she was satisfied.

I would have lost patience with the process, but I was wrapping up one life and starting another, and the search for Molly Hollis was a welcome distraction. In the midst of the tedious details of moving—packing up the house, emptying out the office, searching for babysitters and transporting animals—this exercise in disguise seemed like great fun.

I bought a dowdy Armani suit that was three sizes too large; Claudia insisted that I wear a padded bra and two thick skirts beneath it to give me more girth. I found a proper little purse and Mom's old diamond ring. Bit by bit the clothing came together. It took almost two months before Claudia pronounced the costume complete, but at last she announced that the time had come for Molly's debut. "Make a reservation," she commanded. "Where are you planning to introduce this new woman to the world?"

"You're coming with me, aren't you?" I asked nervously. "I was thinking of starting with a four-star restaurant that has a brand-new chef. Everyone's expecting me to weigh in on him, and if any restaurant in New York is watching for the new critic from the *Times,* this would be at the top of the list. They know I'll be there sooner rather than later."

"Le Cirque!" said Claudia, clapping her hands.

"Yes."

"Perfection," she said. "It's as much theater as restaurant, and it will be a perfect stage for Molly. I will be very pleased to join you."

The reservation was for an early dinner in midsummer. When Claudia arrived at the hotel, makeup lady in tow, I was already dressed. They both burst out laughing when I came to the door, and I realized how ridiculous I must look with my wild hair and Molly's staid suit. Claudia turned to Denise. "We are counting on you," she said, "to make the head match that body."

"I can do that," said Denise, extracting a plastic cape from her bag of tricks. She was a nondescript middle-aged woman who, like so many makeup artists, wore her well-scrubbed face disconcertingly free of lipstick, foundation, powder, or blush. She threw the cape over my suit and began to erase me. First she covered my skin with a thick coat of pancake makeup. Then she made my eyebrows disappear. As she worked, my skin acquired a yellow tone that it has never had, and wrinkles where none had been. She filled out my cheeks so they looked fuller, and the mouth that her pencil drew was smaller than my own. She hesitated over the lipstick, and then chose a rather creepy coral shade that was, she assured me, two years out of fashion.

"Close your eyes," she said, beginning to work on the upper part of my face. Brushes swept across my lids, sponges swatted at the area below. My eyes were still closed when Denise asked me to put on the wig. It had been made to Claudia's exact specifications: straight, short, and ash brown. It was also so tight that I had to wrestle the thing over my bunched-up hair. This was an ordeal, and as I bent down, struggling with it, I had the sensation that two enormous rubber bands were being wrapped around my head.

"It's giving me a headache," I complained, my voice muffled beneath the hair. "I hate it. It's going to be like eating dinner in a bathing cap."

"Darling," said Claudia, "do stop complaining and look up."

I raised my head and opened my eyes. Looking into the mirror, I found a woman I did not recognize staring straight at me.

"Meet Molly," said Claudia. I could not speak. I found myself moving my lips to see if hers would move too. They did. I wiggled my nose; Molly's nose wiggled. I raised my fingers; she raised hers. I waved. She waved back. Claudia tapped my arm and said gently, "I believe it is showtime."

I watched her struggle to keep a smile from escaping, and saw that she was having a Henry Higgins moment. She was about to show her creation to the world; she could hardly wait.

S low down, my darling," said Claudia as we walked out the door. "Take smaller steps. Remember, you are now Molly. Stay in character." She winced when I hailed a taxi. "And do not shout."

That part, at least, was not difficult. It was too hot for speed or noise.

My sensible shoes were sticking to the sidewalk, and beneath the yellow pancake makeup my cheeks were flushed. Claudia, shrouded, despite the heat, in one of the shapeless black dresses she wore everywhere, seemed oblivious.

"I wonder what Molly likes to eat," I said as we settled into the cab. "I wonder what she talks about?"

"That," said Claudia, "is what you are about to find out."

Le Cirque was cool but far from calm. The small, fussy room was crowded with women in shimmering dresses and men in elegant suits who perched on striped silk chairs that seemed too small for them. Huge bouquets of flowers nodded from the corners and little ceramic monkeys frolicked across the tables.

The maître d' was hunched over the reservation book, and when he finally deigned to notice our presence he subjected us to a cool inspection. I found myself patting the wig as he looked me over, hoping no stray dark hairs were escaping.

"Do you have a reservation?" His tone indicated that he considered this a dubious possibility.

"Hollis," I said. He did not acknowledge this, so I said more loudly, "Molly Hollis?" I was surprised to find that my voice had gotten flatter and slower, as if it too had undergone a makeover. The man ran his finger across his book, searching ostentatiously through the names. "Ah yes," he said at last. "Here it is." He sounded disappointed. "A nonsmoking table. I'm afraid there's nothing at the moment. You'll have to wait in the bar." With his head he indicated where that might be found.

It was lonely at the bar, and after we had ordered only water, lonelier still. The wig grew tighter on my head, and I fidgeted in my layers of clothing. The lack of attention was an unmistakable message.

"Do you suppose," asked Claudia, "that they are laboring under the misapprehension that we are going to tire of the wait and go away?"

"Yes," I said.

"I would not dream of granting them that satisfaction," she said.

"Nor I," I said, sticking a finger beneath the wig to scratch my itchy scalp.

Our designated table turned out to be very small, in the back of the dining room, and wreathed in the murk of the surrounding smokers. "But I asked for non-smoking!" I protested in my flat, quiet voice. The man shrugged and pointed around the restaurant as if to say, "Can't you see they're all taken?"

He doled out the menus and beat a hasty retreat. "A wine list?" I asked his departing back, but he was already gone. This, we soon learned, was not going to be a problem; the few inches of banquette to my left were apparently considered storage space, and waiters flung used menus onto it as they dashed past. It was not long before a wine list came flying toward me.

It was a thick tome and as I settled in to read it, I heard my newfound voice say to Claudia, "It is quite a lovely list."

"Good," she said. "I could do with an excellent Burgundy. Do you see one?"

"Pages and pages of them," I replied.

But I had only reached page three when the captain reappeared and held out his hand, saying "I need that wine list" in peremptory tones.

I wavered for a moment, struggling with myself. Then I surrendered the list. "Bravo!" said Claudia. "You stayed in character. Molly is a lady."

"I don't think she's all that happy about it either," I said, noting with fury that my list was now in the hands of a man three tables down the banquette. I was inclined to march over and snatch it out of his hands, but I was determined to stay in character. So poor Molly fluttered her fingers at every passing waiter, saying in a pathetic little voice, "Do you think I might please have a wine list?" Given these timid tactics, it was a full twenty minutes before we were able to order wine.

"I'm going to learn a lot, being someone else," I murmured to Claudia.

"Indeed," she said. "Now when do you suppose that supercilious captain is going to allow us to order?"

Were we invisible because we were women? Or did we look too much like tourists to be worthy of recognition? Maybe the staff was simply over-worked. But when the captain finally came to ask what we would like for dinner, he neglected to mention the special seasonal menu he had so lov-ingly described to the man sitting next to us.

I felt torn between Ruth and Molly. The former was gleeful; this terri-ble treatment was going to make very good copy. But Molly was wonder-ing why anyone would subject herself to this. Molly was wishing she had stayed home in Birmingham, where ordinary people weren't treated shabbily in restaurants. Molly was, in fact, furious.

And so she said, in her very nicest voice, "Did I hear you say something about a special menu to the gentleman over there?"

The captain said sullenly, "It's quite a large meal."

"That will be fine," she said softly. "We'll have that. And a bottle of the 1985 Chambolle-Musigny."

Once the wine came, Claudia relaxed. She swirled the soft garnet liq-uid in her glass and smiled benevolently down at the sautéed foie gras, in-haling the fragrance of the white peach with which it was served.

"White peaches always remind me of Paris," she said happily, and I had a sudden memory of my mother's voice saying, "Poor Claudia," in that tone she reserved for single women. "She did marry once, but her husband was hit by a truck in a freak accident and she never got over his death."

As Claudia cooed over her curried tuna tartare, translucent ruby nuggets surrounded by overlapping circles of sliced radish, I thought how stunned she would be to know that my mother considered her an object of pity. After her husband died Claudia reinvented herself, created a character she could inhabit, and spent the rest of her life showing oth-ers how to do it. She was the only working friend my mother had, and she had obviously supported herself in style; by the third glass of Burgundy she was expounding on her favorite hotel in Beaune.

I listened politely, Molly's best Junior League smile playing across my face. The food was good enough, but it was hard not to notice that everyone around us was receiving considerably more attention than we were.

Then things looked up. The captain came to announce that a table had just become available in the non-smoking section. Would we like to move? As we walked out of the smoke I saw that we were being led to a larger table, and I felt as if the unpleasant part of the meal had come to an end.

But there was no graciousness in the maneuver. The busboy sullenly ferried used water glasses and bread plates across the dining room, shoved our crumpled-up napkins into our hands, and took off. Watching him go, I found myself saying, "You'd think he'd at least refold the napkins!" in Molly's subdued voice.

"Really my darling, what does it matter?" asked Claudia. The waiter had just set a plate of black bass in Barolo sauce before her, and she was looking down at it with a dreamy expression. The fish was wrapped in translucent slices of potato that hugged it like a second skin. She reached out with the tines of her fork and watched, rapt, as the crisp potato coat shattered to reveal the soft, creamy flesh underneath.

"Claudia!" said Molly sharply, "you, of all people, should understand the importance of theater. The food may be good, but the service has been so bad that the evening is destroyed."

"I beg your pardon," said Claudia, setting the fish resolutely aside. "You are quite right."

"I did not come here simply to eat," Molly went on in her slow, serious voice, "I came here for glamour. I am willing to pay for the privilege of feeling rich and important for a few small hours. Is that too much to ask? I have come here looking for a dream, and it has turned into a nightmare. I feel frumpy and powerless. I may be nobody, but I don't like paying to be humiliated. It isn't right."

Claudia was looking at me with a kind of wonder. I was surprised myself. Where had that speech come from? Who was this woman? I found myself toying with the very brown food that was set before me, and when the chocolate soufflé cake arrived, I pushed it away after a few small bites. "I really shouldn't eat dessert," I heard myself saying. "I'd like to lose fifteen pounds." And when I paid the check, I discovered that Molly's signature looked nothing like mine.

Claudia was triumphant. "We did it!" she said when we were back on the sidewalk. "You absolutely fooled them. They had no idea who you were."

"That," I replied, "is certainly true. Even I did not know who I was."

The King of Spain

Arms wide, mouth open, legs pumping, the owner of Le Cirque came bounding toward the table in full cry. "You're Warren Hoge," he wailed reproachfully at my guest.

"Yes," Warren admitted ruefully.

"How could I have seated Warren Hoge *here*?" asked Mr. Maccioni. It was an accusation, as if this lapse were somehow our fault. "You must let me move you to a better table."

Finished with our main courses and already halfway through dessert, we declined the offer. But Sirio Maccioni, stricken at having mistreated such an important person, was insistent. He looked at Michael. He looked at Warren's wife. He looked at me. Failure to recognize a major player was a serious breach of his honor as a restaurateur, and he wanted to remedy the situation. At last he took no for an answer, but when he reluctantly moved off he left behind an army of waiters with strict instructions to bombard us with desserts.

The onslaught of sweets was ferocious. There was a miniature stove with little pots of chocolate, and a troupe of pulled-sugar clowns. There were fabulous cakes and adorably decorated candies. And there was something else. "Look," I said. With my right hand I held up the raspberry tartlet that had just arrived; with my left I held up my old, half-eaten one.

Anyone with eyes could see it: the new raspberries were twice the size of the old ones.

"Do you suppose," asked Michael, "that there is someone in the kitchen who does nothing but sort raspberries for high-status diners?"

"Welcome to New York," I murmured under my breath.

Unaccustomed to the ways of my future employer, I had been charmed when Warren suggested that we meet during one of my trips east. In nine years at the *Los Angeles Times*, I had never gone to dinner with someone on the masthead. "It would be nice to get to know you better before you start the job," he said. When I told him that Michael would also be in New York, working on a Whitewater-related story, he suggested that we include our spouses. "You choose the restaurant," he said. "I wouldn't want you to waste a meal."

I agonized over the choice, knowing that a minor meal would never do. "Le Cirque would be perfect," I said to Michael, "but he must be known there."

"Why don't you ask him?" said Michael, who never beats around the bush. "Maybe they *don't* know him." Then he was struck by another possibility and abruptly changed the subject. "Are you planning to put on that costume for your first meal with your new boss?" he asked. "I don't get the feeling that would be the best way to make a good impression."

I admitted, a little sheepishly, that I was too embarrassed to be Molly for the occasion. "Besides," I added, "Warren's secretary told me that his wife is some sort of Czech countess—or something like that. I have a hard time envisioning Molly dining with royalty; she's going to stay home."

"Can I stay home too?" pleaded Michael. Not for nothing had I dubbed him The Reluctant Gourmet in my Los Angeles columns. "You know I hate that kind of evening: fancy food and polite chitchat. Can't I just stay in the hotel and order room service with Nicky?"

"You don't have to come if you really don't want to," I said unwillingly. "But I really wish you would. I need your support. The idea of dinner in some snooty restaurant with my new boss and his aristocratic wife is not exactly my idea of a jolly evening. Besides, you're the one who got me into this in the first place."

"Don't worry," said Michael, squeezing my hand. "I won't abandon you. I'll put on a tie. I'll charm the countess. I'll eat everything on my plate. I'll even order something in cream sauce if that will make you happy."

Warren assured me that we'd be safe at Le Cirque; he had not, he said, been there in years. It seemed to be true: when we arrived we were paraded past all the important people seated in the front to an ignominious table on the wrong side of the room. The seats were not stellar and the service was not special, but it was far better than what Molly had experienced on her two miserable visits to the restaurant.

Warren was witty and urbane, the countess was full of entertaining stories, and Michael held up our end with admirable fortitude while I concentrated on the food.

I had meanly ordered risotto, a dish few French chefs can master. This one, however, was a masterpiece. It tasted as if a chef had stood at the stove, stirring diligently as he coaxed each grain of rice into soaking up stock. As a finale he had strewn plump little morsels of lobster through the rice, giving it the taste of the ocean. There was rosemary too, just a subtle touch—a fresh wind blowing across the rice and imparting little hints of green fields and verdant forests.

I go silent when food is that good, and I looked up to find Warren watching me. It made me feel naked, as if I were somehow being derelict in my duties. Did he think I was enjoying the meal too much? Then I realized that his focus was not actually on me. He was looking at the veal he had ordered, an entire shank, which was being carried triumphantly into the dining room. As the captain carved, the meat fell from his knife in thin slices, like petals from a rose. The captain gathered up the slices, arranged them on the plate, sprinkled them with sea salt and pepper, and with all eyes in the dining room upon him, set the plate in front of Warren. He liked that.

But I think he liked being recognized even better. When the dessert offensive was finally over and the evening at an end, Warren asked Mr. Maccioni a question. "How did you know me?" he inquired.

"But you're Warren Hoge!" Mr. Maccioni replied, as if the question were absurd. Warren pushed the compliment away modestly, but he looked satisfied. As he bowed us out the door, Mr. Maccioni bestowed his most glittering smile upon us. "I hope," he said in his charmingly accented English, "that you will visit us soon again."

It was a lovely evening and we stood on the sidewalk, saying our farewells, reluctant to part. "That was a very good meal," said Warren.

"Yes," I replied, wishing it had been a little less so. "But was it a great one?"

"That," he said, "is for you to decide. I assume you'll come back?"

"Oh yes," I assured him. "This was only my third visit and I'll be back a few more times before deciding on the stars."

"I look forward to reading the review," said Warren with a solemnity that implied that big things were expected of me.

At the *New York Times,* four stars are serious; they denote luxurious perfection. Bryan had anointed only five restaurants with the coveted quad. Le Cirque's new chef was undeniably talented, but how could I possibly give top billing to the restaurant that Molly had attended? It seemed to be a completely different restaurant depending on who you were. The critics, who undoubtedly got the royal Hoge treatment, all raved about the place. Then the readers showed up and found themselves stuck in some dark corner and ignored. If only there were a way to write about that . . . Suddenly I saw that there was.

What if I simply showed up as me? When an ordinary man turned into Warren Hoge, his raspberries got bigger. Just think what might happen when an ordinary woman turned into the restaurant critic of the *New York Times*. All I would have to do was print two parallel reviews: Molly's meal on one side, Ruth's on the other. My hope was that, like the raspberries, they would speak for themselves.

You sure you don't want to make the reservation in your own name?" Michael asked when I told him my plan. "What if Maccioni doesn't recognize you?"

"Then he's not as smart as I think he is," I said. "Besides, they'd never believe it if I made the reservation in my own name; the restaurant critic of the *Times* would never do that. And I'm pretty sure he must have figured out that Warren was with me that night. This is going to be the most amazing meal!"

A strange look came over Michael's face, and I tried to decipher it. Then it hit me: he didn't want to come.

"I don't," he admitted. "It would be such a waste! Just think of all the people who'd love to be there when the waiters start dancing around the table. I can think of about a thousand people who'd have a better time than I would."

"Like who?" I asked.

"Like Johnny."

It was an inspired idea. My twenty-something nephew was working on Wall Street. Young, handsome, and impeccably dressed, he would go anywhere and eat anything, no matter the hour. He was thrilled when I called and happily volunteered to make the reservation.

Johnny reported back that the earliest table he'd been able to get was at 9:45. "But let's show up early," he suggested. "I bet they won't keep you waiting. This is going to be so much fun!"

We walked in around 9:00 to find a surging crowd pushing and jostling for position at the door. "*Do* something, Gerald," a tight-faced woman was urging her escort. "Our reservation was half an hour ago." The man gave a forlorn little gesture and soldiered reluctantly forward; this was clearly not his first attempt at procuring a table.

"The maître d' says he's doing his best," Gerald was saying sadly when a little flutter went through the throng. Sirio Maccioni was coming through, beaming broadly. He was a majestic figure, gray-haired but still so handsome it was easy to see why Babe Paley once called him "the sexiest man in New York," and the crowd parted before him like the Red Sea. He was heading straight for me. Grasping my hand, he led me jubilantly forward. As the crowd made way for us, I felt like Cinderella with brand-new shoes.

"But we've been waiting half an hour," I heard Gerald's wife whimper. I felt the concussion as she stamped her foot in frustration. "It's not fair," she said.

Utterly ignoring her, Mr. Maccioni turned to me and said regally, "The King of Spain is waiting in the bar, but *your* table is ready." I nudged Johnny. "Keep repeating those words to yourself," I whispered as we followed Mr. Maccioni. "I have to get them exactly right."

Mr. Maccioni, I soon saw, was not leading us to the cheap real estate in the back of the room. We were headed for Boardwalk and Park Place, a table for four in the front of the restaurant. My chair was pulled out. My napkin was unfolded. Mr. Maccioni buzzed about us. "May we make a menu for you?" he asked. "I'd like you to see what Sylvain Portay can do. You know, he was sous-chef to Alain Ducasse in Monte Carlo before he came here."

"We are in your hands," I said grandly.

"And I'll send the sommelier over," he said happily. "He's very young, but his parents run a wonderful restaurant in Italy and they have sent him to me." He went off to see to the arrangements, eager to show New York's newest critic how sweet life can be.

"The King of Spain is waiting in the bar, but *your* table is ready," Johnny intoned. "That's the sentence."

"What a line," I said, writing it down. I didn't even have to hide the pad I was using. "What nonsense!"

"That *is* the King of Spain!" said Johnny, staring at the bar. "He's here to open the Picasso show."

"Are you sure?" I asked.

He turned back to check. "Yes. I saw him on TV last night."

Cinderella sat up a little higher in her seat.

And then fireworks began shooting across the table: black truffles and white ones, foie gras, lobster, turbot, venison. The play of flavors was a symphony, as if we were the only people in the restaurant and fifty chefs were cooking just to please us. Each dish was rushed to the table the instant it was ready; each was served at the peak of perfection. The wines were magnificent, every sip calibrated to improve the flavor of the food. The service was attentive. It was respectful. It was unobtrusive.

It was all a dream. At one point the King of Spain and his entourage sat down at the next table and I could have sworn he smiled directly at me. Or maybe it was just the foie gras and sauternes dancing around in my mouth that was making the world seem so benevolent.

Reviewing that dinner was easy; I started with the line about the King of Spain and the rest just wrote itself. Of course I gave the restaurant four stars.

Writing Molly's review was easy, too. All I had to remember was the humiliation of that first meal with Claudia, when we were sent to the bar like unwanted guests. The food had been good, so despite the misery of the evening I let the restaurant keep one star.

I turned the reviews in early so the editors would have time to find the extra space they'd need for the double review. Perched on a desk next to the copy editor, I went over the pieces, arguing over small details like the *Times*'s ridiculous convention that nothing is ever "lit." At the *New York Times,* dim or bright, it's "lighted." And then I tried not to think about it too much.

That wasn't easy. "They called from downstairs," said Carol Shaw when I went into the office. She eyed me warily, and I began to see that I was making everyone uncomfortable. "They wanted to read your story at the very top. They're all worried."

"Why?" I asked.

"Because," she said, as if I were an idiot, "it's Le Cirque. It's a power place. And not least because Punch loves it."

"Uh oh." I was beginning to understand why everyone was so edgy. Why hadn't anyone told me that Le Cirque was the chairman's favorite restaurant? I began to have a sick, nervous feeling at the pit of my stomach.

I tried to distract myself. I took Nick to the dentist. I had dinner with winemaker Angelo Gaja, who provided very good cover; the people at Felidia were so busy trying to impress him that they totally ignored me. I had lunch with my friend Pat and dinner with my old boss from the *L.A. Times.* And then, on Wednesday night, as I was leaving for dinner, I got a call.

It was an editor on the Culture Desk. "We have a few problems with the piece," he said portentously. I held my breath. "It's been decided that you can't run two reviews. You'll have to combine them."

"I can't do that," I wailed. "The whole point is that Le Cirque is two different restaurants. Which one you get depends upon who you are."

"That's fine with me," he said, "but this comes from the top. You'll have to make the change. I don't think it will be all that difficult; we can keep the essence the same."

"But the rating?" I asked.

"Yes," he said. "The rating. I'm sorry. You'll have to make up your mind. It's been decided. One restaurant, one rating."

And so, over the phone, we figured it out. We combined the two short reviews into one big one. It was easier than I'd thought it would be. And then we came to the rating.

"You want to combine that too?" he asked. "Take an average? Make it three?"

"Maybe it should just be two stars," I suggested.

The editor considered. "It really doesn't matter," he finally decided. "The only thing that people will care about is that you're taking the fourth star away."

Thursday was one of the itchiest days of my life. I went over the piece obsessively, again and again, checking my notes, looking for errors. I had lunch with my friend Donna, the editor of *Metropolitan Home,* at Mad. 61, the new restaurant in Barneys, but I was so sick with fear that I could hardly swallow the food or follow the conversation. "Are you okay?" Donna kept asking. Dinner was even worse.

And then it was bedtime, and I was still going over the piece, still looking for mistakes, even though it was now too late to make changes. I fell into a troubled sleep.

It was 2 A.M. when I sat straight up in bed, electricity racing crazily from my toes to the tips of my ears. "Sea bass?" I asked. "Did I say it was sea bass?"

Fear went shooting through me. I could taste it in my mouth; I could feel it in my fingertips. I had called the restaurant's signature dish sea bass instead of black bass, and it was too late to do a single thing about it.

It was a cold night. Michael was tangled in the covers, fast asleep. The radiator was hissing and the wind was groaning lugubriously through the cracks in the window. Le Cirque was my seventh review in the *New York Times,* and it would surely be my last.

Lying in bed, sleeplessly listening to the wind, I conjured up another mistake. That was not Chambolle-Musigny I was drinking with Claudia; I was now certain it was Mazis-Chambertin. Contemplating this disaster, another popped into my head: What could I have been thinking, saying there were turnips with that tenderloin of lamb when any idiot could see that they were rutabagas? And another: Surely no sensible chef would put rosemary into his lobster risotto. Each new mistake hit me with a jolt of adrenaline, and they were coming at me faster and faster, a veritable hail-storm of errors. I rolled from side to side, trying not to wake Michael as I moaned softly to myself.

Why had I agreed to let them make the change from two reviews to one? Why hadn't I just written a straight review in the first place? Now I was walking around in circles, too nauseated and restless to do anything but prowl the apartment. I stumbled into Nick's bedroom and watched my sweet sleeping four-year-old, wondering how we were going to survive after I lost my job.

I didn't sleep all night—just roamed miserably around the apartment, too ashamed to admit my feelings, even to Michael, too frightened to focus on the book I was trying to read. When the sun came up, it banished the ghosts of the night and I realized that the mistakes were all in my imagination. But I was still shaky with fear, still wondering if I had a job, still too terrified to call in for my messages.

"Are you all right, Mommy?" asked Nicky as I walked him to school. He tucked his hand into mine and looked up at me. "You don't look happy."

"I'm fine, sweetie," I said, squeezing his hand. We joined the others swirling into the pre-kindergarten classroom, with its bright drawings pinned to the walls, and Nicky went running off to join his friends. "I'll see you at three," I promised, blowing him a kiss. And then I turned and walked slowly to the subway.

The train came careening noisily into the station when I pushed through the turnstile, and a wave of terror washed over me. The huge metal thing bellowed toward me, mean and loud. The wheels squealed and it came to a screeching, spitting halt. The doors sprang open.

As I slid into a seat I noticed that the man sitting next to me had the paper open to the Culture section. He was frowning, and I peered over to see what he was reading.

"Restaurants," I read, over his shoulder.

RESTAURANTS
by Ruth Reichl

....

BEING A NEW RESTAURANT CRITIC in town has its drawbacks: there are a lot of restaurants I haven't yet eaten in. But it also has its advantages: there are a lot of restaurants where I am still not recognized. In most places I am just another person who has reserved weeks in advance, and I still have to wait as more important people are waltzed into the dining room. I watch longingly as they are presented with the chef's special dishes, and then I turn and order from the menu just like everybody else.

One of my first interests was to review the cooking of Sylvain Portay, who became chef at Le Cirque late last year. Over the course of five months I ate five meals at the restaurant; it was not until the fourth that the owner, Sirio Maccioni, figured out who I was. When I was discovered, the change was startling. Everything improved: the seating, the service, the size of the portions. We had already reached dessert, but our little plate of petit fours was whisked away to be replaced by a larger, more ostentatious one. An avalanche of sweets descended upon the table, and I was fascinated to note that the raspberries on the new desserts were three times the size of those on the old ones.

Food is important, and Mr. Portay is exceptionally talented. But nobody goes to Le Cirque just to eat. People go for the experience of being in a great restaurant. Sometimes they get it; sometimes they don't. It all depends on who they are.

DINNER AS THE UNKNOWN DINER

"Do you have a reservation?"

This is said so challengingly I instantly feel as if I am an intruder who has wandered into the wrong restaurant. But I nod meekly and give my guest's name. And I am sent to wait in the bar.

And there we sit for half an hour, two women drinking glasses of expensive water. Finally we are led to a table in the smoking section, where we had specifically requested not to be seated. Asked if there is, perhaps, another table, the captain merely gestures at the occupied tables and produces a little shrug.

There is no need to ask for the wine list; there it is, perched right next to me on the banquette where the waiters shove the menus. Every few minutes another waiter comes to fling his used menus in my direction. I don't mind, because I am busy with the wine list, but I have only got to page 3 before the captain reappears.

"I need that wine list," he says peremptorily, holding out his hand. I surrender, and it is 20 minutes before it returns. (Women and wine are an uncomfortable mix at Le Cirque; at a subsequent meal the captain insists that he has only half bottles of the Riesling I've just ordered. When I prove that he's mistaken, he glares at me.)

Still, persistence is rewarded. The list is large and good, and has many rewards for the patient reader. Given a little time, I unearth a delicious 1985 Chambolle-Musigny for $46.

We sip our wine and listen to what is going on at the tables around us. This is easy; those of us seated around the edges of the room have absolutely no privacy. While the captain tells our neighbors about Mr. Portay's $90 dégustation menu ("You know he was the sous-chef of Alain Ducasse at Le Louis XV in Monte Carlo"), we listen eagerly. But ordering it, we are to discover, is not smart.

It is the middle of June, and our "seasonal menu" turns out to be a lot of brown food. The vegetables are mainly carrots, turnips and radishes, and we have potatoes in three out of five courses. Still, the first course, sautéed foie gras with white peaches, is so good that the memory of it carries us through most of the meal. The sweet, soft fruit is a brilliant pairing with the rich meat.

I like the next course, too, curried tuna tartare. Encircling the silky chopped fish, which has just the perfect touch of spice, is a lovely mosaic of radish slices. But would a really great restaurant send out these pale and flabby pieces of "toast"?

We are considering this when the captain appears and informs us that a table has opened up and we will be permitted to leave the smoke zone. The move should make me happy, but when the busboy trails us to our new table, shoves our crumpled old napkins into our hands and dumps our used glasses onto the table, I can't help feeling disgruntled.

Then the parade of brown food begins. First halibut with mushrooms on soggy rounds of potatoes. Atop the fish, a single sprig of chervil waves forlornly, the lone spot of green. I am unimpressed with the dish, but I am baffled when the chef follows it with more fish and potatoes. Potato-wrapped black bass in Barolo sauce has been a standard at Le Cirque since Daniel Boulud's days; in Mr. Portay's hands it is as good as ever, the fish soft and tender inside its crisp coat, the sauce a rounded complement. Unfortunately, this wonderful fish only emphasizes how dull the previous one was.

Next there is tenderloin of lamb on a bed of pureed potatoes. It is a fine dish, if not particularly exciting, but it is certainly not the thing you're dying to eat in the first hot weather.

Desserts don't make any concessions to summer either. The chocolate soufflé cake with whipped cream is excellent, and I like the latte cotto, a sort of light lemon custard served with marinated berries. But watching the people at the next table tucking into tarts filled with summer fruits, and gorgeous sorbets and crème brûlée sheltered beneath an enormous dome of spun sugar, I feel cheated.

The food hasn't been bad, and there was certainly a lot of it. Still, as I pay the bill I find myself wishing that when the maître d' asked if I had a reservation, I had just said no and left.

DINNER AS A MOST FAVORED PATRON
"The King of Spain is waiting in the bar, but your table is ready," says Mr. Maccioni, sweeping us majestically past the waiting masses. Behind us a bejeweled older woman whines, "We've been waiting a half-hour," but nobody pays her any mind. Mr. Mac-

cioni smiles down at us. "Let me get you some Champagne," he says as one of his assistants rushes up with a sparkling pair of flutes.

Who wouldn't be charmed? He has not even checked the book to see if we have reserved (in fact we have, but we are 20 minutes early). My date and I suddenly feel chic, suave and important. And that's before we see that there is a luxurious table for four, a little sea of space in this crowded room, waiting for the two of us.

"We are in your hands tonight," I say. Mr. Maccioni nods happily and goes off to do his magic. A young sommelier appears ("His parents run a wonderful restaurant in Italy," Mr. Maccioni whispers before drifting off) and begs us to let him introduce us to a few of his favorite wines.

The first course comes; it is a luxurious layering of scallops and truffles nestled inside a little dome of pastry. This is not a new dish—it was on the menu before the arrival of Mr. Portay last October—but no chef has ever done it better.

It is followed by more truffles, white ones this time, shaved over an absolutely extraordinary risotto. Risotto is a balancing act that re-

quires perfect timing; there is just one perfect moment when the rice has dissolved into creaminess but you can still bite into each single grain. Few French chefs can make great risotto, but Mr. Portay manages with Italian finesse.

Next there is lobster, intertwined with chanterelles, artichokes and tiny pearl onions. This dish is so tremblingly delicate, so filled with flavor, I feel as if I have never really tasted lobster before. It is followed by turbot, a fine, firm white fish, simply surrounded with zucchini, turnips and red peppers.

Now the captain is coming to the table with tiny glasses of golden sauternes. Is there foie gras in our future? Yes, here comes a slim slice, simply sautéed. Combined with the sweet satiny wine, each bite is an essay on richness. Under the heady influence of the unctuous foie gras, I find myself thinking of all the spectacular dishes I have eaten here over the past months.

One night there was lobster and rosemary risotto, an unlikely combination that really shouldn't work. But the rosemary was just a savory hint, a suggestion of the forest that nudged the lobster into tasting more of the sea. Another night there was jarret de veau, the whole shank of veal carried triumphantly into the dining room before being carved into succulent slices. Sprinkled with cracked pepper and sea salt, it had the true elegance of simplicity.

Mr. Portay does a fine job with the standards, too. His bouillabaisse was practically perfect, a big bowl of intense stock filled with aromatic seafood and served with a powerful rouille. And nobody makes a prettier chicken salad, which came to the table looking like a gift-wrapped package.

When the sommelier appears with the red wine, a mouth-filling Brunello di Montalcino, we discover that it is the perfect choice for venison. Surrounded by chestnuts, apples, a fruity puree of squash, the meat is so delicious that I find myself eating as if it is the first course. When I look down, I realize that I have eaten everything, even the single aromatic grape that decorated the plate.

But there is still dessert. They bring six if you don't count the plate of pastries with its gorgeous ribbon of pulled sugar. Jacques Torres, the pastry chef, likes to play with food, and some of his desserts are sublimely silly; who could resist a miniature chocolate stove holding tiny pots of sauces to pour over a napoleon? Still, my favorite is apple sorbet, the icy essence of fall fruit crowned with a halo of crisped apple rings.

We order espresso. Tiny cups filled with intense little puddles of coffee appear. Each sip takes your breath away; it is the perfect ending to the perfect autumn meal.

I walk reluctantly out into the cool evening air, sorry to leave this fabulous circus. Life in the real world has never been this good.

LE CIRQUE
★ ★ ★

The train pulled into Times Square as I finished reading, but I couldn't make myself get off. The man had moved on to the movie reviews now, and I watched the stations flash past. When we reached Sheridan Square I disembarked, as if pulled by some invisible magnet, and climbed up into the light.

I could not have told you why I was wandering the streets of my old neighborhood, but I had some vague feeling that if I walked through Greenwich Village long enough, I would be consoled. I walked down Bleecker to the Lafayette Bakery and thought about the white bread they used to make, and how my father had loved it. The suckling pig in Ottomannelli's window made me think of my mother, who carried hers home wrapped in pink butcher paper. I walked past Faicco, the sausage store, and inhaled the cheese at Murray's. I turned up Sixth and toward Balducci's, where I bought some of the poppy-seed strudel that my father liked for breakfast. At Gray's Papaya I had a hot dog, and then I had another, wishing my brother was there to share it with me.

I was still eating the second dog as I walked up Greenwich Avenue, past the playground of P.S. 41. At the corner, where Pop's candy store used to be, I found a working pay phone. I dropped a quarter in and started dialing the office. But I still wasn't ready. Instead I called my oldest friend.

All through elementary school Jeanie shared my mother's horrid lunches with me, coming to my house on Mondays and Wednesdays for green sour cream and sandwiches on moldy bread. We went to her house on Tuesdays and Thursdays, and she never told a soul that I always poured the milk her mother made us drink down the drain. I hated milk.

Fortunately, she was free for lunch.

We should have gone someplace familiar, to the Oyster Bar or Peter Luger or Katz's Delicatessen. Instead, I took her to Shin's, a fancy new establishment in the Parker Meridien Hotel. I had second thoughts when I saw the enormous painting of a pink rhinoceros on the wall, but it was not until Jeanie opened her menu and said, "How interesting," in a strange little voice that I knew we were in trouble. I opened my own; the first dish that caught my eye was asparagus-raisin sorbet.

"Maybe it's good," said Jeanie, still an optimist after all these years.

"Yuck," I think I said.

"Well, okay, I see your point," she conceded. She looked around the nearly empty dining room and asked, "Would you like to tell me why we're here?"

I gave her the short answer, the one that didn't mention me drifting helplessly around the Village in a morning-after panic. Instead I told her that the chefs had worked at Matsuhisa, one of my favorite restaurants in Los Angeles, and I was wondering if this sort of innovative Japanese food could make it in New York. I did not say that this might be irrelevant since I might no longer have a job.

We ordered. We talked. Her calm easiness cheered me up, and whole minutes passed when I managed not to think about Le Cirque.

But then Jeanie said, "It's been an awfully long time since we ordered," and I checked my watch. It had been almost an hour. Just then I looked up to see a hostess approaching our table with a quizzical look on her face. "I'm so sorry," she said, "but your waitress has quit. Would you mind giving me your order again?"

"You're joking, right?" I asked.

"Oh no," she said, very seriously. "No joke. Your waitress quit."

"Was it something we did?" I asked.

She did not think that was funny.

"Well," said Jeanie, "look at the bright side. This should make good copy."

And just like that, the review was on my mind again.

The sorbet was one of the worst things I have ever tasted, and the busboy, removing the crumbs from the table, somehow dumped the crumbing tool into my purse. These did not seem like good omens, and when we left the restaurant I was still avoiding the phone booths that beckoned from every corner.

But it was almost time to pick Nick up and I could not put the call off forever. "You have forty-four messages," said the cheery mechanical voice. Attention, clearly, had been paid.

"Shame on you," shouted the first caller. "You have destroyed the finest restaurateur in America. Never fear; a year from now he'll still be here and you won't." He did not leave his name.

The next was another unidentified reader. "You pretentious idiot," she said. "So pleased about being the restaurant critic of the *New York Times* that you have to go bragging about it. Who cares about all the foie gras and truffles that you get to eat? What about the rest of us!"

Another outraged message from a friend of Sirio's. And then another. And one more. And then what sounded like Warren's voice saying, "Ruth?" In a panic, I hung up.

I walked on, replaying the sound of the voice in my head. Was it Warren? Was it cheerful? Or had he called to fire me? I couldn't tell. When I was only a block from Nick's school I finally got the courage to call again. "Ruth?" I heard him say again. It *was* Warren. I played it once more. Cheerful, I decided. He sounded cheerful.

He had called to tell me that the first call the publisher had gotten was from Walter Annenberg, who was applauding the piece. This seemed to make Warren very happy; replaying the message yet again, I could hear the palpable relief in his voice. Apparently I was not the only one who had lost sleep.

The next call was another irate reader, annoyed by what he called my showing off about the way the *Times* got treated. "You restaurant critics are all the same," he snorted. "Corrupt snobs." He was followed by another caller predicting that I would soon be replaced by a more competent critic.

And then, around 10 A.M., the tone of the messages changed. A man called and said simply, "Thank you. I've never been to Le Cirque. I don't expect to ever go there. But it's good to know that we finally have a critic who's on our side." Another said, "Keep up the good work. The silent majority needs you." A third thanked me for being what she called "a spy in the house of food."

I got gleeful messages from other writers at the paper, and one from the publisher himself, who wanted to take me to lunch. But the final word was Claudia's. "My darling," she said, "that was an excellent review. But I do hope that you realize what this means? Now they will be watching for Molly in every restaurant in New York. You will have to become another character. *Think* of the possibilities . . ."

Risotto Primavera

This recipe is my adaptation of the risotto at Le Cirque. I haven't used lobster because while lobster risotto makes perfect sense in a restaurant, where the parts that are not used—the claws, the legs, the shells, and the tomalley—can all go into other dishes or be turned into stock, at home they merely go to waste. And because, frankly, I tend to be a lobster purist who believes that the best lobster is the one that is simply boiled and eaten with a little melted butter.

And on top of that I've replaced the rosemary with saffron. Why? Because I love the way it tastes and it looks gorgeous.

Risotto has a reputation for being difficult. It's not, but it does require good ingredients. Above all, it demands that you use good stock; in my opinion canned broth is not an acceptable substitute. You must use good rice too. (And if you're buying any quantity of Arborio or carnaroli rice, keep it in the refrigerator. It goes bad faster than you would think.) And finally, decide which style of risotto you prefer. Some people like to evaporate all the liquid at the end, which gives the risotto a sort of sticky density. It took me years to realize that I like to add a few final spoonfuls of broth just before the dish is finished, so that it has a looser quality. In Venice this is called *al onda*—wavy—and I find it much more satisfying to eat.

½ *pound asparagus*
5–6 *cups homemade chicken stock*
½ *teaspoon saffron strands, crumbled*
3 *tablespoons butter*
2 *tablespoons olive oil*
1 *medium red onion, diced*
1 *smallish carrot, diced*
2 *small zucchini, diced*
½ *teaspoon salt*
2 *cups Arborio rice*
½ *cup dry white wine*
½ *cup thawed frozen peas*
½ *cup Parmigiano cheese, plus extra for the table*
Salt and pepper to taste

Cut off the tips of the asparagus and set them aside. Dice the top half of the stalks (discard the rest), and set the diced asparagus aside.

Bring the stock to a steady simmer in a saucepan. Remove ¼ cup of the stock. Add saffron and set aside.

Melt 2 tablespoons of the butter with the olive oil in a heavy-bottomed saucepan. Add the onion and cook for about 6 minutes, until it is golden.

Add the carrot and cook for 5 minutes more. Add the zucchini, diced asparagus, and ½ teaspoon salt, and cook for about 5 minutes more.

Add the rice and stir until it is coated with the oil. Add the wine and cook, stirring, until it has evaporated, about 3 minutes. Now slowly add enough simmering stock to cover the rice, and cook, stirring, until it has evaporated. Keep adding, stirring, and evaporating for about 20 minutes. Then add the asparagus tips and peas, along with the saffron stock, and cook for another 5 to 10 minutes, until the rice is soft on the outside and still has a bit of a bite at the center. Add a few more spoonfuls of stock, remove the pan from the heat, and add the remaining 1 tablespoon butter and the cheese. Taste for salt and pepper, and serve with extra cheese for people to add to their own taste.

Serves 4

Looking for Umami

I have an idea," said Claudia. Over the phone her voice was rich as velvet, steeped in mystery and vibrant with dramatic possibility. "I know exactly who you must now become."

"Who?" I asked.

"Miriam," she replied.

"Who?" I asked.

"Your mother. We shall turn you into your mother."

A shiver went down my back and I found I was unable to speak. Undaunted by my silence, Claudia continued. "It will not be difficult. Have you noticed how much you are beginning to resemble her?"

"No," I said shortly. "I don't look the least bit like her."

"You do indeed," Claudia insisted. "A short silver wig, a few wrinkles, a bit of makeup . . . We will make you much older than Molly, which will be extremely effective. Nobody notices old ladies." She said it so casually that it occurred to me that she did not consider herself one of them.

"I hope," she went on, "that you have saved some of Miriam's clothing? And a few of those dreadfully gaudy jewels?"

"Who else would want them?" I muttered, mentally reviewing some of my mother's more exuberant purchases. Mom liked her jewelry to provoke conversation; she was not at all put out when people told her how "interesting" it was. Her favorite necklace was a large gold-plated Indian affair that resembled a breastplate and covered her chest from neck to navel. Her earrings dangled, her watches talked, her rings extended to the first knuckle. Cleaning out her closets, I had found tie racks strung with ropes of semi-precious rocks in every conceivable color. There were bags of the stuff. Oh yes, I had everything I needed to turn into a replica of my mother. Just the thought of it gave me the creeps.

"I don't think I need another disguise right now," I hedged. "I'm concentrating on ethnic restaurants and they couldn't care less who I am. Bryan didn't pay much attention to Asian food, but I want to change that. I've been eating in Chinese, Japanese, and Korean places. Believe me, not one of them has my picture in the kitchen."

"Laudable, I'm sure," Claudia replied. "But you cannot spend all your time eating in minor restaurants."

"Minor?" I said. "Minor? A thousand years ago the Chinese had an entirely codified kitchen while the French were still gnawing on bones. Chopsticks have been around since the fourth century B.C. Forks didn't show up in England until 1611, and even then they weren't meant for eating but just to hold the meat still while you hacked at it with your knife."

"Quite true, I am certain," said Claudia. "I applaud your knowledge. But that does not change the fact that Molly will soon require replacement and we must be prepared."

I could see that Claudia was determined to make me into Mom. "All right," I said, sighing, "let's discuss it over dinner."

As it turned out, we did not discuss it over dinner. When Claudia discovered that I expected her to eat raw fish and naked noodles she was so offended that the only thing she would discuss was her plight. She began complaining before she even opened the menu.

"Up there?" she asked when I pulled open the door to Honmura An. She glared accusingly at the stairs. "And the elevator?"

"Does not exist," I replied.

"Impossible!" she exclaimed, planting her feet on the solid ground.

"It's not exactly Mount Everest," I pointed out, noting that the flight was wide and rather modest. "Look, from here you can even see the tables."

She groaned and reached for the banister. "I hope," she protested as she pulled herself painfully upward, "it is not your intention to begin your tenure at America's most prestigious newspaper by introducing your readers to bizarre food requiring strenuous exercise. No matter how many stars you bestow upon this place, no one will come. Your career will end before it has begun."

"You are not the first to say that," I said, sniffing the clean fragrance of the air. I found it sensuous and refreshing, this mixture of seashore and cedar with the clear high note of ginger singing through it, and for a moment it gave me hope that the spare, elegant room would have a calming effect upon Claudia.

But she was unmoved. Still panting from the exertion of her climb, she sat on the edge of her seat, peered suspiciously down at the long gray menu, and said despairingly, "I find it impossible to pronounce these words."

"Have some green tea," I suggested soothingly, certain that the tranquility of the restaurant would soon take effect.

The cool, peaceful aura of Honmura An is so profound that most people reach the top of the stairs and lower their voices, as if entering a temple. The dining room is deceptively spare and artfully devoid of ugliness. The decorations—a single piece of fruit balanced on a platter or a tangle of branches captured in a bronze bowl—look more like offerings than ornaments, and even the view seems part of the plan. Seen at an oblique angle, the sidewalk below looks like a scene captured in a glass paperweight, the frantic activity on the street part of some noisier, less serene world. I picked up the smooth black stone my chopsticks were resting upon and caressed its worn surface.

Suddenly, as if the images were being conjured by the stone, I remembered the last time I had seen a room like this one. I had been walking on a hillside in Kyoto when my feet found a little pathway. Feeling my way along it, I passed simple fountains that splashed and gurgled, leading me to a door. Pulling aside a bamboo curtain, I discovered a small room much like this one.

When I sat down on a tatami mat, a waitress wordlessly brought me water in a rough ceramic vessel. I tipped the liquid into my mouth and it was instantly flooded with icy coldness and a deep, ancient flavor, as if the water had come bubbling up from the middle of the earth.

"Soba?" asked the waitress. It was not really a question and she was gone before I could answer. Almost immediately she returned with a lacquered tray holding a bamboo mat covered with short, thin noodles the color of bark. On one side was a dish with scallions, grated radish, and wasabi; on the other, a cup filled with a faintly briny broth. She pointed to the dish with the condiments and mimed dropping them into the broth. Choosing a small speckled quail egg from the bowl on the table, she cracked it into the dish and made a mixing gesture.

Now she picked up imaginary chopsticks, held them over the noodles and swooped them into the broth. Pursing her lips as if she were about to whistle, she inhaled with a surprisingly loud, sucking sound.

I did just as she had shown me, but even after all the theater I was not prepared for the feel of the noodles in my mouth, or the purity of the taste. I had been in Japan for almost a month, but I had never experienced anything like this. The noodles quivered as if they were alive, and leapt into my mouth where they vibrated as if playing inaudible music.

"It takes a magician to make soba," I explained to Claudia, as I showed her how to eat the noodles. "They are made of buckwheat, which has no gluten. That means that getting them to hold together is an act of will. They say it takes a year to learn to mix the dough, another year to learn to roll it, a third to learn the correct cut. In Japan they like soba because they taste good. But they like them even more because they are difficult to make. You have to understand that if you are going to understand anything about Japanese food."

"May I please have a fork?" Claudia replied.

The soba at Honmura An were as good as the ones I had eaten in Japan, but their allure was lost on Claudia, who would have been much happier with a plate of pasta primavera. The restaurant's sea urchins were fabulous too: great soft piles of orange roe as succulent and perfumed as hunks of ripe mango. Claudia refused to taste them. She merely shuddered when I offered her raw shrimps, which melted beneath the teeth with the lush generosity of milk chocolate. And eating seaweed salad, she said, was absolutely out of the question.

Given all that, I was not surprised when Claudia was the first to call on the day my review of Honmura An appeared. "Are you mad?" she asked without preamble. "Raving about that miserable little restaurant you took me to? Do you know what they are saying?"

She was happy to enlighten me. "People are scandalized that you have given that little noodle joint three stars. Three stars! They are saying that you will never last." She paused for a moment and then added her final thought. "And just wait until they realize that the restaurant is on the second floor and lacks such modern amenities as elevators!"

RESTAURANTS
by Ruth Reichl

....

IN JAPAN an expensive object is prized because of its price. This explains why people actually buy those $100 melons you sometimes see in Tokyo. It also helps explain why all my Japanese friends are so taken with Honmura An. "Very expensive soba?" they ask when they hear of the SoHo noodle parlor. "They must be good."

They are. The buckwheat noodles known as soba have been eaten in Japan for 400 years. As soba restaurants multiplied, the Japanese urge for perfection set in, and soba masters began competing to see who could make the purest soba. This is not easy. Buckwheat is extremely nutritious, but it resists turning into malleable dough. Ordinary soba noodles are made mostly of wheat: to make pure buckwheat noodles that do not shatter and crack apart requires the hand of a true master. The Japanese say it takes a year just to learn to mix the dough, another year to learn to roll it, a third to learn the correct cut. The soba chefs at Honmura An have clearly put in their time.

Knowing this can put you in the proper spirit. The room will certainly put you in the mood: it is a spare, almost severe, quietly soothing space. It is so peaceful that just walking in the door makes you slow down and lower your voice. Even the air seems purer here, and when you look around, you see that every object has been carefully chosen to harmonize with the rest. From up here on the second floor, you find yourself looking down with amused detachment at the people scurrying along the frantic streets of SoHo.

A good beginning. Then there are warm towels to help you wipe away the outside world, and the perfect drink, cold sake in a cedar box with salt along the edge. The icy alcohol picks up the sweetness of the wood, the salt offsets it, and the flavor of the sake comes singing through, cold and pure.

With the sake I like a little bowl of edamame—fresh soybeans—slightly salted and still in the pod. You pick them up and pop the beans into your mouth. (If you try to eat the pods, you will find that they are rather tough.) At first taste, they are slightly salty, and then the buttery richness of the beans comes through. If you think of soybeans as boring, these will change your mind.

Other appetizers worth trying include tori dango, lightly fried balls of ground chicken that are crisp outside, soft inside and intriguingly flavorful. There are fine small bowls of marinated wild greens and seaweed that give new meaning to the word salad. And iso age: shrimp that are rolled in noodles, topped with prickly leaves of pungent shiso, wrapped in seaweed and deep-fried. There is also tempura, which is good. But nothing is remotely on a par with the noodles.

To really appreciate how fine these noodles are, you must eat them cold. Seiro soba come on a square lacquered tray, the beige noodles arrayed across a bamboo mat. On the side is a bowl of dashi, a dipping sauce made of soy sauce, rice wine, kelp, dried bonito flakes and sugar. In ordinary restaurants this is a salty bore; here it is mellow, rich, slightly smoky and incredibly delicious. Next to it are condiments—grated daikon, scallions, wasabi—to mix into the dashi according to your own taste. Now you pick some strands of soba off the mat with your chopsticks, dip them into the dashi, and inhale them as noisily as possible. (Slurping is de rigueur.) The noodles are earthy and elastic, soft and slightly firm to the tooth, and when you dip them into the briny bowl of dashi it is as if land and sea were coming, briefly, together.

You can also order soba with various toppings: seaweed, mushrooms, even giant fried prawns. And you can get them hot, the noodles submerged in a bowl of soup with chicken, seafood or greens floating on the top. In the version called kamonan, the strands of soba luxuriate in an intensely fragrant duck stock, with slices of duck covering the top of the bowl, making this one of the restaurant's more substantial dishes. It is an immensely satisfying bowl of food, but the true soba aficionado eats soba plain and cold, especially in the late fall, when buckwheat is harvested and tastes especially fine.

Honmura An also makes its own extraordinary udon, the fat wheat noodles that, in ordinary noodle shops, are about as exciting as slugs. Not nearly so difficult to make, and therefore not nearly so prized by the true cognoscenti, udon are easy to overlook. But the udon at Honmura An are the best I've ever eaten. Served cold with a sesame dipping sauce, they are so resilient that they seem to snap when you bite into them. Served hot, in the dish called nabeyaki (a staple of cheap noodle shops), they virtually redefine the dish.

You can have dessert here if you insist. On the other hand, if you're still hungry, you could always have another tray of noodles.

HONMURA AN

★ ★ ★

I had known that many readers would be upset by the review; after nine years of Bryan's frankly French sensibility, three stars to a Japanese soba restaurant was a big change. But I began to notice that Bryan himself seemed offended. Almost overnight his attitude toward me changed.

On my first day at the paper Bryan had come strolling by my desk to tell me how glad he was that I had accepted the job. He was the best-looking man at the paper, and as I watched him walk, I knew that he knew it. His thick gray hair somehow emphasized the boyishness of his face and the lankiness of his body; in any room he would turn heads, and looking at him, I wondered how he had managed to be anonymous.

"I wish you luck," he'd said, smiling down on me with an avuncular air. "It can be rocky at the beginning, and if there's anything I can do to help, just say the word."

I had not availed myself of this offer, which may be why he became so distant. As time went on he grew colder and colder, and before long he stopped talking to me altogether.

"What have I done to offend Bryan?" I asked Carol Shaw. She fiddled with the pencils on her desk, reluctant to meet my eye. "It's not you," she finally replied, looking up at me. "But Bryan is having a hard time adjusting to ordinary life. He just can't believe that he's turned back into a frog."

"Excuse me?" I said, not understanding.

"He got used to being the Prince of New York," she said. "*Sixty Minutes* was on the phone. Gérard Depardieu wanted to play him in the movies. After nine years he thought it was all about him, that the paper was holding him back. When he gave up the beat, he thought the offers would come pouring in."

"What happened?" I asked.

"*Le Roi est mort,*" she said, her face crinkling into a smile. "*Vive la Reine.*"

"I don't get it," I said.

"He's not the critic anymore," she said. "You are. The offers stopped." Her eyes locked onto mine, and I could see that she was weighing whether or not to say what was on her mind. I stared back, willing her to say it. "It's not your fault," she said finally, "but he's never going to forgive you. He was a nice man when he was a critic, but he made a stupid move, and now it's too late."

Carol hesitated again, and I sensed that there was something more she wanted to tell me. I waited for her to continue. She pointed over to the desk where Bryan's head was just visible above the partition of the pod he shared with Frank Prial. "Watch your back," she said. "And later, when everyone's telling you how *wonderful* you are, don't forget this. Remember that no matter how well you do the job, the power is not yours. It all, every scrap of it, belongs to this institution. You're just a byline. Take a good look. The minute you give up the job, you become a nobody. Like him."

"Thanks," I said. I waited for her to say more; I could feel that there was something else, something she still had to say. But she remained silent and after a moment, not knowing what else to do, I said, "I think that's my phone ringing," and retreated.

"I have the Secretary of State for you," said a faraway voice when I picked up the receiver. It was, indeed, Warren Christopher calling from Washington. He was on his way to New York and wanted advice on where to eat. We chatted about restaurants for a while and then the other line begin to ring. I picked it up to hear Gregory Peck's unmistakable voice. He wanted to discuss steak. Then Mike Nichols called in urgent need of a vegetarian cook. No wonder Bryan was sorry he had given up the job, I thought; these calls once came to him.

But Bryan was not alone in wishing he was still the critic. The city was filled with people who did not think that Shanghai dumpling parlors, Korean barbecue places, and sushi bars merited serious consideration. They did not want these restaurants taking up the space that properly belonged to the French, Italian, and Continental establishments they were accustomed to seeing reviewed in their Friday morning paper. "Bring back Bryan Miller!" they howled in their letters to the editor.

But I was determined to give Asian, Indian, and Latino restaurants the respect that they deserved. I would certainly not be the first *New York*

Times critic to do so. Mimi Sheraton had not reserved her stars for fancy restaurants, and I had once heard rumors that Raymond Sokolov, who had been the food editor of the *Times* in the early seventies, had been pushed out because of his excessive fondness for ethnic food. He was now the culture editor of the *Wall Street Journal,* and I decided to ask him about it.

"Of course I'll have lunch with you," he said when I reached him on the phone. "Why don't we go to my favorite Korean restaurant? It's just a few blocks from your office."

I walked through the depressing ghost of Times Square, the dreariest section of Manhattan. The renaissance of the area was still a few years off, and when you exited the *Times* building and navigated the grimy streets it did not seem possible that this unlovely part of the city could ever be brought back to life. The movie theaters sat empty and disconsolate, and the boarded-up girlie parlors shouted out ancient invitations. Occasionally I'd pass a broken-down bar that burped alcohol into the street when the door swung open, or a cheap deli redolent of old grease and garlic. Grim shops selling bogus electronic equipment stood on every corner. The streets felt raw and dangerous, and I clutched my purse each time a person shuffled past.

Things got better below Forty-second Street, where the boutiques overflowed with discount dresses and the coffee shops were filled with the people who sewed them. The city's pulse quickened even more as I approached Macy's. By the time I reached Thirty-fourth Street, Manhattan had changed back into the city it wanted to be.

And then I turned onto Thirty-second Street and found myself transported to a completely foreign place, a teeming Asian metropolis where all the signs bellowed incomprehensible phrases. It was as if an entire Korean city—barbers, butchers, florists, pharmacies, and accountants—had been picked up by a tornado, swirled halfway around the world, and restacked into a single crowded block.

Entranced, I walked slowly from Sixth Avenue to Fifth, following the seductive aroma of beef grilling on charcoal. The scent pulled me along, past shops displaying beautiful little pastries and herb emporiums whose windows were forests of twisted ginseng and reindeer horns. I crossed the street and doubled back, losing myself among the kiosks selling newspapers with indecipherable letters and the restaurants offering homemade tofu and big bowls of milky white soup.

In this vertical city every inch was made to count; looking up, I saw signs offering massages, spiritualism, translation, and twenty-four-hour doctors. This compact little enclave offered everything you could possibly need. How had I missed it all these years?

I found Ray near Sixth Avenue, standing in front of a restaurant called Kang Suh, tapping a rolled-up paper against his palm. He would have been hard to miss even if he hadn't been the only other Caucasian on the block. An elfin man with a head slightly too large for his body, he seemed perpetually amused, as if life were a private joke that the rest of us don't get. "Wonderful, isn't it?" he said, waving his arms proprietarily up the street as if he had just conjured it up.

We went inside, passed a dark sushi bar, and climbed the stairs. On the second floor the air was thick with smoke as young men scurried about with buckets of glowing coals to fuel the braziers at each table. Slim, dark-eyed women carrying platters of marinated raw meat and little dishes of mysterious condiments pushed brusquely past us.

I slid into a booth as a waitress set six little bowls of *panchan,* the cold dishes that Korean restaurants offer free with every meal, on our table. I picked up pointed steel chopsticks that looked like knitting needles and took a bite of marinated cucumber; it was cool and delicate, shimmering with sesame oil. I held it in my mouth for a moment, savoring its musky, familiar flavor. "I thought that you had to go to Flushing if you wanted Korean food in New York," I said. Now my mouth was on fire from the cabbage kimchi laced with red chilies.

"Strange, isn't it?" said Ray, spearing a bit of marinated watercress. "It's right here, right in midtown. The food is wonderful and cheap, and you'd think there would be lines of people out the door. But you never see anyone here but Koreans."

I picked up the menu, which went on for pages offering fiery stews and rich soups and half a dozen different kinds of grilled beef. "Americans should love this food," I said. "It's got every flavor we most admire. The meat is beef, it's salty and sweet at the same time, and you get to cook it right at the table. I don't understand why Korean barbecue doesn't have a huge following."

Ray shrugged. "You could change that," he said. "You're the restaurant critic of the *New York Times*. At least you could try."

This was my opening. "Ask him what happened when he was at the *Times*," I urged myself, but I couldn't get the words out of my mouth. It seemed so impertinent. Instead I said, "It might help if they translated the menu. Especially if they played with the language a little. You know, they could call *gul pajun* 'our version of Hangtown Fry.'"

"'Try our omelet,'" he intoned. "'Made of farm-fresh eggs and tender oysters from Blue Point, Long Island, it is the Korean version of the San Francisco classic. Ours, however, replaces the bacon with sprightly just-picked spring onions from the Union Square Greenmarket.' Who could resist?"

"*Bulgoki*," I said, getting into it, "the barbecued beef of the Far East. Our highly trained chefs cut prime steak into strips, marinate them in an irresistible mixture of soy sauce, sugar, garlic, and chilies, and bring them to your table where they are seared to perfection over glowing coals."

"*Jap chae*," he said, "intriguingly transparent strands of spaghetti in a light and lively meat sauce."

"*Jo gae tang*." My turn now. "Clams from the shores of New England steamed in a crystal clear broth." I studied the menu for another minute and then asked, "Do you think we could come up with any euphemism that would make grilled tripe enticing to an American audience?"

Ray shook his head. "That," he said, "would be asking the impossible."

He was a champion eater, matching me bite for bite, and we sat for hours drinking Korean sweet potato vodka and languidly eating the fiery food. Ray spent a long time telling me what was wrong with the paper's cultural coverage, which offended his ferocious intellect. I nodded, slightly sleepy from the heat of the coals still glowing in front of me, as I munched on the last crisp bits of meat from the grill.

It was time for the check and I still hadn't worked up the courage to ask Ray why he had left the *Times*. I had a sudden, vivid memory of my mother reading his review of Sammy's Roumanian in the early seventies and deciding to try it. When we got there, she was horrified by everything: the gritty Lower East Side location, the bottles of schmaltz on the table, the coarseness of the food. "To think that the *New York Times* is endorsing this," she said, looking disdainfully down at the length of tough skirt steak on her plate. "They should sell this meat by the yard. I'll never believe another word that paper writes."

And then I realized that I didn't need to ask Ray why he'd left. Twenty-five years later, nothing had changed.

M y first caller on the morning my review of Kang Suh ran was Claudia. Her voice was dramatic as she began to read it out loud. "'The sweet smell of garlic and sugar and chilies still clinging to your hair . . .' How extremely unappetizing. My darling, are you determined to lose this job? What can you possibly be thinking?"

Claudia went on and on, appalled by what she insisted on calling my "reckless disregard for people's true feelings about food."

"Just come with me, once," I cried. "I'm sure you'd like it."

"Absolutely not!" she said.

"But the food's wonderful," I protested.

"Fine," she said. "I am certain that you have many friends who will enjoy it. But I am not among them."

"Look," I said, desperate, "I make this really great Americanized version of Thai noodles. Everyone loves it. Will you come to our house and at least try it?"

"No!" cried Claudia. "Thai food is filled with garlic. It is not for me. Please, my darling, let me be. After all, it is only food."

I was suddenly angry. "It is not 'only' food," I said heatedly. "There's meaning hidden underneath each dish. Why do you think politicians go around munching on pizza, knishes, and egg rolls on the campaign trail? We all understand the subtext; with each bite they're trying to tell us how much they like Italians, Jews, and Chinese people. Maybe New Yorkers really won't like *bulgoki* and chicken *mole* and sushi, but how are they going to find out if they don't at least try them?"

Claudia drew a deep breath, and even through the phone I could sense her standing up very straight. "You will *never* get me to eat raw fish!" she declared. "Never! No matter how hard you try."

Here was a challenge I could not resist. That night, as I stood in the kitchen making Thai noodles, I thought that if I could just get this recalcitrant old lady to eat sushi, I could probably get anyone to eat it.

Sort-of-Thai Noodles

½ *pound very thin rice noodles (I prefer Thai rice sticks,*
    but Dynasty brand noodles found in supermarkets are
    perfectly acceptable)
¼ *cup sugar*
¼ *cup Asian fish sauce (Vietnamese* nuoc mam *or*
    Thai naam pla*)*
¼ *cup white vinegar or unseasoned rice vinegar*
2 *tablespoons peanut oil*
½ *pound medium shrimp, shelled*
2 *cloves garlic, minced*
½ *pound ground pork*
4 *scallions, sliced into* ½-*inch lengths (including about half*
    of the green part)

2 eggs
1 teaspoon dried, crushed red pepper flakes
¼ cup fresh lime juice (about 2 limes)
½ cup salted peanuts, ground or chopped fine
1 lime, cut into 6 wedges
Sriracha chili sauce

Soak the noodles in hot water to cover for about 20 minutes, until soft; then drain and set aside.

Mix the sugar, fish sauce, and vinegar together and set aside.

Heat the oil in a wok or skillet until it is very hot, and sauté the shrimp just until they change color, about 1 minute. Remove them from the wok and set aside.

Add the garlic to the wok, and as soon as it starts to color and get fragrant, add the pork and half of the scallions. Sauté just until the pork loses its redness; then add the drained noodles and mix quickly. Add the reserved fish sauce mixture, reduce the heat to medium, and cook until the noodles have absorbed all the liquid, about 5–8 minutes.

Move the noodles aside and break 1 egg into the wok, breaking the yolk. Tilt the wok so you get as thin a sheet of egg as possible, and scramble just until set. Then mix the egg into the noodles. Do the same with the remaining egg.

Add the shrimp, remaining scallions, and red pepper flakes and mix thoroughly. Add the lime juice and cook, stirring for another minute.

Transfer the noodles to a platter, and top with a sprinkling of peanuts. Serve the lime wedges, remaining peanuts, and chili sauce alongside.

Serves 4

I spent the better part of a year looking for the perfect sushi bar, the one that would persuade Claudia to try raw fish. Then, in the spring of 1995, it found me.

It was one of those days when the sky looks as if it has been washed clean and the air is so pure it pulls you along, forcing you to stay outside. I walked across Central Park, past all the delirious children on the carousel, exited at Fifth Avenue, and continued downtown. Just as I passed Bergdorf Goodman, the door opened to disgorge a stylish Japanese fashion plate. From her Manolo Blahnik shoes to her Hermès scarf, she was dressed entirely in designer clothing. As she tripped elegantly along I found myself following her, and when she turned west on Fifty-fifth Street, some impulse made me turn with her. Her destination, it turned out, was a modest restaurant I had never noticed halfway down the block.

I blinked when I walked in; it was quite dark, and quite empty. When my vision cleared I saw two Japanese men at one end of the sushi bar, and a bearded American wearing Birkenstocks in the middle. Vacant seats stretched between them.

The sushi chef was an older man, and when he looked up and saw the fashion plate, his lined round face was illuminated with fierce joy. He bowed very deeply and intoned, *"Hajimemashite."*

The woman bowed back, but much less deeply. *"Genki-Desu,"* she said, tucking herself into a seat directly in front of the chef and carefully arranging her legs.

An older woman in a kimono appeared from behind a curtain and bowed to the new customer. Then she noticed me standing in the doorway, and said discouragingly, "Only sushi."

"That will be fine," I replied.

"No tempura. No noodles. Only sushi," she reiterated in a voice that held no invitation.

"Only sushi," I agreed. "Fine." She led me to the far end of the bar, the one that was not occupied. "Only sushi," she said again, warningly.

"May I have tea?" I asked, giving a sidelong glance to the chic woman, who was now engaged in what seemed like polite Japanese chitchat with the old man.

He had laid a long bamboo leaf in front of her and was grating a pale green wasabi root against a traditional sharkskin grater. Seeing this, I suddenly understood that this was going to be an expensive meal; ordinary sushi bars do not use fresh wasabi.

It took me a while to convince the waitress that I wanted whatever the chic woman was having. It took me even longer to persuade her that I could afford it. "Very expensive," she said, shaking her head. I said that would be fine. She shook her head and went down the counter to convey my wishes to the chef, who turned to give me a long appraising stare.

He ambled down the bar toward me, smiled, and stared frankly into my face. Then he asked, "You have eaten sushi before?"

I told him that I had, and struggled to say something that would reassure him. I knew that he was worried that when the bill came I would not be able to pay it, that he was embarrassed to tell me that when he said "expensive" he meant that my lunch was likely to cost more than a hundred dollars. What could I say to him? I tried this: "I have spent time in Japan."

This did not seem to reassure him. I tried again. I bowed and said, "*Omakase*, I am in your hands."

A broad smile moved across his face. I had found the code. He spread the bamboo leaf in front of me and, leaning forward, said softly, "Sashimi first?"

"Of course," I said, and he began grating the wasabi. Patting it into a pale green pyramid, he placed it precisely on the leaf, added pickled ginger, and retreated to the center of the counter to survey his fish.

From a drawer beneath the counter he extracted a wrapped rectangle and began peeling off the plastic to reveal a pale pink slab of tuna belly. As his knife moved unerringly through the flesh, the waitress glided up to me. "Notice," she said, "that Mr. Uezu does not cut toro as other chefs do. He cuts only *with* the grain of the fish, never across it." I scrutinized the squares of fish the chef placed on the leaf. They were the pale pink of pencil erasers, with no telltale traces of white sinew snaking through them. When I put the first slice on my tongue it was light, with the texture of whipped cream. It was in my mouth—and then it had simply vanished, faded away leaving nothing but the sweet richness of the fish behind. "Oooh," I found myself moaning, and the waitress allowed herself a tight little smile.

The chic woman said something to the sushi chef, and he grinned and said *"Hai,"* as he bent to take something from the glass case before him. It was a small silvery fish, only a few inches long, that I had never seen before. He filleted it quickly, pulled the shining skin back in one quick zipping motion, and chopped the fish into little slivers that he scooped into two hollowed-out lemons. He placed one lemon before her, along with a little dish of chopped ginger and scallions, and then he came to my end of the bar and did the same.

"Sayori," he said.

"No wasabi," said a voice in my ear. The waitress had glided up so silently that I had not heard her. She pointed to the soy sauce. "Sayori is very delicate and Mr. Uezu does not want you to eat wasabi with this fish."

I picked up a cool sliver, dipped it into the ginger mixture, and placed it in my mouth. It was smooth and slick against my tongue, with a clear, transparent flavor and the taut crispness of a tart green apple.

"Oh," I murmured in surprise, and again the waitress gave a tight little smile.

"You have not had this before," she said. "Mr. Uezu has secret ways of obtaining fish that no one else can get." I had a fleeting vision of the small, sweet-faced man rampaging through the Fulton Fish Market with a snub-nosed pistol.

"No," I agreed, "I have not had this before." As I said it a look of horror, quickly replaced by a less potent look of mere disapproval, flashed across her face. Following her glance I saw the man in Birkenstocks plunk his sushi rice-side-down into the soy sauce, and as he put it in his mouth we could both see that the rice had turned a deep brown. The waitress made a quick, sharp intake of breath and turned away.

Mr. Uezu was in front of the fashion plate now, prying a tiny abalone out of its thick shell and slicing it so thinly you could practically see light through the slices. He was creating a little still life, his knife slashing through the long neck of a geoduck clam until he had created little stars snuggling next to the abalone. Now he laid a bright red Japanese Aogi clam beside it, and next to that two tiny octopuses the size of marbles. Finally an assistant handed him a pair of minuscule crabs, no larger than my thumbnail, on a little square of white paper; he placed them on the plate. The woman became more animated, smiling and bowing in a way that let me know that something he had given her was really out of the ordinary. I wondered if he would deign to repeat the still life for me.

He did. The abalone was like no creature I've ever eaten, hard and smooth, more like some exotic mushroom than something from the ocean, with a slightly musky flavor that made me think of ferns. Beside it the geoduck was pure ocean—crisp and briny and incredibly clean—so that what I thought of was the deep turquoise waters of the Caribbean. Next to the pure austerity of these two, the Japanese clam seemed lush and almost baroque in its sensuality.

Mr. Uezu pointed to the miniature crabs. "*Sawagani*," he said. "One bite, one bite. Whole thing."

I picked up one of the crabs with the tips of my chopsticks. They had been deep-fried, and they crunched and crackled in my mouth like some extraordinary popcorn of the sea. When the noise stopped, my mouth was filled with the faint sweet richness of crabmeat, lingering like some fabulously sensual echo.

"More?" asked Mr. Uezu. And I suddenly realized that no matter what the beautiful woman might be eating, I did not want more, that I wanted to keep these tastes in my mouth, to savor them as the day wore on. And so I shook my head no, I was finished. "One handroll?" he asked. How could I resist?

He filled a crisp sheet of nori with warm rice and spread it with umeboshi, the plum paste that is actually made from wild apricots. Then he covered that with little sticks of yama imo, the odd, sticky vegetable the Japanese call "mountain yam." It tastes as if a potato had been crossed with Cream of Wheat—changing, in an instant, from crisp to gooey in your mouth. The chef added a julienne of shiso leaf, wrapped it all up, and handed it across the counter.

It was an extraordinary sensation, the brittle snap of the seaweed wrapper giving way to the easy warmth of the rice and then the crunch of the yama imo, which almost instantly turned into something smooth and sexy. Meanwhile the flavors were doing somersaults in my mouth: the salt of the plum, the sharp of the vinegar, and the feral flavor of the herb.

"Umami," the waitress whispered in my ear. Again she had glided silently up.

"Excuse me?" I asked.

"Umami," she said again. "It is the Japanese taste that cannot be described. It is when something is exactly right for the moment. Mr. Uezu," she continued proudly, "knows umami."

Paying the bill, I held the tastes in my mouth, along with the knowledge that this was, absolutely, the place to bring Claudia.

RESTAURANTS
by Ruth Reichl

....

"SUSHI?" SAID A DUBIOUS VOICE on the other end of the line. "Must we? I've never tried it."

That is not the answer I'd been hoping for; introducing your friends to sushi is an awesome responsibility. But when trendy restaurants like Match, T and Judson Grill start serving sushi and others like Blue Ribbon sprout actual sushi bars, it is time to take a look at tradition. Which brings me to Kurumazushi, one of New York City's most venerable sushi bars.

"But," my friend's voice dropped to a whisper, "what if I don't like it? Can I eat something else?"

This, I had to admit, was a problem. Kurumazushi, like the classic Japanese restaurant it is, serves only sushi and sashimi. There are no noodles, no teriyaki, no tempura. I hedged a bit. "The fish is so fine," I heard myself saying, "that any person who likes to eat as much as you do ought to appreciate it." I could feel her wavering.

"It's very expensive," I urged. "It might cost $100 a person, and I'm paying."

That did it.

Still, when I arrived at the restaurant she was standing in the deserted bar looking crestfallen. "It doesn't look particularly fancy," she whispered loudly, disappointment dripping from her voice. She stared accusingly at the plain wooden counter and the glass case filled with fish. Just then all the men behind the bar let out a boisterous chorus. "Hello!" they boomed in unison. My friend jumped. "Hello!" a waitress in a long Japanese robe echoed more softly. "Would you like to sit at the sushi bar?" She led us to seats in front of the proprietor, who gave us a gentle smile.

Toshihiro Uezu arrived in New York City in 1972 to work at Saito. Five years later, he opened his own restaurant, developing a loyal following long before the current craze for sushi. At night he serves a mostly Japanese clientele, but during the day most of the seats at the sushi bar are occupied by Americans. Nobody knows better than Mr. Uezu how to introduce people to the pleasures of sushi.

"The toro is very fine tonight," he began.

"Omakase," I said, "we are in your hands." And then I added that my friend had never tasted sushi.

He smiled broadly as if this were a pleasure and turned to say something in Japanese. The man beside us swiveled in his seat, looked at my friend and said, "You are very lucky."

And so she was. "First," Mr. Uezu asked, "sashimi?"

The answer to this was yes; serious sushi eaters always start with sashimi. Mr. Uezu set a pair of boards in front of us, heaped them with shiny, frilly green and purple bits of seaweed and began slicing fish. Next to him an underling was scraping a long, pale green root across a flat metal grater.

"What's he doing?" my friend asked.

"Grating fresh wasabi," I replied. "Very few places use fresh wasabi, but the flavor is much subtler and more delicate than the usual powdered sort." The man scooped up little green hillocks and set one on each board. Beside them Mr. Uezu placed pale pink rectangles of toro.

I showed my friend how to mix the hot wasabi with soy sauce and dip the edge of her fish into the mixture. She picked up a slice of the fatty tuna and put it in her mouth. She gasped. "I never imagined that a piece of fish could taste like this," she said. "It is so soft and luxurious." She liked the rich, cream-colored yellowtail almost as well. Then Mr. Uezu put slices of fluke on our boards; we dipped them into a citrus-scented ponzu sauce, admiring the clean, lean flavor of the fish.

"Spanish mackerel," said Mr. Uezu, holding up silver-edged slices of fish as the waitress set down dishes of ginger-scented sauce. The mackerel had an amazingly sumptuous texture, almost like whipped cream in the mouth. "It just dissolves when I take a bite," my friend said, amazed.

"Now sushi?" Mr. Uezu asked.

"Yes," my friend said. "Yes, yes." She was clearly hooked.

"One piece each?" Mr. Uezu asked. "In Japan we always serve sushi in pairs, but I like to serve sushi one piece at a time so you can taste more." His hands hovered over the fish in the case, selecting Japanese red snapper, crisp giant clam, small sweet scallops. "Can I use my fingers?" whispered my friend.

"Yes," I said. "But be sure to dip each piece into the soy sauce fish side first; it would be an insult to saturate the rice with soy and ruin the balance of flavors."

Raw shrimp as soft as strawberries was followed by marinated herring roe, which popped eerily beneath our teeth. Gently smoked salmon gleamed like coral. Then Mr. Uezu pillowed some sea urchin on pads of rice.

"It looks like scrambled eggs," my friend said. She took a bite. "I think," she said finally, groping for words, "that this is the sexiest thing I've ever eaten. Let's stop now."

"You must have a little green tea ice cream with red bean sauce for dessert," the waitress behind us said. "Mr. Uezu makes it himself. He makes everything."

Of course, we had to have that. It was barely sweet but very appealing. My friend looked down at the Christmas-colored dessert and said, "Who would have thought I'd find myself liking raw fish and bean sundaes?"

And then she was struck by an awful thought. "It's not always this good, is it?" she asked accusingly.

I had to admit that it is not.

There is nothing flashy about Mr. Uezu, and his restaurant has a deceptive simplicity. But after eating at Kurumazushi it is very hard to go back to ordinary fish.

KURUMAZUSHI

★ ★ ★

Miriam

My mother's blue silk dress fell over my shoulders and settled against my hips with eerie perfection. Smoothing the skirt, I reached up to clasp her pearls around my neck. As they clicked into place I could feel them nestle into my skin and begin to gently warm themselves. I wrapped myself in a robe and sat down to let Denise work her magic, keeping a wary eye on Claudia, who was slumped alarmingly into her seat.

"Are you all right?" I asked when Denise's work was nearly done. "You look as if you've seen a ghost."

"I have," said Claudia, going even paler. "I suggested this, but I was not expecting the transformation to be quite so dramatic. With the dress, the jewelry . . ." Her voice grew faint and she gestured helplessly toward the mirror.

I had found the dress in the back of my mother's closet after she died, hanging between the fake Pucci shifts and the jackets from Loehmann's; the scent of Joy still clung faintly to the fabric. It was beautifully cut, with a straight skirt and high neckline, and Mom had worn it for years. As I sorted piles for Goodwill, heaping up the bold prints and bright colors that my mother favored, I found myself putting the blue dress aside, along with the pearls that had belonged to my grandmother.

"Pearls like to be worn," Mom said every time she fastened them around her neck. "I hope you'll remember that when these are yours. Every time you wear them, they grow more beautiful." The pearls gave off a warm glow against the silky blueness of the dress, an effect that was far too quiet for my mother, who always completed the ensemble by splashing bright green eye shadow across her eyelids and pressing a tiny silver star onto each one.

"Like this?" asked Denise as she put the stars on my eyes. She had painted my short nails with the deep blue-red polish my mother always used; when I slipped on Mom's large moonstone ring, even my hands were playing the part. "Now look," she commanded, whirling the chair to face the mirror.

"My God" was all I could muster. And then we all went silent, staring at the reflection.

Claudia had been right: I had never noticed the resemblance, but if you dressed me up in my mother's clothes, hid my hair beneath a silver wig, and covered my face with wrinkles, I turned into a virtual replica of Miriam Brudno. "Are you aware," asked Claudia at last, "that when you said *gawd* it was in that Cleveland accent of your mother's? You even *sound* like her."

Molly had been a costume; putting it on made me realize that we all become actors, to some extent, when we go out to eat. Every restaurant is a theater, and the truly great ones allow us to indulge in the fantasy that we are rich and powerful. When restaurants hold up their end of the bargain, they give us the illusion of being surrounded by servants intent on ensuring our happiness and offering extraordinary food.

But even modest restaurants offer the opportunity to become someone else, at least for a little while. Restaurants free us from mundane reality; that is part of their charm. When you walk through the door, you are entering neutral territory where you are free to be whoever you choose for the duration of the meal.

When I became Molly, I merely took the theater of restaurants to the next logical step. Becoming my mother, on the other hand, was taking a giant leap beyond. The only thing I can compare it to is being so absorbed in a novel that you disappear into the fiction and feel emotions that are not your own. The moment the silver wig went on my head, I turned into someone else. It was stunningly unnerving.

I am nothing like my mother. No one is. She was a commanding figure who did not have a timid bone in her body. Frank, fearless, and totally tactless, she was a woman who said what she felt, did what she pleased, and let the chips fall where they might. Having spent most of my life being embarrassed by Mom, I was shocked to discover how easily I slipped into her shoes.

Finding out that it was fun was even more frightening. Becoming my mother was like getting cosmic permission to abandon my superego, act without considering the consequences, behave badly. It wasn't me, after all, doing these bold things, but it gave me an extraordinary sense of exhilaration.

"What are you doing?" asked Claudia, her voice rising when I went to the phone. She was still chalk white, and talking fast as if attempting to keep herself from fainting.

"Making a reservation," I said. My mother never walked; she advanced upon the world as if she were an invading army intent upon conquest. My rhythm, I found, had changed too. When Mom made calls she punched the numbers into the phone, as if the very pressure would speed the connection. And I was punching now.

"But this was just a dress rehearsal," wailed Claudia. "We're not going out tonight."

"Oh yes we are," I heard my voice saying. "I'm all dressed up and I want to go out." I punctuated this by thumping my foot firmly onto the floor. "Right now! I've always longed to go to 21, but Ernst felt we couldn't afford it. I've dreamed of this for years. Tonight's the night."

"I am not dressed for 21," mumbled Claudia, who was still the color of an egg. "Why don't you take Michael?"

"I would gladly take him if he were here," I replied, "but he's not. He's in Arkansas, working on another Whitewater piece."

"I am certain you must have some other friend who would like to go to dinner with you," Claudia said.

"I'm sure I do," I said, "but I don't want to wait. I want to do it right this minute. We're going to go to 21 and we're going to spend a great deal of money. We'll have cocktails. We'll have caviar. I've already made the reservation. Put on your coat, dear, we're going out."

My mother had been an irresistible force. Feeling her inside me, I swept Claudia up and propelled her out the door, paying no heed to signs of resistance.

Claudia shakily navigated the narrow steps that lead to 21, and she walked through the door with uncharacteristic diffidence. She was still lagging behind as we traversed the staid little lobby, tugging on my arm as if to hold me back.

But inside the dining room she emitted a little cry of protest. "*This* is 21?" she asked. It was a moan of disappointment. She looked at the red-and-white-checked napkins on the table, the long bar, and the low ceiling hung with thousands of toy trucks, airplanes, and football helmets. Her mouth formed a large circle of discontent. "It looks like a parody of an inexpensive Italian restaurant," she wailed. "It looks like a suburban recreation room. It looks as if it has not changed since it was a speakeasy."

"I don't think it *has* changed," I said as a maître d' led us inexorably toward the dim reaches of the rear. "I think that's supposed to be part of its charm."

Claudia snuffled unhappily. "This must be the worst table in the entire room," she noted when the maître d' finally came to a halt. "I am certain that all the important people are seated in the front."

She was right. What would Mom do? I surveyed the situation. "We need a martini," I decided, and let my mother take charge, waving my hand imperiously about to summon a waiter. When he finally materialized I firmly delineated our requirements. "Gin," I said. "Dry. With olives. Shaken, if you please, not stirred. I like them very, very cold."

Eating out with my mother was a terrible trial. Soup was never hot enough, meat was always too well done, salads were overdressed or underdressed or served at the wrong temperature. She sent everything back. Each time Mom went into her routine, I wanted to crawl under the table, but here I was, in a restaurant with her once again, and this time I was enjoying it. I watched the waiter approach with the martini and noted, with a kind of glee, that it was not in the distinctive triangular glass.

Suddenly I heard my mother's voice issuing from my mouth. "Martinis," it said, "never taste as good when they are served in wineglasses. But that can't be helped. But this one isn't cold, and that can. Take it back, please, and fetch me a cold one."

The waiter started to give me a who-do-you-think-you-are look, but I swept him with one of my mother's queenly glares and he changed his mind. "Yes, madam," he said.

Claudia watched this with bewildered fascination. But Miriam hadn't finished. "This menu," I allowed her to note, "is shocking. An appetizer of cold asparagus for sixteen dollars! Who spends this kind of money anymore?"

"My darling," Claudia pointed out, rousing herself, "it is not your money. Would you mind very much if I had oysters instead of caviar?"

"If you must," I said. "What will you have as an entrée?"

"Steak?" she asked. "Would that be acceptable?"

"Ask the waiter for his recommendation," I said. "Make him work for his tip. I think I'll have Caesar salad and steak tartare; they'll both have to be made at the table. That should be entertaining."

The waiter did his best to make us understand his limited interest in two old ladies. "You don't want that," he said curtly when I ordered the steak tartare. "It's raw."

This was extremely unwise. "I do, indeed," I told him, "but only if the meat is hand-chopped. Please inform the chef that if he tries to send me tartare that has been turned to mush in a food processor I will send it straight back."

"Yes, madam," he said for the second time.

Next we had to endure the sommelier's condescension. "Ponzi Reserve Pinot Noir?" he intoned in a slow, lugubrious voice. I had deliberately ordered one of the least expensive wines on the list. He sighed loudly. "Very well, madame." His manner was meant to convey the information that persons spending a mere fifty dollars were unworthy of his attention. Mournfully, he shuffled off. I watched him go with a look my mother had perfected, one that did not bode well for the next person approaching the table.

That turned out to be the waiter, with a tray of oysters. "Oh," I said as he set them on the table, "Malpeques." I sniffed. "Served with catsup and horseradish—what were they thinking?" I picked up my fork and poked one of the unhappy mollusks. "You can't eat these," I announced to Claudia as I summoned the waiter. "They've been out of the water too long."

"How can you tell?" asked Claudia.

I prodded the soft gray lips of the oyster. I thrust a tine straight into its rounded belly and watched it quiver. "See how dry it is?" I noted. "An oyster should have abundant liquid in the shell. This dryness could be the result of chipping, or the oyster might have been ineptly opened, but it's not a good sign. The real giveaway is the color. See how dull it is? When an oyster first comes out of the water, it is shiny, luminescent. It looks like"—I searched for something to compare it to—"this moonstone," I said, waving my mother's ring at her. "But the longer an oyster is out of the water, the duller it becomes. This, as you can see, has no shine at all." I sent the oysters back. Claudia bleakly watched them depart.

Then I dipped an exploratory spoon into my lobster–butternut squash bisque, noted that it was thin and sweet, and took another bite. No soup was ever hot enough for my mother, and this was no exception. Once again I summoned the waiter. "Tepid soup is not worth eating," I told him. "Please take it back and do not return until it is steaming." He started to pick up the bowl when I was struck by another thought. "And see that they take those chunks of lobster out beforehand. It would be a shame if they were to become tough."

He nodded and removed the offending soup.

Mom would have rejoiced in rejecting the asparagus as well. Unfortunately, other than the fact that the spears cost three dollars apiece, I could find no fault with them. But when the waiter made a Caesar salad, the Mom in me decided that he had overdone the anchovies. "I'm so sorry," I said sweetly, "but it's a bit fishy. Would you mind making me another?"

He glared at me. Then he cleared the plate and recommenced the operation. "Stop!" I cried. The waiter came to attention, salad fork in the air. "Are you sure that egg is coddled?" I asked.

"Yes, madam," he said. His voice now betrayed exasperation tinged with grudging respect. "It has been cooked exactly one minute."

"Very well," I said, keeping him under surveillance as he warily mixed the dressing. "Be careful with that cheese," I cautioned when he was nearing the end. "Too much will ruin your creation." Lifting his eyes to mine, he cautiously dusted the lettuce with grated Parmesan until I indicated that he was welcome to stop.

"Is it to your liking?" he asked anxiously as I took the first bite.

I felt one of my mother's triumphant little smiles cross my lips. I inclined my head, as she would have done. "Perfectly," I said. "You have outdone yourself." I waved him off and took another bite. As he rolled the cart from the table, relief was etched in every muscle of his back.

"Being an old lady can be extremely useful," my mother used to say. "I can get tickets to any Broadway show, even if it's sold out. When they tell me there are none, I simply stand there. The box office *always* has a couple of tickets, and in the end they let me have them, just so I'll go away. What else are they going to do?" I had known that Mom was proud of this talent, just as she was proud of her ability to put a waiter in his place. What I had not known was that, unbeknownst to me, I had absorbed every one of her tricks.

The onion rings were cold; I sent them back. There was too much

Worcestershire sauce in the steak tartare, and I considered rejecting it. "Don't, I implore you," Claudia pleaded. "This is starting to feel like the second act of *Taming of the Shrew,* and it has always made me uncomfortable."

"But you can't let them get away with treating you shabbily," I said. "If you don't insist on good service in restaurants, you have only yourself to blame."

Claudia said nothing. But when I decided that the fudge on my sundae was not sufficiently hot, I understood the look that crossed her face. She wanted to put the poor waiter out of his misery, if only to end her own.

The moment we were out the door, I pulled the wig from my head and released my hair from the nylon net. I ran my fingers through my curls, over and over, shaking myself out. "Free at last," I said.

Claudia looked at me. "Tell me," she asked, "did you actually believe any of those things you said in there?"

"No," I said, happy to hear that my own voice was back. "That was all Mom. She made a scene at every restaurant we ever ate in, and it always made me miserable. I'll eat almost anything rather than endure the trauma of sending it back."

"Your father felt the same way," said Claudia. "He once told me how uncomfortable he became when she started in."

"Lots of people feel that way," I said. "Last week I had lunch with the paper's wine critic, Frank Prial. When he tasted the wine he hesitated, and then rejected it with obvious reluctance. It was clearly corked, but when the sommelier went off for a replacement, Frank told me that even if the next bottle was off he planned to accept it. And then he said something that made great sense: 'What's the point in taking people out only to make them wish they weren't there?'"

"If only you had kept that in mind during dinner," lamented Claudia. "I would have preferred to be almost anywhere else on this earth." She closed her mouth and looked at me, and then her shoulders began to shake. I watched the laughter move into her face and then slowly begin to escape. Soon great peals of mirth were rolling down the dark street and I was laughing with her, although I wasn't quite sure why.

"It was rich," gasped Claudia when she had finally stopped long enough to breathe. She held her stomach and said, "Tonight we scored one for every old lady in New York." Then she gave in, once again, to the laughter. When it was over she grabbed my arms and looked squarely into my face. "If I were being entirely truthful, I would have to admit that I would not have missed that for the world."

"I'm glad you feel that way," I replied, "because tomorrow we're going to tackle a more difficult target."

"We are?"

"Oh yes," I said. "Tomorrow we lunch at the Four Seasons!"

I woke up the next morning with a sense of anticipation. Groping through the sleepiness, I tried to remember my plans for the day. And then it hit me: I was going to dress up like my mother. The notion pleased me just a little too much, and I realized that sometime in the near future I was going to have to think about why this disguise was such fun. But first I had to practice putting on Mom's makeup. I didn't want Nicky to wake up and discover that his mother had been replaced by a stranger—it would probably terrify him. But if I worked fast I could get the makeup on, and off, before he was out of bed. I went into the bathroom, taped the diagram Denise had given me to the mirror, spread the pots and brushes across the sink, and started in.

It was awkward work. Covering my face and eyebrows with the foundation was more difficult than I'd expected, and the more I began to look like my mother, the clumsier I became. I had been working for almost an hour when I realized that it was time to wake Nicky up. I reached for the tissues and the cold cream and then my heart stopped: the bathroom door had swung open and my son was standing there, watching me.

I caught his eye and he came padding into the bathroom in his electric blue Superman pajamas, red cape flying out behind him. He stared for a moment at the person I had become. And then he said simply, "Mommy, you look very silly," and left the room.

So much for terror. I turned back to the mirror and went on with the makeup. My colleagues had been begging me to show them one of my costumes, and today might be a good time to do it. I put on the blue dress, squirmed into the wig, and went to make breakfast. Nicky wrinkled up his nose at the strong smell of Joy. "What's your name?" he asked, as if it were the most natural thing in the world to see your mother dressed up in someone else's clothes.

"Miriam, Miriam, Miriam," he chanted when I told him. He was still chanting when we left the apartment. As the elevator door opened he turned to Gene, our large Irish elevator man, and said, "This is my friend Miriam."

Gene tipped his hat. He looked at me. "Morning ma'am," he said. "You must have arrived very early, before I started my shift."

"Yes," I said, "very early indeed."

Nicky stifled a giggle.

There is no place colder than a Number 5 bus stop in the middle of winter. The wind howls off the Hudson, sneaking down your collar and whistling up your sleeves. We jumped up and down; we rubbed our hands; we prayed the bus would show up. And here it came, slowly and majestically sailing down Riverside Drive, taking its time to kneel for the old people who lived in the neighborhood.

"Mommy, there are icicles in my hair!" Nicky cried, tears in his eyes from the stinging wind. "I'm so cold. Can't we go back to L.A.?"

"Look," I said, pointing down the street. I wrapped myself around him to provide a little warmth. "The bus is only two blocks away. It will be here soon. And there aren't really icicles in your hair."

"It feels like there are," he said reproachfully. "And if we were in Los Angeles, it wouldn't."

"If we were in L.A. I wouldn't be wearing this wig," I muttered as the door opened and an enormous woman lumbered slowly down the steps while we stood, shivering and helpless, watching her progress. She took her time. When she finally reached the ground and cleared the doorway, we rushed toward the bus, Nicky dancing up the steps, happy to reach the steamy warmth of the interior.

He dropped our coins into the box, listening to the satisfying pings, and then skipped toward the back of the bus. I followed, more slowly. When I reached the halfway point a man jumped up. Pointing to the place he had just vacated, he said politely, "Please ma'am, take my seat. You need it more than I do." Blushing furiously, I kept moving.

"Mommy," said Nicky loudly, "that man thought you were *old*."

I dropped Nicky at school and went on to the office, slipping and sliding through New York's winter mush in my mother's oversized shoes. Debris skittered up the street before me, crumpled cups, broken combs, and forlorn papers swirling in the icy air. Times Square seemed tired and sad, and walking these streets in my mother's clothes made me feel as if I were trespassing on a set for *The Twilight Zone*.

At the corner of Forty-third and Broadway I stopped to buy a donut. The man inside the cart was the unofficial mayor of the neighborhood; he knew everyone's order by heart. He did not have to be told that the woman in front of me wanted black coffee and a cruller, and by the time I reached him he was already spooning out extra sugar for the man behind me on the line. Normally he handed me a jelly donut and coffee without a word, but now he looked straight at me and asked, "What can I get you?"

Clutching the brown paper bag, I walked up the block and into the lobby. The guards, Al and Joe, were standing there as they did every morning. They were a study in contrasts: Al was rotund, balding, with a lifetime of meatball heroes spilling out of his uniform, while Joe was small and spare, with an economical face. Most mornings they unleashed a chorus of hellos when I walked in, but now Joe gave me an unfriendly look and pointed to the bank of phones. "Call the person you've come to see," he said mechanically.

"Don't you recognize me?" I asked.

"Just call upstairs," he said wearily, as if he had heard this a thousand times. "Even if I did recognize you, I'd need authorization."

"But I work here," I said.

"New, huh?" his partner piped up. "We haven't met. I'm Al. Got your i.d.?"

I pulled the card out of my purse and flashed it at him. Al peered at the picture. "You're not her," he said.

"I am," I insisted.

He looked at me more closely.

"It's a wig," I said.

He turned to Joe. "She says she's the restaurant critic."

"Nah," said Joe.

"Yes!" I reiterated.

Al stared hard at me. "Look," I said, pulling the wig up enough to pull out a lock of my own brown hair.

"I think it *is* her," said Al. "Whaddaya know about that!"

Joe was not convinced. "What's in the bag?" he asked suspiciously.

"You know what's in the bag," I said. "It's what's always in the bag." I opened the top and pulled out the donut.

"Jesus," said Joe. "It *is*."

They both gaped at me, shaking their heads. And then, finally, Al said what he said every morning. "You're the food critic. How can you eat those things?"

The leaden donuts were not only bad, they were bad for my reputation. But I loved the coffee cart guy, loved the New York ritual of stopping on the corner to exchange a few words. It made the paper, not the friendliest of places, feel more like home. The donut was truly terrible, but every morning I tore it in half, ate the jelly out of the middle, and threw the rest away.

If Bryan was there, I altered my routine and dumped the bag in the garbage unopened. I could easily imagine him marching into Warren's office, asking why the paper had a critic with taste so terrible that she ate fifty-cent donuts from the corner cart.

Bryan was not there, so I strolled self-consciously over to my desk, certain that all eyes were on me, sat down, opened the bag, and extracted the leaden lump of dough. But my entrance had gone unremarked. I took a bite and waited to see what would happen.

The Style section was an odd little enclave. We did not have much contact with the reporters downstairs in the newsroom, and we never saw the columnists who occupied the offices upstairs. And even though we shared quarters with Sports and Fashion, we food folk didn't see much of them either (although we did get to enjoy the parade of flowers delivered to Fashion on a daily basis).

My colleagues tended to make themselves scarce. Molly O'Neill worked mostly at home, so her pod was almost always empty. Marian Burros spent half her time in Washington, and Florence Fabricant was freelance and prohibited by union rules from having a desk of her own. Eric Asimov had the $25-and-under column to keep him out of the office, and Frank Prial came in so rarely that he and Bryan shared a single computer.

That left Trish Hall, who was too busy editing copy to have noticed my arrival. When I looked up from my donut, I found only four pairs of eyes focused upon me. One pair belonged to Alexandra Palmer, who sat across the aisle. She'd been the secretary in the Living section since the fifties, and she was dressed, as always, in a straight tweed skirt, her substantial bosom encased in a t-shirt, her feet clad in sensible running shoes. She had pulled her auburn hair severely back, but that could not disguise the extraordinary sweetness of her face.

As Alex thoughtfully examined me, I realized that nothing fazed her. I suspected she disliked her boss, but she never said a nasty word about him (or anyone else). She was a single woman with what looked like a miserable job, but she found dignity in everything she did and somehow seemed to enjoy her life more than the rest of us.

I wondered what her secret was and I openly eavesdropped on her conversations, hoping to discover it. It was, I think, selflessness; she lived a few blocks away, in one of New York's seedier neighborhoods, and appeared to have adopted every young person on her block. She was constantly counseling, cajoling, and commiserating with this odd cast of characters and I suspected she was about to add Miriam to her list of good works.

Elaine Louie was staring at me too. That worried me; I had known Elaine long before coming to the paper, and admired the pieces she wrote on design, fashion, and food. She, I was certain, would see through the disguise, and she would waste no time in unmasking me. I expected her to come up, laughing, at any moment and rip the wig from my head.

Suzanne Richie was worrisome too. The photo editor had a keen eye and would surely see the real Ruth lurking beneath the costume. But she went on talking into the telephone as if some weird white-haired person had not just plunked herself down at a desk.

In the end it was Carol Shaw who got up. Of course, I thought, as she walked toward me, how could I possibly fool Carol? She was a restaurant critic's dream, an adventurous eater willing to go anywhere and eat anything on a moment's notice, and she had become one of my eating companions. Unlike the editors, who wanted to be taken to fancy restaurants, Carol actually preferred the little Korean and Mexican joints around the office, and she was always ready to jump onto the Number 7 train and take a ride.

Now she was bearing down on me. I could feel my cheeks getting hot beneath the makeup. Then I noticed Alex hovering protectively behind her, a pair of scissors in her hand.

Carol cleared her throat. "Excuse me," she said. She was standing right over me now. "You can't sit here. You will have to move. I don't know who you are, but this desk belongs to our restaurant critic."

·   ·   ·

In the end they made me take off my wig and tell them about Claudia. It was all done with such good humor that I began to feel, for the first time, as if I might actually fit in at the paper. "Come back and tell us how it goes," Carol called as I left for lunch. "I can't wait to hear what happens at the Four Seasons."

Claudia lived on West Fifty-fourth Street, so I picked her up on the way. Yesterday she had come near fainting at the sight of her old friend, but today when she climbed into the taxi she seemed entirely comfortable. If she remembered that Miriam was no longer with us, she gave no sign. Today we were both playing a part.

As we drew up to the restaurant, I turned and said, "Before we go in, there's something I need to tell you."

"What?" she asked.

"We don't have a reservation."

"You failed to make a reservation?" she asked. "May I ask why?"

I gave my mother's meanest little laugh. "It's an experiment," I said. "I want to see how New York's most elegant restaurant behaves when two old ladies show up at the door."

"But it will be so embarrassing!" cried Claudia.

"Not to me," I replied. The little disturbances of life held no terrors for Miriam. "Besides, there are two rooms at the Four Seasons and they will surely have a table in the wrong one."

"Do you know which one is wrong?' asked Claudia as I helped her from the taxi.

My mother had not been an avid student of New York society in vain. "At lunch," I said, standing under the restaurant's awning, "you want to be in the Grill Room, so you can watch Henry Kissinger and Barbara Walters and Vernon Jordan work the power room. But at night you want to be in the Pool Room, because it's so much more romantic. I'm surprised you don't know that, dear."

"I certainly wish you had informed me of this plan," said Claudia.

"Would you have come?" I asked.

"Certainly not!"

"That's why I didn't."

"This," she said with a sigh, "feels lamentably familiar."

Claudia in tow, I traversed the cool lobby of the Seagram building. It looked the same as it had when I was ten, wearing the soft blue velvet dress my mother made me wear when we went out. "They have real Picassos!" she had insisted, "and a Richard Lippold sculpture hanging over the bar. Think of it as a museum. We'll have a drink, see who's there, and then go have dinner in a restaurant we can afford."

Passing the door to the ladies' room, I remembered my childhood confusion when the attendant held a towel out to me, offering cologne, lipstick, a hairbrush, for a final touch-up. I had wondered then what it was like to spend your life in a bathroom, offering towels to rich people, and I had been embarrassed for the woman, and embarrassed for myself when I took it from her hand. I wondered if there was still a woman standing in there by the sink, and made a note to check before the day was out.

But then I put my foot onto the first step and the attendant faded from my thoughts. I was feeling what my mother would have felt if she had been there, knowing that she was staying through the meal. I felt my mother's joy as I swept up the stairs, breathing in the affluent air. By the time I arrived at the top I was seeing it as she would, thrilling to the chains rippling seductively across the windows and the deep, private, underwater feel of the room. The Lippold sculpture still hung like bronze icicles above the bar, and my eyes swept across the vast carpeted floor, noting the enormous diamond here, the fabulous pocketbook there, as my ears adjusted to the luxurious murmur of money. With all my mother's confidence I marched up to the pale, cool man behind the reservation desk.

"We have no reservations," I said in my mother's coyest voice, "but we thought you might be able to find a seat in the Pool Room for two old ladies."

He glanced down at the scribbled names in the book and then he looked me over appraisingly. I gave him one of those flirtatious smiles my mother had perfected late in her life, the one that said, "I have lived a rich life and there are many things I could show you."

Our eyes held for a moment and then he made up his mind. "Of course," he said. "If you two young ladies will follow me?" And he led us down the hall, past the huge Picasso tapestry, and into the Promised Land.

It might have had something to do with the recently published Le Cirque review. I may have reminded him of his mother. Perhaps the management of the Four Seasons occasionally amuses itself by lavishing attention on perfect strangers. Or maybe he saw through the disguise. Whatever the reason, this was our day.

The maître d' led us to one of the tables that edges up against the square expanse of the pool. I put my hand on the white marble ledge, appreciating its cool smoothness as he pulled out my chair. As I folded myself into it he said, "Please allow me to send you some champagne." The tone of his voice implied that in accepting we would be doing him a great favor.

"Thank you," I said. The Miriam in me had expected no less. I languidly extracted a croissant from the silver curve of a bowl and perused the menu.

Across the table Claudia produced a deep sigh of contentment. When the champagne was poured, she picked up her flute and took a tentative sip. She smiled and took another.

Our appetizer appeared, a little roulade of silky smoked salmon cleverly wrapped around cream cheese so that it looked like a giant piece of orange taffy. The frilly green salad on the side was small and adorable, like something that belonged on a fancy Easter bonnet.

"Lovely!" said Claudia, as she pushed her empty plate away. "Truly lovely."

"I have something lovelier for you," said a man standing by our table with a plate in either hand. His face was all points—sharp chin, long nose, a crescent of hair falling into humorous black eyes that danced with fun. He juggled the plates so that they wiggled suggestively and then set one in front of each of us. "Risotto," he said, rolling the *r* so that his Italian accent became pronounced. A waiter hovered attentively next to him, holding a tray. "Since you are here at the height of truffle season," said the man, selecting a gnarled tuber from the tray, "you must celebrate with us."

"Truffles," said Claudia. "Oh, truffles, truffles, truffles." As the word came rolling from her throat it sounded rich enough to eat. "Truffles," she said once again in her deep voice. She clasped her hands like a diva at center stage and said dramatically, "The most divine food on earth."

She watched hungrily as the man began to shave curls of creamy white truffle over the top of her risotto. The aroma was so rich and damp that I was not surprised when Claudia leaned over the plate and inhaled. "Divine!" she said again, performing.

The man was amused. "Which do you prefer," he asked her, "black truffles or white ones?"

"White, most definitely," she said. "They have the most elusive fragrance on earth. And a flavor so subtle you can only detect it when you concentrate all your faculties."

"And you?" he asked, turning to me.

"Black," I heard myself saying. It wasn't true; I've always considered black truffles overrated. But it's what my mother would have said. I doubt that she had an opinion on the subject, but she would have liked contradicting Claudia; it made a more interesting story. And so I said, "Black truffles are so much earthier than white ones."

The man gave a shout of laughter. "Ah yes, earthy, very earthy," he said seductively. Was he flirting with me?

"I think that was Julian Niccolini," I whispered to Claudia. "He's one of the owners."

"I should hope he is!" she replied with some asperity. "I cannot think that the owners would be very happy to find their staff being so profligate with the truffles. Do you have *any* idea what they cost?"

"A vague inkling," I said, smiling. "Don't worry. If everything I've read about this place is correct, we'll be billed for every morsel. They may be nice, but they're not *that* nice!"

After the busboy whisked the plates away, the angular man returned. "You cannot leave the Four Seasons without tasting our foie gras," he said, motioning to a waiter who held out two small plates. "Tell me how you find the pears as an accompaniment," he continued as the waiter set a plate in front of each of us.

Claudia seemed to have gone into sensual overdrive. "To think," she said, taking a bite, "of all the years we did not come here . . ." Her voice was a dirge, a lament for lost meals she might have eaten.

When we were finished, the angular man returned, insisting that we taste the restaurant's newest dish, peppered loin of bison. "Just one bite," I said, "to be polite. I really cannot manage more."

But I was enjoying the moment for my mother, thinking how much pleasure it would have given her. One meal like this would have thrilled her for years. She didn't care about food, but she craved this feeling of being special, important, well cared for. She would have enjoyed what she was eating because of the way it was served. And so I took another bite and tasted it, really tasted it, with all my mind. The meat was wild, like the steaks of my childhood. It had heft and chew; it tasted like grass and sky and the Wild West, something strong and powerful in my mouth. And suddenly I uttered my mother's classic phrase, the one she used every time she found some food she really liked. "This," I said, "is the best thing I've ever eaten."

"Oh my darling," said Claudia. Her eyes filled with tears. "Oh my darling, how she would have adored being here."

Much more, I thought, than I ever would. And suddenly it came to me what being Miriam meant: it had allowed me to experience this meal in an entirely new way. My mother could be difficult, but when she was happy she was uniquely capable of abandoning herself to the moment. By becoming her I had shed the critic, abandoned the appraiser who sat at a distance, weighing each bite, measuring each dish.

I had originally put on a disguise as a way of fooling the restaurants, but now I saw that it was also a way of fooling myself. I had been ready, eager even, to know what it felt like to walk in someone else's shoes. And I had enjoyed it. The previous night I had relished every minute of my obnoxious performance. And now, reveling in the sheer luxury of this lunch, I began to wonder what other disguises were out there waiting for me, and what lessons I would learn from the women I would become.

Moules Marinières

When I think about my mother in the kitchen, I think about the two dishes she did really well. This was one. Most Americans didn't eat mussels in the fifties, and serving them made Mom feel sophisticated and slightly superior (not a bad trick for such an inexpensive dish).

In those days mussels were big, barnacle-encrusted things gathered at the shore, with long beards gripped tightly between their clamped shells. It always fell to me to scrub off the barnacles and remove the beards—a thankless task that took hours.

Today mussels are still cheap, but now they're easy as well. Farmed mussels are small, delicious, and so clean that all you have to do is rinse them and dump them into a pot. I don't know a faster or more satisfying meal.

4 pounds mussels
1 onion, diced

2 shallots, diced
1 cup dry white wine
3 tablespoons unsalted butter
Chopped parsley
Salt and pepper to taste

Wash the mussels.

Combine the onion, shallots, and wine in a large pot and simmer for 5 minutes. Add the mussels, cover, and cook over high heat, shaking from time to time, for about 4 minutes, or until all the mussels have opened. Discard unopened mussels.

Add the butter and chopped parsley. Season the broth to taste with salt and pepper. Serve in individual bowls, with an extra bowl for empty shells and a loaf of crusty bread to mop up the sauce.

Serves 4

Meat and Potatoes

When you made a mistake at the *L.A. Times,* an editor would take you aside, politely discuss where you had gone wrong, and suggest ways to avoid it in the future. When you made a mistake at the *N.Y. Times,* you were held up to public ridicule.

We all lived in mortal fear of "the greenies," the paper's exercise in self-criticism. Since the seventies, Al Siegal had been sifting through the paper every day, ferreting out mistakes. At one point he had written his pointed criticisms in bright green ink, but now when "the best of the greenies" were distributed throughout the newsroom, they were the work of many people and they were in plain black and white. We pored over the pages, eager to see who had committed crimes against journalism. Occasionally approving comments—"This is a sentence that makes a great paper proud!" or "Fine head; whose?"—appeared, but more often the comments were scathing. "Dull!" might appear next to an obituary, or an article on the former regime in Argentina might elicit a reproving "We prefer 'left' to 'departed.'" The ostensible idea was to learn from our colleagues' mistakes, but this fooled no one: we all knew that humiliation was the main object.

"What are you worried about?" Carol asked each time I mentioned my terror of showing up in the greenies. "Are you afraid you'll misidentify an herb? That word will spread throughout the city that the great and powerful critic of the *New York Times* doesn't know basil from marjoram?"

"Yes," I said, "that's exactly what I'm afraid of. Remember the flap when Bryan misidentified the color of a tablecloth?"

"Oh," she said confidently, "you'd never make a mistake like that."

But she was wrong. I did manage to elude the greenies—for all of five months. And then I wrote about steak.

In 1993 the city of New York was wallowing in steakhouses. For twenty years the combined forces of political correctness, a down economy, guilt, and California cuisine had conspired against this great American institution. Now the opposing forces of greed-is-good, an up economy, and pride in regional American food brought it back. In my first year at the *Times* half a dozen steak places set up shop. It was only the beginning: as New Yorkers grew richer, they began to see steak as a birthright and the consumption of red meat as their patriotic duty. Revised government grading standards had moved truly fine meat out of the supermarket, and restaurants rushed in to fill the void. It would have been impossible to be a restaurant critic in New York City and *not* write about steak.

I spent months researching a steakhouse roundup, eating at venerable old places and shiny new ones. I ate oceans of shrimp cocktails and acres of potatoes. I tasted every possible cut of steak, faithfully toting the leftovers home so I could retaste the meat in the morning. I called butchers all over the country to quiz them on their aging techniques. And as always, I agonized at the end, poring over the piece, looking for possible errors. I deleted the color of the napkins at one restaurant (Were they beige or brown? Better not to say at all) and the spice in the spinach at another (Nutmeg, I thought, but maybe there was also mace?). However, the lead sentence that read "If you are a native New Yorker, steak is in your blood" completely escaped my scrutiny.

The word police pounced. There, circled in the greenies, was the offending sentence. Next to it, written in a precise, angular script, was this comment: "What if you are Chinese? Latino? Beware of generalizations."

Mortified, I went slinking through the newsroom, wishing I had never written those words. Why hadn't I simply said what I meant? Which was: "Growing up in New York City, steak was an important part of my childhood." It was the truth, and no one could possibly have objected.

Every Saturday morning my father and I got up early to walk the sleepy streets of Greenwich Village, searching for a perfect piece of meat. We walked down Tenth Street to Greenwich Avenue, slowing to listen to the inmates in the Women's House of Detention call to their boyfriends in the street below. Sometimes when we turned into Sutter's Bakery on the corner, a raucous voice would shout, "Get some for me, baby," and I'd think how sad it was to be locked up. But then the warm brown smell of butter and sugar would wrap itself around me, chasing everything from my mind as I stood breathing deeply, thinking how good it was to be alive. By the time we left, munching on jam tarts, I'd forgotten all about prison and was as happy as I knew how to be.

We'd pass Balducci's and sometimes the grocer would come out to show us the glamorous strawberries that had just arrived, or the fine figs that were exclusively his, and the day would get even brighter. Together Dad and I would stop to read the slogan printed on Prexy's window: "The hamburger with a college education." Occasionally we'd press our noses against the plate glass at the Ideal Cheese Shop next door, and go in to buy a slice of real Gruyère to take home to Mom.

But no matter which route we took, our journey always ended at the narrow butcher shop on Jones Street, with its sawdust floor and its fine mineral aroma. The cases were filled with the bacon that they smoked themselves, pink and white strips spread out like gorgeous fabric, and a few pretty little lamb chops, red circles of meat clinging to elegantly long bones and decorated with frilly paper caps.

"Good morning, Jimmy," my father would say.

And Jimmy would look up and smile and seem delighted to see us.

He'd hand me a slice of salami, or some of the liverwurst he brought down from Yorkville, or sometimes the dried beef that he made when business was slow. "Fine morning," he'd say, even when it wasn't.

"We need a porterhouse, please," my father would say. And Jimmy would reply, "The finest steak there is!" as if the thought had occurred to him for the very first time. Then he would pull open the heavy wooden door, with its huge slab of a handle, and disappear into the cooler in the back. When he reappeared he was carrying what looked to me like half a steer, although it was really just the short loins that had been hanging for a few weeks, acquiring a fine patina of age.

Picking up a hacksaw, he'd indicate a cut: "This much?" And no matter how thick it was, my father always said, "A little thicker, please." And Jimmy would nod and cut off a substantial steak, humming as he worked. When he was done he'd hold up the steak and point out the fine veins of white tracing a pattern through the dense red meat. "Good marbling," he said admiringly every week, as if this steak was a special star. "All the flavor's in the fat. Cut off the fat, you can't tell the difference between beef, pork, and lamb. That's a fact. Did you know that?"

Then he'd thump the steak onto the chopping block and begin the ritual of trimming. First he'd cut the thick blue-black layer of mold from the outside of the steak, scraping it until the bright red flesh beneath the crust had been revealed. Then he'd carefully remove a few inches of fat from the edges so that only a creamy white frame remained. Carefully folding in the little tail end, he'd lay the meat on a piece of pink paper and heave it onto the scale.

"You're going to have a fine dinner," he'd say, as if the compliment were to the cook and not the cutter. "Don't be afraid of the salt."

"That's the secret!" my father always replied, carefully tucking the parcel under his arm. Waving cheerily, we'd walk out the door.

At home we had another ritual. Three hours before it was time to eat, my father would jump up from his chair and say, "No point in cooking cold meat." Together we'd go into the kitchen, remove the porterhouse from the refrigerator, carefully unwrap the package, and set the steak on a platter lined with wax paper. When it had thrown off the chill, Dad would salt it, releasing a small blizzard over the meat. "The secret to a great steak," he always said, "is that when you think you have enough salt, you add some more. The other secret," he'd say as he got out the big cast-iron skillet, "is to heat the pan until it's blazing hot and cook the meat exactly eight minutes on each side."

"And the final secret," I'd add, doing my bit, "is the butter." My job was to plunk a lump of sweet butter onto the sizzling steak just as my father set it on the platter.

My father carved the steak with long, precise strokes of the knife, carefully separating the sirloin that he and my brother preferred from the tenderloin that my mother favored. The bone was mine.

While they plied their forks like civilized people I'd bring the bone up to my face until the aroma—animal and mineral, dirt and rock—was flooding my senses. Then I'd bite into the meat, soft and chewy at the same time, rolling it around in my mouth. It was juicy, powerful, primal, and I'd take another bite, and another. The meat closest to the bone was smooth as satin, and sweet. It tasted like nothing else on earth, and I would gnaw happily until the bone was stripped naked and my face was covered with a satisfying layer of grease.

Could you still find a steak that good? Myron Rosen, the Weekend editor, was thrilled when I said I wanted to try; he promised me the front page of his section for my steakhouse roundup.

"Great! We can take Nicky with us," said Michael when I told him that massive amounts of meat were in our immediate future. "Steakhouses are loud and fast—perfect for a five-year-old."

"Yeah," I said, "and every one of them serves French fries."

I'm helping Mommy with her work," Nicky confided to Gene as we set off for the first steakhouse.

"Are you now?" asked Gene, stepping aside so Nicky could drive us down to the ground floor. "What might you be doing?"

"I'm the potato man," he said proudly, bringing the elevator in for a bumpy landing.

"Good for you, buddy," said Gene, taking over the controls, "important work. New York is depending on you! Bundle up, now—it's wicked out there."

The city was having its bitterest winter on record, and the icy dampness crept through your boots and entered your bones. We stepped outside to find the wind howling angrily off the river. The moon hung above us, aloof and silver in the noisy night, as we struggled up the street.

I had wrapped Nicky in so many layers that he looked like a walking snowball. As he stood next to Michael in the frozen slush, trying to flag down a taxi, his face glowed and his nose dripped.

"If we don't find a cab in three minutes, we're going home," muttered Michael. "It's too cold. Besides, I hate the Palm; the waiters can be such jerks."

"My mother felt the same way," I said. "She always said they threw the food at you."

"Really?" asked Nicky, perking up at this news. "Do they get extra points for hitting you in good places?"

A taxi came sputtering and sliding, skidding to a stop in front of us, so I was not obliged to answer this question. And by the time we were settled, Nicky had moved on to French fries. "Do they have the fat kind or the skinny kind?" he wanted to know.

"Something even better," I promised. "Hash browns."

"What's that?" he said.

"Just wait," I said. "You're going to like them. They're like a cake made out of potatoes, and nobody does them better than the Palm."

Nicky considered this as we rode, snuggled together in the back of the cab, happy to be warm. There wasn't much traffic on this frigid night, and we went shooting through the streets at rocket speed.

The Palm smelled of hope and garlic and grilling meat. Vast crowds stood in the sawdust, clawing their way to the front of the line, desperate to lay claim to one of the uncomfortable chairs. Waiters rushed past, bearing enormous platters of food.

Michael put Nicky on his shoulders so he could see the action. "Nobody's throwing food!" Nicky reported disconsolately, "and I can't see the palm trees."

"There aren't any," I said, happy that I'd read up on the restaurant's history. "The name was a mistake. When they opened in 1926 the owners wanted to call it 'Parma.' But they had thick Italian accents, and when they registered the name the clerk thought they were trying to say 'Palm.'"

"That was lucky, wasn't it," said the consummate Los Angeles kid as he climbed down from Michael's shoulders. "They got a better name."

Our waiter started frowning when he saw three people approaching his prime four-top, and he looked even unhappier when he realized that one of us was only three feet tall. I could see him mentally calculating the tip and not liking the equation. Still, he perked up when Michael and I each ordered steak. And when Nicky asked for lobster he tried to be nonchalant as he mentioned that the smallest one they had weighed five pounds.

"That's okay," I said.

I watched him struggle with himself a moment, and then his better nature won. "You sure?" he asked. He pointed his chin at Nicky. "It's bigger than him."

"That's okay," I said again. "Whatever he can't eat we'll take home." The man recalculated his tip and grew visibly warmer.

"Hash browns?" he asked. If he wondered why two adults and one small child were ordering a mountain of food, he kept the question to himself.

The steaks were good enough, but the meat couldn't hold a candle to the steaks that Jimmy used to cut for Dad. But then, I hadn't expected them to. The hash browns, however, which spilled sloppily across the plate, were a major disappointment.

"You said it was a cake!" said Nicky accusingly.

"Something wrong?" asked the waiter.

I held up the messy pile. The man picked up a fork and prodded the potatoes. His lip curled. He looked down at Nicky. "Ever have hash browns before?" he asked.

"No," said Nicky, "but my mommy said that yours are the best in the whole world." In a smaller voice he added, "I think I'd rather have French fries?"

"Now wait a minute," said the waiter, his pride obviously wounded. "Our hash browns *are* the best. Let me get some fresh ones." He turned, reconsidered, came back, and asked, "Would you like to see how they're made?"

Nicky nodded. The waiter took his hand. "Come with me." And together they trotted off to the kitchen.

Great steaks aren't cooked, they're bought; the important work is done before you ever leave the shop. Hash browns, however, are a different matter: They give a cook the chance to shine. Done well, they are a textbook on texture. Perfect hash browns are simultaneously crisp and tender, salty and sweet, black and white. When Nicky returned, he was carefully carrying the potatoes beneath the waiter's watchful eye. Settling in at the table, he took a bite. Then he took another. And one more. Soon every morsel of potato had disappeared.

"You were right, Mommy." He sighed happily. "Hash browns are *much* better than French fries." He smiled and said, "Do you want to know the secret?"

"Oh no, young man," said the waiter solemnly. He wagged his finger. "You must never tell. Remember? The recipe goes with you to the grave."

Nicky looked up. "Cross my heart," he said.

Hash Browns

Making these remain in a cake is very difficult and requires a fair amount of practice. But they're delicious even when they fall apart, so keep trying.

A few hints: I use a Spanish tortilla plate, which is made precisely for the turning maneuver (it has a knob on the bottom), which makes things easier. And if you have a short-sided skillet, it is much easier to slide the cake out; the high sides of an ordinary cast-iron skillet mean that you have to turn quickly in one smooth fast motion. And that requires strength.

8 small waxy potatoes (new potatoes), 2¼ pounds
6 tablespoons unsalted butter
½ small onion, very finely diced
Salt and pepper
Coarse salt for sprinkling on top

Bring a saucepan of water to a boil, add the potatoes, and boil about 10 minutes, or until they are cooked about halfway through. Drain, and allow them to cool to warm; then peel and chop into about 1-inch squares.

Melt the butter over medium heat in a well-seasoned 8- to 10-inch cast-iron skillet. Remove about a quarter of the butter and set aside. Add the potatoes to the skillet, forming them into a flat cake and pressing down on it with a spatula. Cook, uncovered, over medium heat for about 6 minutes, until a good crust has formed on the bottom. Keep pressing with the spatula, and run it around the edges a bit so the potatoes don't stick.

Scatter the diced onions over the top, along with a good shake of salt and a good grinding of pepper. Remove the skillet from the heat and cover with a large plate; leave for 2 minutes, allowing the potatoes to steam. Using oven mitts, hold the plate and a skillet together and invert together, so the potatoes drop onto the plate.

Put the skillet back over medium heat and add the remaining melted butter. Carefully slide the entire potato cake into the skillet, trying not to break it. Add more salt and pepper, turn the heat up to medium high, and brown the potatoes for another 5 minutes, until a crust forms.

Slide the potato cake onto a hot platter, sprinkle with the coarse sea salt and serve immediately.

Serves 4

Note: You can use bacon fat or duck fat, or, if you are very lucky, goose fat for these potatoes as well. You can also gussy them up a bit by adding diced parsley or diced garlic at the very end, as they do at L'Ami Louis in Paris.

Palm's potatoes were a hard act to follow, and as we ate our way through the steakhouses of the city—through Gallagher's, where the waiters were extraordinarily kind to children, and Christ Cella, where they were not, through Pietro's, and Pen and Pencil, and Smith and Wollensky—I watched my son struggle with the memory of his first hash browns. He soon expanded his repertoire to include cottage fries and steak fries and potatoes O'Brien, but none measured up to the masterful hash brown. He went on to sample the potatoes at the Old Homestead, Ruth's Chris, Ben Benson's, and Frank's. But at the end, when we were beginning to wrap up our research, he discovered a whole new class of potato.

It happened at the brand-new Morton's in midtown, where we watched with rapt attention as a cart laden with raw meat was trundled toward us. Nicky listened intently as the waitress held up one plastic-wrapped piece of meat after another. In her hands each filet, strip steak, and porterhouse became an actor auditioning for an important part in our meal. When she had finished showing off the meat, she allowed the potatoes their shot at stardom.

Nicky was entertained, but Michael and I both found this show so silly that we started looking around the room, trying to find some distraction to keep us from laughing out loud. While Michael stifled his mirth by focusing on the LeRoy Neiman prints, I peered through the expensive gloom at my fellow diners and began to experience a prickly sense of déjà vu.

"Look, Mommy," said Nicky, tugging at my sleeve, "look at the potatoes. See how big they are!"

The waitress was holding up giant tubers, magnificent spuds of Falstaffian proportions. I'd never seen anything like them. "Those will make good hash browns," Nicky said confidently. "Can I go into the kitchen and watch them cook?"

"Probably not," I said without thinking. "The kitchen's pretty small."

Michael and Nicky both looked at me quizzically. "How do you know that?" Michael asked. "You said this was your first visit."

"It *is*," I said, puzzled myself. "But it feels so familiar." And suddenly I had it! "I *have* been here before—but it was a long, long time ago."

"Before I was born?" asked Nicky. "That long ago?"

"Yes, sweetie," I said. "Way before you were born. The last time I was here, I was just about your age."

Manhattan in the fifties was paved with dim little French restaurants with red velvet walls. They were everywhere. They looked the same, they smelled the same, their menus were interchangeable. They all served coq au vin, filet of sole, and consommé à la something or other.

The chefs in these establishments came and went; the waiters came and stayed. You chose your restaurant for the waiter. And my parents chose the Dubonnet for Max, visiting him two or three times a week.

Probably it was an ordinary restaurant, but I remember it as a magical place of endless treats: Max gave me whole glasses filled with maraschino cherries and bowls of chocolate mousse large enough to drown in. Sometimes he showed up with adorable white bunnies that turned out to be made of mashed potatoes, or rare tidbits of tenderloin cut into tiny squares that fit perfectly into my mouth. But the biggest treat of all was when Max took me to the kitchen.

Together we would parade across the crimson carpet, past all the ordinary people doomed to spend their ordinary evening in the dining room, and push through the swinging doors into the warm, bright domain of the cooks.

"Get that brat out of here," the chef always shouted when he saw me. "You know I hate children." But as he spoke a sautéed mushroom or a slice of apple was flying toward me, the first of the many little gifts he would bestow upon me before evening's end.

If it was a slow night he and the sous-chef would tie an apron around my waist and demonstrate the art of making radishes into roses, or turning potatoes into perfect rounds. As Max hovered watchfully in the background they would have omelet races, arguing over who could flip his higher into the air. On busy nights they sat me on the counter, handed me a dishcloth, and had me carefully clean the edge of each plate just before it left the kitchen.

Sometimes my parents lingered after the other guests had gone, and the chef would say, "Let's play the spice game." He'd wrap a dishcloth around my eyes and hold one canister after another beneath my nose. "Tarragon," I'd cry when the dark licorice scent assaulted my senses, and the cooks would cheer. When a dusty smell hit the back of my throat before it hit my nose I knew it was the turmeric they used to color their curries, and when the smell was wild and musty and brown I recognized the juniper berries used in game stews. They held bottles of rum extract (like butterscotch), cooking sherry (nutty, slightly sour), and Worcestershire sauce (sweet, tangy, mysterious) under my nostrils and if I identified them all correctly, they'd thump each other on the back and fête me with lemon cookies.

But what I liked even better were the times Max took me into the private dining room where the waiters went to smoke. We'd sit in that tangle of extra chairs and scarred wooden tables as he and Bruno and Jacques traded stories, reaching back farther and farther into their memories.

The best stories always began "When my father was a waiter . . ." Hearing that, Bruno would light a cigarette, Jacques would sip his wine, and I would cross my legs beneath me and hold my breath.

"When my father was a waiter," Max said, clearing his throat, "people did not receive remuneration from the restaurant. No, no, my friends, it was not as it is today. Back then people paid for the privilege of collecting tips. And let me tell you, the competition for the grand establishments, for Sherry's and Delmonico's and Rector's, was fierce.

"But those were different days, a time when the word 'diet' had not spread its blight across the land to ruin everybody's appetite. Today your average diner indulges in an appetizer, an entrée, and maybe, just maybe, if he's feeling flush, a tiny tidbit of dessert. But in those days? Oh yes, my friends, back then people knew how to eat. Why, Diamond Jim would eat four dozen oysters and a gallon of orange juice before he even ordered dinner. And those were manly oysters, six inches from one end to the other, not these puny little creatures that huddle in their modern shells. And Miss Lillie Langtry, why, she would match him oyster for oyster, swig for swig, as if her honor was in it. That was, you understand, just a little snack to wet their whistles, provide them with the fortitude to contemplate the menu. Theirs, my friends, was a table worth waiting on. The eating lasted through the night: whole herds of cattle and braces of birds were demolished before the evening ended. And on good nights my father would come home with silver jingling in his pockets and ducks dangling from his fingertips. Oh yes, my friends, in those days, being a waiter was a wonderful thing."

"It's good now too, Max, isn't it?" I'd ask, slipping my hand anxiously into his. "Think of all the people you make happy!"

And Max would twinkle down at me and say, in his most courtly manner, "Thank you very much. Sometimes I need reminding." And then, very gently, he would lead me back into the kitchen and through the swinging doors into the dark, hushed, perfumed air of the Dubonnet, where my parents were still sipping wine and talking in the low voices that meant that they were having a very good time.

And on those nights, with my mother smiling and my father looking at her as if she was the best thing in the whole world, I wished that we could live at the Dubonnet, where nobody worried about money, the food was never burnt, and only good things ever happened.

I hadn't thought about the Dubonnet for many years, but now I could feel the ghost of Max hovering in the room, and I was grateful to Morton's for restoring him to me. And a few days later I went to Peter Luger and discovered an entirely different doorway to the past.

As the waiter walked across that great barn of a restaurant, the meat aroma grew so intense that I was suddenly back in Jimmy's shop. The scent of steak was like the sound of a trumpet cutting through the air, so high and clear that it triumphed over every other sense. Then the soft richness was filling my mouth, and it was a taste as old as I was and for a moment I merged with the flavor so that I had disappeared completely. *This* was a great steak. I had found what I was looking for. I had another piece, and then I was chewing on the bones and picking out the marrow and chasing all the tender little bits that hide between the fat and the bone.

By the time we were done with dinner I was covered in meat juice from head to foot. But I didn't care: I had discovered that I could go back in time whenever I wanted. All it took was an old-fashioned piece of steak.

· · ·

Working on the steak roundup piece made me happier than I remembered feeling since we'd moved to New York. But being in the greenies ruined it, and it was a long time until I wrote about another steakhouse. Now and then I took Nicky to the Palm for hash browns, and I sometimes sneaked back to Peter Luger for a taste of the past, but I kept that to myself. It was not until a few years later, when a reporter asked where I spent my own money, that it came to me that Peter Luger deserved a full review. Of course I gave it three stars.

That set off another flap. I may have been unaware that Bryan Miller had considered the restaurant worthy of no more than a single star, but his fans were not. Taking my review as one more sign of my unsuitability, they wrote in to remind my editors of this fact.

I didn't mind: controversy is good for a critic. Little did I know that my steak problems were not behind me.

One day near the end of my tenure, my boss motioned me into his office. John Montorio's title was Style Editor, but his style was decidedly un-*Times*ian. Brash, noisy, and very smart, he was the son of a bricklayer and took up more emotional space than the paper generally allotted its editors. He was funny and gossipy, stormed through the newsroom like a bull in a china shop, and made no bones about the fact that he had come up the hard way. His editorial sense was impeccable, but he seemed to spend a fair amount of time thinking of ways to get promoted. Now he looked me straight in the eye and said, "You're making my life miserable."

"How?" I asked, watching him run a hand across his head and wondering, as we all did, whether he was wearing a toupee.

He gave his hair a final tug and said, "Last year I had to go have lunch with one of the paper's bigger advertisers to explain why, even though you are always writing about steak, you never choose to write about the steak in *his* restaurants. That's okay, that's my job, I don't mind. But you go five years without a single correction, and then you make a mistake about Sparks. Sparks!"

"Oooh," I said, beginning to understand.

"That's not a good place to make a mistake about!" he said.

"I'm sorry," I said, feeling a little sick. The greenies are bad; corrections are worse.

"And it wasn't even about food!" he fumed. "It was about art!"

"I'm sorry," I said again.

"Don't criticize the art if you don't know what you're talking about!"

"Have you seen the paintings they have hanging in there?" I asked, trying to make John smile. He was not in the mood.

"You could have called them ugly," he said. "That's an opinion, and you have a right to it. You could have called them atrocious, or repulsive, or even ludicrous. But you cannot call them ersatz, for Christ's sake. That is not a judgment. That's a fact."

"I know," I said, "but ersatz is such a great word."

He groaned.

In a Diner's Journal article about the newly expanded Sparks, I had written this: "The new restaurant is huge and slightly tacky, so filled with ersatz old things that it looks more like a steakhouse designed by Disney than one in the beating heart of Manhattan."

The owners were furious. They sent a registered letter assuring us that all the antiques were genuine and could be documented. They said that their Hudson River School paintings had been characterized as one of the better collections. They insisted that all the ugly old cabinets were made by Horner, who was not only one of the greatest American furniture makers of all time, but a New Yorker to boot. They demanded a correction.

They got one. "I'll do even better," I promised John. "I like the place. They serve good steak. I'll write a full review."

"Fine idea," he said.

And so, for the first time in my life I set out to review a restaurant with my mind already made up.

Giving Sparks a good review should have been easy. It is, after all, a perennial favorite with New York critics, who are charmed by its meat, its wine list, and its background. Although Sparks is an infant in the venerable pantheon of New York steakhouses, it acquired instant history in 1985 when mob boss Paul Castellano was gunned down right in front. New Yorkers love a Mafia connection, and the restaurant's reputation was made.

"You're going to like this place," I promised Nicky as we opened the door. He was older now, and it took more than hash browns to win his endorsement. "They do this thing with the tablecloths, a sort of magic act where they whip them off without removing the plates."

"I *am* going to like that," he replied confidently.

But by the time we got to the magic plates, Nicky was fast asleep with his head on the table. We had spent forty-five minutes waiting to be seated, jostled by an ever-increasing crowd of growingly disgruntled people. The maître d', who glared at us when he saw that we had a child in tow, had no sympathy for our distress.

"This is ridiculous," said Michael after twenty minutes. "Let's leave."

"We can't," I pointed out. "I've *got* to review this place."

"But I'm so hungry," he said morosely. "If we aren't seated in fifteen minutes I'm going to call and order a pizza. I'll have it delivered right here."

"You can't," I pleaded, thinking of John. "Please don't."

Fortunately our table beat the deadline. Unfortunately the service was terrible, the steaks were worse, and Nicky found the hash browns so sad that they put him to sleep. He woke up in time to taste the tartufo, took one bite, and put his head back down on the table.

"Are you telling me," said Michael as he carried our sleeping son out the door, "that you're going to write a good review of an ugly restaurant that doesn't honor reservations and serves terrible food?"

"This was just a bad night," I said optimistically. "Every restaurant's entitled to one. It's usually much better."

"Okay," he said, "we'll give them another chance."

But things got worse. One night we were seated next to a group of drunken stockbrokers. Another night I showed up for my confirmed reservation only to find the restaurant closed. At other times the food came undercooked, overcooked, and overdressed. In the end I took a fellow critic along, hoping that he'd be recognized and get a great steak. He was, and he did—but mine was terrible. The two of us sat there, tasting the two steaks side by side, completely flummoxed by the experience.

"You told me that you liked the place!" cried John when he read the review.

"I thought I did," I said, "but further investigation proved me wrong. You wouldn't want me to pull my punches, would you?"

"Of course not." He sighed and let the matter drop.

But a few months later John called me back into his office. "I just had a meeting with the owner of Sparks," he said.

"Uh-oh."

"You can say that again. He told me to, and this is a direct quote, 'order up a positive story and put it on the fucking front of Dining.'"

"You're kidding!" I said.

"No," he said, "I'm not. He even had the chutzpah to tell me when to do it. He said I should blame it on 'the old man.'"

"The old man?"

"Yeah, to tell my subordinates that the senior Mr. Sulzberger told me to do it."

"What did you tell him?"

"After I caught my breath and counted to ten," said John, "I told him we simply don't operate like that. And you know what he said? He said, 'Oh yeah? Don't be fucking naive.'"

"What are you going to do?" I asked.

"Nothing," he replied wearily. "But do me a favor, okay? From now on, stay away from steak."

WHERE STEAK IS BOTH KING AND JESTER
by Ruth Reichl

....

KURT VONNEGUT JR. does not seem happy. The author has been hanging around the entryway of Sparks with the actor Albert Finney and about 20 other hopeful diners. The maitre d'hotel does not seem in the least concerned that we are squashed into an uncomfortable crowd, and he is brusque with those of us who ask when our tables will be ready. After about 20 minutes, Mr. Vonnegut's party leaves, and as I watch the men walk through the door, I find myself wondering if there is another restaurant in America where people of such stature would be kept cooling their heels.

In the end, we wait 40 minutes for our reservation, but it is some consolation to know that Sparks does not play favorites.

The problem is that it does not play favorites with the steaks either. I have had terrific steaks at Sparks. I have had mediocre ones, too. Sometimes on the same evening. And although lobster is usually excellent, there have been nights when it was a disaster. Late last year, Sparks expanded into the space next door, once occupied by Arcimboldo, and the kitchen seems to be struggling. Hash browns are not always crisp, meat is often overcooked, and almost everything is oversalted. But there are two things of which you can be absolutely certain when you are finally seated: the service will be cheerful, and the wine list will make up for almost everything else.

It is, however, possible to improve your odds of getting a great meal at Sparks. I hereby offer these guidelines.

• Dine on Saturday night. At Sparks, unlike other restaurants, Saturdays seem slow. You are more likely to be seated immediately, and you are unlikely to be seated next to a group of 13 drunken stockbrokers celebrating their bonuses, as I was one Wednesday night. "How much did they spend?" I asked our waiter when the table terrorizing us finally departed, "Oh, not much," he said, flipping open his order pad. "They only had four double magnums and a bottle of port. Just a couple grand."

• Don't bring a crowd. Maybe it is just coincidence, but the best meal I had at Sparks was the night I took only one guest. Everything came out piping hot, and both the steak and the lobster were superb.

• Watch what others eat. You don't see anyone around you eating hot seafood appetizers, and there is a reason for that. The baked clams are very bready and not very baked. You don't see anyone eating melon either. The appetizers of choice are shrimp cocktail (served butterflied and flat on the plate), lump crab-meat, and a sliced tomato and onion salad. The cognoscenti, you will note, ask to have their tomato salads chopped and topped with Roquefort dressing, which makes a very American and curiously deli-cious treat. You will also find that many around you are eating as-paragus vinaigrette. It is not on the menu, but it is very good.

• Stick to plain steak and chops. The menu is filled with froufrou food like medallions of beef in bordelaise sauce, steak fromage (topped with Roquefort cheese) and beef scalop-pine (sliced filet with peppers and mushrooms). The kitchen seems to have utter contempt for someone wanting anything so effete, and nei-ther the meat nor the sauce is on the same level as the straightforward dishes. Incidentally, the most reli-able dish I have found is lamb chops, which are always delicious.

• It you want seafood, have lobster. Lobster at Sparks is usually reli-able, although once it was so tough I wish I had sent it back. Fish are treated as if they were silly intrud-ers, and those who order chunks of lobster meat and broiled shrimp in lemon butter sauce are going to get what they deserve. This is, after all, a steakhouse.

• Don't be embarrassed to send it back. The steaks are prime and aged in a combination of wet and dry aging. The quality varies, and you can only pray you will get one of the great ones. But you don't have to pray about the cooking; if it is not as you like it, ask the waiter to take it back to the kitchen. If you ordered rare meat, you shouldn't have to eat it well done.

• Don't expect much from the hash browns. Unfortunately, I have never had a great plate of hash browns at Sparks. They should be crisp on the outside, soft within and very hot. I wonder if the kitchen even knows how to make them? Buttered spinach, on the other hand, is bright green and delicious.

- Drink your dessert (unless you're having cheesecake). Skip the tartufo, the berries and the ice cream, and note that there are terrific ports, Sauternes and late-harvest wines that would make a very sweet ending to the meal.
- Confirm your reservation. Sparks can be very casual when you call.

I once made a reservation for Sunday night only to show up and discover that the restaurant was closed. Sparks, it turns out, is never open on Sunday.

SPARKS STEAK HOUSE

★

Chloe

I liked the black satin suit the minute I saw it at Michael's Resale. The jacket was simple, tight, cut low, with a little flare at the bottom. The skirt was short, with three tiers. It fit me perfectly—more than perfectly. It made me look elegant, thin, put together. Glancing in the mirror, I caught a flash of leg. Then my eyes moved upward and I witnessed an instant metamorphosis. What I saw was a woman who stood up very straight, so she appeared taller. Her hands had long red fingernails and her smooth, pale face was framed by silky, champagne-colored hair. As I watched, the person who belonged inside that suit invented herself. She even told me her name. When I took off the jacket, it said "Chloe."

I went straight from Michael's to the wig shop on Fifty-seventh Street. I'd never been inside, but I'd often walked past the elegant showroom, with its long spills of human hair, and I felt that Chloe deserved the best of everything.

Inside it was all sunshine and glass, with the smell of oranges and fresh wax wafting through the air. The wigs were artfully displayed on mannequins all around the room. Some wore jewelry and a few had lovely hats to set them off, but one was unadorned, long honey-color tresses that rippled in the light like liquid butterscotch. I reached to touch the soft strands, but before I could make contact a salesman sauntered purposefully toward me. He looked me over coldly, hooked his fingers into his belt loops, and said curtly, "That's not for you."

I stopped, my hand in midair, looking longingly at the wig. The man kept his eyes fixed on me as he removed his fingers from his belt and crossed his arms over his chest so that his entire body was a giant *no*. "Trust me," he said, "you'd look ridiculous." His lips curved downward into a sour smile as his cold gray eyes considered me. "Why is it that you girls with frizzy hair all dream of being blondes?" For a moment I was back in high school, a loser, watching the sleek blonde cheerleaders from the sidelines. I longed to try the butterscotch wig on, but I couldn't seem to get the appropriate words out of my mouth.

The man knew exactly what I was thinking. "Believe me," he said, and now his voice had changed and there was a glimmer of what might be sympathy in his eyes, "the silky one's not for you." His voice was gentler, and I thought perhaps we understood each other; the high school blondes had not been kind to him, either. "When your hair starts falling out," he continued, "you'll be much happier with a more natural look."

I stared at him, nonplussed. As I began to apprehend his meaning, I wondered if I should take advantage of the mistake. But before I could say anything, he added, "I know, I know, you're thinking that it sometimes grows back straight. I'm not saying it doesn't occasionally happen, but you won't know for a while, will you?"

He moved to his left and picked up a short black wig, its stick-straight hair cut into a Louise Brooks bob. "You could try something like this," he said, looking dubiously down at the wig as he twirled it on the end of his finger, "but I don't recommend it."

I had yet to open my mouth, and now the freight of his assumptions had piled up until my skin was crawling with embarrassment. I went back to the butterscotch wig, caressed the glossy hair, and finally found some words. "I don't have cancer," I said. "I'm not about to undergo chemotherapy."

The man's face went slack and I watched all the compassion drain out, like water from a sink whose plug has just been pulled. "You're not?" he said sullenly. "I just assumed." He reached to touch my hair, fingered it, and announced, "Well, if you want to wear a wig, you'll have to lose this one way or another. You can't put a wig on top of a bush."

"I'm not cutting my hair," I said.

"Then you're not getting a wig," he replied. "At least," he added, placing Louise Brooks firmly back on the bald mannequin, "you're not getting one here." And then he turned around and walked away. No longer a sympathy case, I had been dismissed.

I went outside and considered my next move. I could go down to the little cubbyhole on West Fourteenth Street where the transvestites shopped for hair. The Chinese couple who ran the crowded shop didn't care what you tried on, so long as you bought a wig cap before you began. The shop was filled with hair in every imaginable hue and shape, but it was all so cheap that I was afraid the wigs would self-destruct as I ate, leaving the strands swimming in my soup.

And then I remembered what the paper's gorgeous new fashion reporter had told me. Amy Spindler had stopped at my desk one day to say that I would look great in Romeo Gigli dresses. When I said I couldn't afford designer fashions, she offered to take me shopping at a discount department store down by the World Trade Center. As we talked she absently stroked Molly's wig, which was lying on my desk. "You can probably do better than this," she said. "Have you tried the wig shops in the thirties?"

This was my chance.

The garment district was laced with hair emporiums, and I walked up one block and down another, peering into their windows. The uptown experience had made me skittish, but all the windows here were caked with grime and filled with dusty wigs perched on Styrofoam heads, and one looked so much like another that it was impossible to choose between them. When I got to Thirty-seventh Street I took a breath and just walked into the nearest shop.

The door groaned as I pushed it open, and one of those old-fashioned bells rang out. The place looked weary, the unvarnished wooden floors exuding an odor of dust and age. A counter ran along the right wall, and behind it sat a large and amiable-looking woman, her girth spread across two stools. She smiled widely at me, displaying a gap between her front teeth. "In the market for a wig, dearie?" she asked, grinning like an enormous toad. She gave me a pitying look, touched her tongue noisily to her teeth, and said, "Oh, look at your head. What a shame to lose all those curls!"

I debated for a moment, reluctant to lose her goodwill. But it is unwise to tempt fate. "I don't have cancer," I said, and waited for the smile to fade.

Instead, it grew. "I'm glad to hear that," said the woman. "Forgive me—these days when I see a new customer, I assume she's come from the oncologist. So many recommend us. I'm happy to know that you're here for another reason. Do you care to tell me what it is?"

Her smile was so warm, so encouraging, that I blurted out, "I want to be a blonde."

"Don't we all, dearie, don't we all. What color did you have in mind?"

"Champagne?" I asked hesitantly. "Unless you have a better idea?"

She lumbered down from her stool and reached for a drawer behind her. "Let's just start out and see where the hair takes us," she replied. She pulled the drawer open. "I'm Shirley. I hope you're not in a hurry? It might take a while to find the right wig. But believe me, we will."

Shirley filled her arms, spilling hair in a dozen different shades of blond until it looked as if she were holding a bizarre pet. "You just have to keep trying," she said. "You'll know right off when you find the one. Try this." She held out a hank of yellow hair that looked as if it had been worn by Marilyn Monroe on the set of *Some Like It Hot*. "Synthetic," she said, giving it a vigorous shake. "Inexpensive. Let's just have a look." With her other hand she held out a wig cap.

I had learned to divide my hair into sections and pin each one flat to my scalp before squeezing my head into the tight, flesh-colored stocking. Shirley watched as I did this, and I waited for her to comment on the volume of my hair. But she looked on impassively, silently spreading the wig with her hands, readying it. When the cap was finally in place, I bent forward and she eased Marilyn onto my head. I shook it as I looked up and faced the mirror.

The wig just sat there, making my features go pasty and flat. I was clearly not meant to be a blonde.

"Take it off, take it off," cried Shirley, waving her arms. "Believe me, we'll find one. But for sure that's not it." She laughed, and as the mirth spread across her broad nose and wide mouth, her plain face was transformed until she was almost pretty. "Don't be discouraged," she soothed, pawing through the pile on the desk. She held up a longer yellow model with big fat curls. "Let's try Farah."

That was even worse. Dolly made me look like a forlorn poodle, and Mia, a pale pixie cut, gave me the air of a jail warden in drag.

"No, no, and no," said Shirley. She was enjoying herself. Her conviction that I would find something was encouraging, but as I tried on gold wigs and white ones, yellow ones and brass one, wigs with a faint strawberry tint and some that were almost pink, I began to despair. Shirley Temple, Alice in Wonderland, Faye Dunaway . . . they all looked terrible on me.

"Do you have a special occasion you want this for?" Shirley asked after a while. "It might help me if I knew."

"I'm a restaurant critic," I began.

"That's a new one on me," she said as my story came to a close. "And are you working on someplace special at the moment?"

"Lespinasse," I said. "The chef is amazing. I keep going back and every time he just blows me away. I've been thinking about giving him four stars, but it's not something I could do casually. Not only would it be my first four-star review, but it would also be the first time a hotel restaurant ever got four stars from the *New York Times*. I can't make a mistake with this. And here's the thing: I think they made me, even when I was there in disguise. Everything's been just a little too perfect. So I'm trying to create a new disguise, one that is foolproof."

"Gotcha," said Shirley, moving to a deep, wide drawer, "I have an idea." As she opened the drawer, her bulk blocked my view, so I couldn't see what she was holding until she turned around with a cascade of hair the color of Dom Perignon spilling from her hands. As the wig caught the light, the color changed from pearl to buttercup. "Try this," said Shirley.

The wig felt different in my hands—lighter, cooler—and when I put it on, the hair fell across my face as gently as silk. I squeezed my eyes tight, not wanting to look until it was seated right, holding my breath, wanting this to be the one. I could feel it settle into place, feel the soft strands graze my shoulders just below my ears.

"Wait!" said Shirley as I started to open my eyes, and she leaned forward and began tugging at the wig, adjusting it. She slid the hair on my left side behind my ear and pulled the hair on the right forward so that it fell across one eye. Her hand cradled the hair under my cheek, then let it fall. "Okay," she said at last, "you can open your eyes now."

The champagne blonde in the mirror did not seem to be wearing a wig. The hair looked real, as if it were growing out of the scalp. Even the dark eyebrows looked right, as if this woman had so much confidence, she didn't care who knew that she dyed her hair. My mouth dropped open. "Oh!" I said stupidly. "Oh, my."

In the mirror Shirley caught my eye. "I *told* you there was a right wig for everyone!" she said, but her face did not match her matter-of-fact tone. "You look absolutely fabulous!" she said, looking absolutely amazed.

I don't think I would have recognized myself if we had met walking down the street, and I had yet to put on any makeup. Somehow this cut, this color, made my cheeks pink, my eyes almost violet, my lips seem redder than they had ever been.

"You were meant to be a blonde!" cried Shirley. And then, as I watched, her face fell.

"What's the matter?" I asked.

She hesitated for a moment, and I was afraid she was going to tell me that the wig was already sold. "It's real hair," she whispered sadly, and I was so relieved I burst out laughing.

"Is that all?" I asked.

Then she told me the price. It was shocking, but even if Lespinasse had not been in my future, I could never have left without the wig. I felt new, glamorous, bursting with curiosity. What would life be like for the woman in the mirror?

"I wish I could let you have it for less," said Shirley apologetically. "But it's very good hair, and I've just quoted you the price that I paid."

"I have a feeling it's going to be worth every penny," I said.

Shirley packed the wig into an old-fashioned hatbox and handed it to me. "You'll come back and tell me what happens, won't you?" she asked wistfully.

"You mean whether I fool the restaurant?" I asked.

"Well," she said, "that too. But what I mostly want to know is, when you're a blonde, do you have more fun?"

Carrying the box very carefully, I went to Ricky's, one of the cheap cosmetic shops that stands on every Manhattan corner holding out promises of instant beauty. I bought beige foundation, pink lipstick, brown eyeliner, and eyeshadow in various shades of pale. Then, eager to create Chloe, I went home.

Nick was at his friend Gabe's house and Michael was at work, so there was no one to watch me slip on the wig and pat on the foundation. The makeup was easy; the wig on my head dictated the colors. But as I stroked lavender shadow across my eyes, I saw that my hands were wrong; Chloe needed nails. An amateur job would never do.

"I haf time," said the large woman behind the desk at the nail shop on Seventy-eighth Street, "I take you now." Her nametag identified her as Rosa. Behind her sat a row of women with their hands buried in bowls of suds and their feet propped on the plump laps of polish-wielding women. Rosa filled a little bowl with soapy water and pushed my left hand into it. "Soak," she said as she clucked over my right. "Such mess!" she scolded. "What is beautiful girl like you doing with dirt on hands? What do feet look like?"

"Worse," I said.

"Pedicure," she insisted. "Is must."

While Rosa clipped and pushed and glued, she extracted Chloe's life story. I was curious as well; Molly had been made up in a moment. I supposed Chloe could be too.

"My husband is a doctor," I began, hesitantly. I faltered. "Or, rather, my husband was a doctor. He's still a doctor; he's just not my husband anymore."

"Another voman," said Rosa. It was not a question, and her voice vibrated with sympathy.

"Yes," I said. Why not?

"Younger voman," Rosa declared, her head moving back and forth as she contemplated the perfidy of men. "And doctor!" She sucked in her breath three times, sounding like an angry vacuum cleaner.

Yes, of course it was a younger woman. "She's his nurse," I said. "Well, she was his nurse. He won't let her work anymore." I closed my eyes for a moment, picturing the white blouse buttoned tight across big breasts, the slim skirt clinging to a small waist, the long legs. The nurse had pale stockings, and when I looked down, expecting sensible crepe-soled shoes, I saw that she was wearing pumps with very high heels. "She's a real blonde," I announced. "Dan likes blond hair. He made me dye mine when we met. Everywhere." I gestured down.

"Is very pretty," Rosa said, ignoring my hand and steadfastly eyeing my head. "All men like. You keep."

But now that I was getting the images, I didn't want to be interrupted, so I rushed on, afraid to lose them. "Dan doesn't like his women to work. He thinks they should be available to him at all times. 'I want to be able to take a plane to Paris for the weekend on the spur of the moment,' he always said. That's why he didn't want children; he wouldn't even let me have a dog. Nothing was supposed to interfere with his freedom. I'm an interior decorator, but when I met him I dropped everything and dedicated my life to him."

"Interior decorator!" said Rosa, clearly impressed. "Is fine."

"I loved it!" I said passionately, and as I spoke I really could see myself hunched over a big stuffed chair with fat wooden legs, swatches of fabric in my hands as I made crucial design decisions. I actually visualized the apartment I had designed for Dan, saw the little powder room with its black-and-white-patterned wallpaper of Minute Men marching toward Concord, saw the Early American waiting room I had filled with pine furniture and kerosene lanterns, cleverly wired for electricity. I saw the green dining room in our apartment, with its bouquets of dried flowers that made my nose prickle, and the handsome living room, all wood and horse paintings and deep pile carpet. I smelled the Lemon Pledge that the maid applied to the tops of the tables every day, and the slight residue of the one cigar Dan liked after dinner, blowing the smoke out in large, self-satisfied puffs.

"I created a kingdom for him," I cried, "but now I'm going to redo the apartment and make it my own." In one grand gesture I swept it all away, replacing the horses with something vaguely Monet lily–like, the walls stripped down and painted a delicate lavender that changed as the sunlight moved through the room.

My family, who know my utter ineptitude at home décor, were going to find this fantasy highly entertaining. If not for Michael, we would sit on broken chairs and walk across frayed carpets. He is the decorator, the one who cares about lamps and sofas and the color of the walls, the person who has made every house we've had worth living in. But no one has ever faulted my imagination; I was Chloe at this moment, and I uttered every word with real conviction. "I'm going back to work," I told Rosa. "I got the apartment in the settlement, but the mortgage is so steep that unless I start making money, I won't be able to keep it."

"Men!" said Rosa with disgust; she was now massaging cream into my feet. "I give you red toes," she decided, brandishing her brush as if it were a tool of liberation. "So sexy." She swiped the polish savagely across my nails, leaving a trail of bright crimson in its wake. She wove a length of cotton between my toes, and as we waited for the paint to dry, she outlined a plan of action. "You will find better man," she promised, urging me to begin the chase at once. No time, she said, like the present.

"I don't think I'm quite ready," I demurred, squirming at the thought of walking into a bar alone.

"You must!" said Rosa, shooing me out the door. "Go." She gave me a last look and sighed. "So pretty. So blonde!"

She had said the magic words. The overweight teenager who still lived inside me, the one with thick glasses and frizzy brown hair, the one who never had a date for the prom, was intrigued. I took one last look in the mirror, feeling the same reckless exhilaration I had felt when I first saw Miriam. Now I had created an alter ego who was my direct opposite, and I was eager to start living her life.

I tipped Rosa lavishly and left the shop, intent on finding a taxi. This, in past experience, involved stepping into the street and hurling myself into the path of oncoming cabs in an attempt to attract their attention. For Chloe, on the other hand, things were different. I stepped out the door, raised my hand, and two taxis came screeching to a halt, avoiding a collision by mere inches.

The effect at the far end of the journey was no less gratifying. As my taxi came gliding to a stop on Fifty-second Street, a tall man in an overcoat rushed over hopefully, eager to catch the cab before someone else could snag it. But when my platinum hair swung into sight, followed by my pink lips and red nails, he hesitated, and for a moment I could see him struggle. In the end he smiled, helped me out of the cab, and climbed in himself. But I could feel his eyes still on me as I pushed open the door of the bar.

· · ·

Palio is a small square room, so hermetically sealed off from the city that it is its own little world. Murals cover all four walls, and no matter where you sit, heroic horses come thundering toward you, so vivid you can almost feel their breath. In Siena, at the actual race, people pack into the square until they are so dense that the air grows thin. The crowd sings and sweats and cheers as the horses careen about in crazy circles and the atmosphere becomes electric with colors of dizzy-making intensity.

I sat down, ordered a martini, and looked up, losing myself in the painting, remembering the heat of summer in Siena, the sounds, the smells.

"Come here often?"

I blinked and looked around. A small man with a neat gray beard had taken possession of the stool next to mine. As my eyes swung toward him I saw that he was extremely good-looking, and then I caught the pale helmet of my hair reflected in the martini glass and remembered where I was, and why.

"No," I said, my voice softer than I had known it could be, "this is my first time."

"They're beautiful, aren't they?" he asked, gesturing toward the paintings.

"Oh, yes," I said in my new whispery little voice, "I think they may be the most beautiful paintings I have ever seen."

"They're by Sandro Chia," he told me, "and I was so excited when I first saw them that I went out and bought a few of his drawings."

"Was it a good investment?" I asked.

"Very," he replied, "collecting art is one of my hobbies." He gestured to the bartender for another snifter of single malt, and raised his eyebrows in the direction of my glass, indicating that he would like to buy me a refill.

"Oh, I couldn't possibly," I said demurely. "One is more than enough for me." And then I asked the question he obviously wanted to answer.

"Yes, many hobbies," he replied. "I have a large wine collection and I spend a great deal of time going to auctions. I also travel a good bit, and I guess you might call me a collector of restaurants as well." He wiped his rather corpulent lips with a handkerchief and added, with a self-deprecating laugh, "My friends consider me something of a connoisseur."

"Really?" I asked breathlessly, as if this was the most rare and fascinating knowledge.

"Oh yes," he replied, and his hand came up again to stroke the beard. "I actually put out a little restaurant guide for my friends every Christmas, telling them about my discoveries. It's strictly for fun, of course, but they've come to depend upon it. The year I decided not to do it they were furious."

"I'm sure they must have been," I said in that little-girl whisper. I suddenly saw that I was doing a bad imitation of Marilyn Monroe, but he didn't seem to notice. "I don't actually know much about food myself," I added. Gesturing down at the black suit, I said, "Fashion and food don't mix very well. But"—and here I sighed and let my eyes go misty, wondering if he was going to fall for this—"maybe it doesn't matter anymore."

He did! "Troubles, my dear?" he asked, picking up my metaphorical handkerchief. And so, reluctantly, I told him the story of the dastardly doctor.

"What a coincidence," cried my new friend. "My name is Daniel too. Dan Green." He patted my hand and added, "But, believe me, I have no interest in young women. And if you don't mind my saying so, I find it hard to imagine leaving someone as charming as you are for—well, for anyone."

Dashiell Hammett," Lillian Hellman once told an interviewer, "used to say I had the meanest jealousy of all. I had no jealousy of work, no jealousy of money. I was just jealous of women who took advantage of men, because I didn't know how to do it." I was about twenty when I first read that, but I copied it into my journal because I recognized myself. It is that jealousy that made Chloe different from Molly and Miriam.

I was never able to disappear into the role. I sat back, watching Chloe with amazed distaste, this blonde who seemed to know just what men wanted to hear and didn't mind saying it. The most astonishing thing was discovering, at the age of forty-five, that I did know how to take advantage of a man after all. When had I learned this? And what was I going to do about it?

Dan excused himself for a minute, and as I watched him walk away I saw that he had an incipient potbelly and moved with a short man's swagger. But he seemed very sure of himself and I did not think it would be long before he asked me to dinner. I knew I would be tempted: it was such a perfect ploy. My friends were usually so titillated by the disguises that they gave me away. Here was an opportunity for complete anonymity, a chance to have dinner with someone who truly believed I was the person I was pretending to be. The restaurant would never know I was there!

But could I go through with it? Dan returned and I watched, fascinated, as Chloe extracted the information she needed. He was a lawyer, he lived in Los Angeles, and he had never been married. Business brought him to New York a few times a month. At last he glanced at his watch and said he must be going. "I'm already late," he said with obvious regret. "If it wasn't an important business meeting I'd blow it off. But . . ."

Here it came, the invitation. Looking earnestly into my eyes he said, "Tomorrow night I have a reservation at what I consider New York's best restaurant, and I'd be honored if you'd join me."

I couldn't go through with it after all. "Thank you so much, but it's impossible."

"Nothing's impossible, Chloe," he said, giving me a soulful look. He pressed on. "One of the world's great chefs is right here in New York, and the locals have yet to discover him."

"Really?" I replied. And then, because I just couldn't help myself, I added, "Not even that new critic at the *Times*?"

"Her?" He let out a contemptuous little snort. "What an idiot. All she seems to know about are Japanese noodle shops. The critic before her was a man who knew what he was talking about, but this one wouldn't know a great restaurant if it bit her."

Is that so, I thought, beginning to reconsider. Dan caught my hesitation. "You seem like a woman of discernment," he urged. "Please join me at Lespinasse. Gray Kunz is as talented as any chef working in France right now. It would give me such pleasure to introduce you to his food."

It was too delicious. There was the delicate matter of money, so I put on my breathiest little voice and told Dan that I would join him for dinner, but only if he would allow me to pay.

In the end we compromised: we would go Dutch. We agreed to meet at the restaurant at eight. Then I went home to wrestle with my conscience. I had twenty-five hours to change my mind.

R uth?" said Michael when I walked into the apartment. He recoiled as if I were an intruder. "Ruth?" Although I had opened the door with my key, he assumed a threatening stance and eyed my blond head uncertainly. I could see him searching for identifying marks, watched him note my familiar shoes and then saw his eyes move up, looking for my wedding ring. I had taken it off. Only when Nicky hurled himself into my arms, shouting, "Mommy! Mommy! Mommy!" did the doubt leave his face.

"Pretty," said Nicky, stroking the soft blond hair. And then, ever the diplomat, he added, "But I think I like brown curly hair best."

"Are we staying home for dinner?" asked Michael.

"Yes," I said, and they looked at each other and smiled. "I've done enough today. We're going to have salad and spaghetti carbonara. But first I have to change."

The guys went into the kitchen to put the pasta water on to boil while I went to the bedroom and began peeling Chloe off, layer by layer. When I joined them, Michael was washing lettuce and Nicky was sitting on the kitchen counter, drying it.

"My teacher wants to know if you'll come on our class trip," Nicky said as I removed the bacon from the refrigerator. He puffed out his chest and added importantly, "We're going to the Metropolitan Museum to draw the Temple of Dendur."

"Do you want me to come?" I asked, thinking how miserable it made me when my mother came to class.

He nodded solemnly. "Please?" he asked.

"Of course I'll come," I said, putting the spaghetti into the pot. I turned to Michael and said, "What a day! You're not going to believe it; I've got a lot to report."

Spaghetti Carbonara

Contrary to the recipe so often used in restaurants, real carbonara contains no cream. The real thing also uses *guanciale*, cured pork jowl, but to be honest, I like bacon better. I think of this as bacon and eggs with pasta instead of toast. It's the perfect last-minute dinner, and I've yet to meet a child who doesn't like it.

1 pound spaghetti
¼ to ½ pound thickly sliced good-quality bacon (I prefer Nueske's)
2 cloves garlic, peeled
2 large eggs
Black pepper
½ cup grated Parmigiano cheese, plus extra for the table

Bring a large pot of salted water to a boil. When it is boiling, throw the spaghetti in. Most dried spaghetti takes 9 to 10 minutes to cook, and you can make the sauce in that time.

Cut the bacon crosswise into pieces about ½ inch wide. Put them in a skillet and cook for 2 minutes, until fat begins to render.

Add the whole cloves of garlic and cook another 5 minutes, until the edges of the bacon just begin to get crisp. Do not overcook; if they get too crisp, they won't meld with the pasta.

Meanwhile, break the eggs into the bowl you will serve the pasta in, and beat them with a fork. Add some grindings of pepper.

Remove the garlic from the bacon pan. If it looks like too much fat to you, discard some, but you're going to toss the bacon with most of its fat into the pasta.

When it is cooked, drain the pasta and immediately throw it into the beaten eggs. Mix thoroughly. The heat of the spaghetti will cook the eggs and turn them into a sauce. Add the bacon with its fat, toss again, add cheese and serve.

Serves 3

At the office the next morning I found myself telling Carol Shaw about meeting Dan at Palio. She was instantly amused. But when I told her that I was going to dinner with him, she frowned.

"You sure you want to do that?" she asked. "It would serve the guy right, but it seems sort of risky."

"What could possibly happen?" I asked. "I'm meeting him in the restaurant, and he can hardly attack me there. I'm paying my way, so he can't think I owe him anything. And when dinner's over I'll jump into a cab and go home."

She shook her head. "I don't know why it makes me nervous, but it does. What did Michael say?"

"It makes him nervous too," I admitted. "He wanted to come and sit at the next table just to make sure I was okay. I talked him out of that, but he said that if I wasn't home by midnight he was coming to get me."

"Good," she said. "That makes me feel better. But I sort of wish he was going to be there."

"Don't even think it," I said. "It took me hours to talk him out of that scheme."

The doorman at the St. Regis greeted me with a warmth I was sure he saved for blondes. I got out, sailed through the door, and heard my heels click along the hotel's marble floor as I watched the maître d' scrutinize my approach. I was positive he did not recognize me. Relieving me of my coat, he murmured, "Welcome to Lespinasse. Are you joining someone?"

As he led me into the dining room I saw how perfectly Chloe suited this cream and gilt décor, which seemed to have been designed to show her off. Or perhaps it was the other way around: as Dan stood up and the maître d' held my chair, I wondered if I had unconsciously designed the perfect patron for this Louis XIV fantasy.

"I'm relieved that you're here," said Dan. In his neat black suit and starched white shirt, he looked less handsome than he had the night before; what he brought to mind was a prosperous penguin. "I was a little afraid that you might stand me up."

I said nothing and he continued, "I've been going over the wine list—" He stopped, looked at the maître d', and said, "If you'd be good enough to send the sommelier?"

A little robin of a man came bouncing to the table and stood, balancing expectantly on the balls of his feet. I could feel him assessing Daniel Green, could sense him estimating how much money this particular customer was worth. "Perhaps a little Champagne?" he offered.

Dan shook his head. "No," he said, and I had the feeling that he would have rejected any suggestion, just to get the upper hand. "I think we'll begin with a white Burgundy."

"Excellent, excellent!" approved the sommelier, and I saw that he knew exactly how to handle his customers. Last week, when I had shown a disinclination to engage him in discussion, our transaction had been brief and businesslike. Now he said, "I assume you'd prefer the Côte de Beaune?"

"On the contrary," said Dan, and although it might have been my imagination, I thought I detected a small smile flit briefly across the sommelier's face. "I see you have an '89 Musigny here, which interests me very much. I consider a good white from the Côte de Nuits a thing of great beauty."

"Very wise," said the sommelier, his head cocked to one side. His voice rich with admiration, he added, "So few recognize the merits of the whites from the north." Unspoken, but surely there, was the phrase "but you are obviously among the discerning few."

"As for the red," he asked, "will we stay in France?" It was not lost on me that he was now employing the royal we.

"Certainly," said Daniel Green. "Chef Kunz's food is so subtle. It would be criminal to assault the delicacy of his flavors with the brashness of American wine." I made a note to try to remember these phrases for later use; they might come in handy. I liked the idea of wine assaulting food with criminal intent.

The sommelier nodded respectfully. "How right you are!" he said, and I wondered if he was not overdoing it just a little. I sneaked a glance at Dan; apparently not. I hoped my face was wearing an appropriately admiring smile. "Will we continue with Burgundy?"

Dan indicated that this was exactly what we would do. "I wonder," said the sommelier, "if your eyes had wandered toward Le Corton?"

"Precisely!" cried Dan happily. "You have read my mind!"

Not all that difficult, I was thinking to myself. A man who chose whites from a region known for reds might be reasonably expected to choose a red from a region known for white wines. And since Le Corton was the only *grand cru* on the list from the Côte de Beaune, it hadn't taken Sherlock Holmes to make that guess. But now the sommelier was coughing diffidently; he was still in the game.

"Might I venture to say that the wine isn't drinking at its best just now?" he said hesitantly. "It is having a small awkward period. Might I suggest this Clos St.-Denis?"

"An '86?" cried Dan. "You're suggesting an '86 over an '88? I'm intrigued."

The sommelier gave a timid shrug. "The wine is lovely," he said. "I tasted it only yesterday and I was most impressed."

"We'll take your advice," said Dan. There was just the slightest hint of threat in his voice.

"If you don't like it," soothed the sommelier, "I will drink it myself. With pleasure." He bowed and walked away.

"The remarkable thing," said Dan when he had moved out of earshot, "is that the red wine he's suggested is considerably less expensive than the one I was going to order. That is a very good sommelier!"

We still had the tasting ritual before us, and Dan dragged that out for fifteen minutes. He wanted the white plucked from the ice so that the red could be "brought up to cellar temperature." This initiated a conversation about American restaurants always serving their red wine too warm, which somehow led to a discussion of root stock and vintage years. This was man talk, and I was not invited to join the conversation. The minutes ticked by. Finally it was over. Or so I thought.

Dan raised his glass and took a sip. "Violets," he said. "Silver. A cool brook babbling in a forest. Sunshine on rippling leaves." I looked across the table and saw that his eyes were closed as he took rapid little sips of wine. He opened them and said, "When I first taste, I like to concentrate and just let images come. It helps me remember. Try it yourself."

I obediently closed my eyes and took a sip. "Grapes," I thought. "Chardonnay. A bit of oak." I tried to come up with something more romantic, just to please him, but all I could see was the grapes hanging on the vine. I pulled back the focus and looked again. "A village," I said. "A little stone village with roads twisting through ancient green hills."

"Good," he said, "very good. You see, I have a method for filing flavors so that I can access them later. To me wine is more than mere enjoyment; I'm attempting to build a mental encyclopedia that I can recall at will. The next time I encounter a Musigny, I'll need to compare it to this one."

"Fascinating!" I said. This time I meant it.

It was time to consider the menu. I was tempted by the foie gras with quince and lentil salad but then the shimeji broth leapt out at me. It seemed like just the thing that Chloe would order.

"And for your main course?" asked Dan.

"Steamed black bass with lime?" I said, realizing that I had just ordered what amounted to a diet dinner.

Dan frowned. "That's going to be difficult with the red wine," he said.

"Of course," I said. "What if I tried the salmon braised in Syrah?"

He smiled approvingly. "Much better!" he said, beginning to debate the merits of short ribs versus squab ragout; the ribs won.

"I have an idea," he said happily. "Why don't we share the steamed bass as a mid-course?" I stole a glance at my watch. It was only three hours until midnight, and at this rate we'd never be done with dinner. He'd probably insist on cheese before dessert and cognac after. I hadn't reckoned on an endless feast.

"Tell me some more about your wine filing system," I said when the decisions were finally behind us. "It's so fascinating." I was sincere about this, and he sensed that and relaxed.

"It's an ancient trick," he said. "A device for memorization. You pick something—anything—as a way of differentiating the intangible to yourself. How do you define flavor? Some people might do it chemically, but that seems too cold; it would never work for me. Some might try colors, but my imagination doesn't run that way. So I ascribe an image to each wine and file it away in a sort of mental photo album. Take this Musigny . . ." He lifted his glass and held the pale wine up to the light. I followed his gaze. "Take a sip," he urged. "Close your eyes. I am going to describe what I see."

I closed my eyes and heard him take a sip. Then his words began to wash over me. "I am standing deep in the forest," he said. "It's early spring, and the leaves are just changing from little buds to leaves. They're still that tender green they have when they're new, and a little breeze is rippling across them so that they catch the light and are faintly silver." He took another sip. "It's cool here, and there is a brook at our feet, which murmurs softly. Violets are poking their heads up, between fiddlehead ferns." I put my glass to my lips, and as the cold wine splashed into my mouth I could see what he was describing very clearly. It was beautiful in that forest, the air fresh and delicious.

"Incredible!" I said, my voice soft and awestruck. But then I opened my eyes and the image disappeared, leaving me back in the pseudo-palace on the ground floor of the St. Regis Hotel. I quickly squeezed them shut and asked, "Can you remember the last Musigny you tasted?"

I could sense him flipping through an invisible file. "In the woods, definitely," he said. "No violets, though, just fiddlehead ferns. The brook is still, the leaves darker. It's later in the year, a wine with less delicacy, less finesse. Yes," he pondered for a moment, lost in his forest, "it's an '88. Not as good a year, and a bit clumsier in the mouth."

I was trying to taste it in my mind when his voice changed and he said, "Here's our first course!"

I opened my eyes and watched the waiter approach, holding a tapered Japanese bowl, very narrow at the bottom and wide at the top, an inverted pyramid balanced on the plate. It seemed oddly modern in the formal antiquity of the room, but when I leaned over and let the steam bathe my face, I forgot everything but the surprisingly fragrant aroma. I dipped my spoon into the broth and tasted lemongrass, kaffir lime, mushroom, and something else, something that hovered at the edge of my mind, familiar but elusive. I took another taste and it was there again, hiding just behind the citrus.

The shimeji mushrooms went sliding sensuously across my tongue with the lush texture of custard. The sensation was first sour, then spicy, and then, there it was again, something sweet but not sugary that came whirling into my consciousness and then slid maddeningly away before I could identify it. What was it?

"I can see that you like your broth," said Dan, and I blushed, realizing that I had not said a word in many minutes. "Chloe, please don't apologize," he said, noting my embarrassment. "I like to see a woman enjoy her food. And my tuna is excellent! Would you like to try it?"

"You must taste my soup," I said, pushing the bowl toward him so that he had no choice but to hand his own plate, reluctantly I thought, across the table. "I have never tasted anything quite like it."

But I'd never had anything like his raw tuna either. The clear, almost translucent fish had been tumbled with caviar so that it glowed deep red, like rubies among black pearls. A garland woven from leeks was twined around it, interspersed with mysterious little dark dots.

"That aceto balsamico is excellent," said Dan. I touched my fork to one of the dots and put it in my mouth, expecting the musty sweetness of the vinegar. But my mouth closed across something funkier and more mysterious, and I almost blurted out, "This isn't balsamic."

Instead, I managed to make myself say, "How clever of you to know what it is," as I took another taste. It was definitely not balsamic vinegar.

"Good balsamic," he said, "is a wonderful ingredient. It's unfortunate that so few Americans know how to use it right."

"Oh?" I said, still trying to figure out what it was. Black, I kept thinking, what's black in nature? Could it be Chinese black vinegar? I tasted again. Definitely not.

"They use that industrial product on salads," he said contemptuously. "Nobody in Modena would ever do such a thing. This is the correct use of real balsamico, which as you can see is much thicker than ordinary vinegar. It should be used as a condiment, just like this, something to punctuate flavor. This chef is brilliant! Brilliant!"

I took another taste, as if I were tasting the balsamic to confirm his verdict. And suddenly I had it. Squid ink! It was squid ink! "Wonderful balsamic," I said quietly. "And what do you think is the sweet flavor in the soup?"

"I don't taste anything sweet," he said, taking another spoonful. Then he reached across the table to reclaim his plate. I took my bowl back and tried again. The flavors tiptoed quietly into my mouth and then suddenly picked up the pace, so powerful that they were reverberating in a little tap dance of taste. The sweetness came and then disappeared as I tried to separate the flavors.

"Still taste something sweet?" asked Dan.

"Would you mind asking what's in the soup?" I pleaded.

"Of course not." He raised his hand and summoned the waiter. "The lady thinks that she is tasting a sweet element in the soup," he said, as if urging the waiter to forgive what he knew was an error. "Is there some secret ingredient?"

The waiter smiled. "Pineapple juice," he said.

I should have gotten that! But even though I knew it now, when I took another bite it was there and then gone, so elusive that it was like the ghost of the fruit, merely haunting the bowl.

"I'm impressed," said Dan, but he was not pleased. He, after all, was the one with the flavor file. Clearly it was time to play dumb again.

When the salmon arrived, a fat slash of bright orange fish in a deep purple sauce, I looked down at the sprig of chervil and said, "The colors are gorgeous, and the parsley looks so pretty on the orange fish."

"Chervil," he corrected me. "Take a taste. See—it has a faint anise flavor."

"You know so much!" I said, and felt his knee creep over to touch mine.

I took a bite and immediately forgot his knee. I forgot everything but what was going on in my mouth, the fish doing a little tango with crunchy strips of artichoke. The softness of the fish was sandwiched between layers of crunch—the artichoke on the bottom, bread crumbs on top, the flavors appearing and vanishing in a maddening way. I thought I tasted chestnut, and then it was gone, absorbed into the deep musky flavor of the wine. I tasted again and discerned something sour and completely unfamiliar. "I can see that you like your fish," said Dan, who had, apparently, been watching me. "It's such a pleasure to be with a woman who appreciates food."

"This chef," I said sincerely, "is astonishingly good. How's your beef?"

"Superb!" he said, looking down at the little sculpture on his plate, a single boned rib set upright on a bed of pureed potatoes. "The chef has cooked it in a ginger-spiked sauce. But what is most impressive is the way he has laced the mousseline with shreds of fried potato—" He stopped with a horrified look and I realized that I had unconsciously scooped some potatoes off his plate.

The knee withdrew. "You might have asked," he snapped.

I knew that contrition was in order, but I was too taken with the fireworks in my mouth to pay it much mind. The potatoes—more potato-laced butter than the other way around—were studded with the crisp strands of fried potato, which went off like little sparks. No matter how prepared you thought you were, each encounter was a little shock of electricity. Without thinking I stretched my fork out and took a bit of meat from his plate. It had melted into something so soft it simply slid down your throat. "Mmmm," I murmured.

"Try mine," I said, pushing my plate toward him. "Maybe you can tell me what that faintly sour flavor is?"

He tasted noisily. "Olive?" he asked. His lips chattered against the fish again and he said, "No, it's not salty. What could it be?"

"You would know better than I," I replied demurely.

"I taste the Syrah," he said. "And the artichokes. But you're right, there *is* something else." He raised his hand and a waiter came skidding to a halt. "Sir?" he intoned.

"We've been wondering what the unusual flavor in this dish is," said Dan.

"Kokum," said the waiter. "It's the dried peel of a fruit that is used a great deal in Indian cooking."

"Amazing!" I said. "I've learned so much tonight."

It was true. But I was tired and the wig was digging maddeningly into my head, making my temples throb. I was beginning to feel the wine. Glancing down at my watch, I saw that it was past eleven, that we had been in our seats for three and a half hours, that I would soon turn into a pumpkin. It was time to go.

A wave of desperation washed over me, and then I caught my own reflection in a knife and realized that Chloe would know exactly how to handle this situation. And so I let her handle it.

I put one hand over Dan's and said, so softly that he had to lean in to hear me, "Would you mind terribly if we skipped dessert?"

The knee pressed harder against mine and I realized that he had misunderstood. Undaunted, I gently rolled my legs away and said, "I'm rather tired, and it's very late, and I have a big day tomorrow."

"Of course," he said, putting his other hand over mine so that our fingers formed a little stack on the table. "There will be other meals. Many other meals, I hope. This has been so enjoyable."

We paid our respective checks and he walked me to the door. By the time we reached it, the maître d' was already holding out my coat. I slipped into it, Dan took my arm, and together we strolled out across the marble floors.

"What a delightful evening," he said. He held the door of the taxi for me, and leaned over to brush my cheek with his lips. His beard tickled as he pressed his card into my hands. "Call me. I'll be back in New York in a few weeks, and I hope we can share another meal."

"Good night," I said, making no promises. I slipped the card into my pocketbook and the door closed. The taxi pulled away from the curb. I turned to take one last look at Dan Green, wondering what he would think when he read the review.

RESTAURANTS
by Ruth Reichl

....

Pow!

The food at Lespinasse comes out shooting. With your first bite you know that you are in for an exciting adventure. These are flavors you have never tasted before.

This aggressive food is particularly shocking because it is served in such sedate surroundings. The dining room, all soaring ceilings, creamy gilded columns, chandeliers and luxurious chairs, makes you feel that you have walked into an 18th-century chateau, and the service makes you feel that you belong there. The restaurant, which was named for a French literary patron, overlooks no opportunity to pamper its own patrons.

"You don't need a check," says the hostess as she relieves you of your coat. Sure enough, when you leave, there she is, standing at the door with your coat in her arms. An evening here is constructed of so many small, considerate gestures that by the time it ends you feel entirely relaxed.

Waiters work unobtrusively, anticipating every wish. Cutlery comes and goes in the elegant ballet of fine service. Wine is quietly put in and out of the wine bucket to keep it at the perfect temperature. When Lespinasse (pronounced less-peen-AHSS) opened in 1991, there were complaints about the service, but the restaurant now runs seamlessly. The staff has become so familiar with the food that in five visits I never came up with a single question the waiters were unable to answer.

If you care about food, you will ask a lot of them; nothing at Lespinasse ever tastes the way you expect it to. Sour-spicy shimeji mushroom broth arrives looking like an austere Japanese still life. It is a surprise to dip your spoon into this mild-mannered soup and experience an explosion of flavor. Mushroom is at the base of the taste sensation, but it is haunted by citric tones—lemongrass, lime perhaps—and high at the top, a resonant note of sweetness. What is it?

"Pineapple juice," says the waiter. We dip our spoons again, taste. Yes, of course, there it is. Then, even though we know it is there, the elusive flavor begins to fade and disappear into the mushroom broth.

Silky bits of raw tuna are tumbled with two kinds of caviar that add an intensity to the flavor and an edge to the texture. The fish sits on a disk of diced vegetables surrounded by spears of leek and colorful dots that get brighter as they dance around the plate. Between the colors are little dabs of black. Balsamic vinegar? No; you taste again. They are dense, unctuous, vaguely mysterious. And then it hits you: squid ink!

Braised salmon and crisped artichokes with a syrah wine reduction sounds like a dish you may have tasted before. It even looks vaguely familiar, a fat slice of salmon on a bed of crisply fried strips of artichoke in a deep purple sauce. There are bread crumbs on top and a sprig of chervil. Take a taste, however, and you know you are in new territory. Yes, there is a bit of chestnut, and you can taste the wine and the tricky flavor of artichokes. But there is something else. You taste it again. Olive? Not quite. So you ask.

"Oh," says the waiter offhandedly. "That is kokum. It is a fruit used a great deal in Indian cooking."

Crisply coated snapper arrives in a shallow bowl of broth. The first taste is tarragon. It is replaced by fennel, which gives way to something that is definitely Chinese. You taste again. The tarragon is gone and what comes through is the elusive flavor of five-spice powder. In a minute all these flavors have come together so that you cannot separate them. You take another bite, and then another. Suddenly, disappointingly, the fish is gone.

It is no surprise, of course, to find Thai, Chinese and Indian foods turning up in your favorite French restaurant. They have become so chic that chefs sprinkle them ostentatiously through their dishes. But Gray Kunz, the chef at Lespinasse, is ahead of the curve. A Singapore-born Swiss who trained in the kitchen of Frédy Girardet near Lausanne, Mr. Kunz uses these herbs and spices with extraordinary confidence. His cooking was impressive at his last post, Adrienne in the Peninsula Hotel in Manhattan, but it has matured; he now cooks as if he had an instinctive understanding of each of his ingredients. He combines them, coaxes new tastes from them and yet maintains such firm control that no single flavor ever dominates a dish. At first you find yourself searching for flavors in this complex tapestry, fascinated by the way they are woven together. In the end, you just give in and allow yourself to be seduced; these dishes are too delicious to dissect.

Each meal is a roller coaster of sensations. Mr. Kunz has an almost Asian fascination with texture, and he loves to play with temperature as well. His risotto always comes with a contrasting dish: one night the creamy rice was slicked with white truffle oil and served with a tiny casserole of sliced salsify and black truffles. The creaminess of the rice was emphasized by the crunchiness of the black truffles just as the delicate perfume of the white truffles emphasized the deep musky flavor of the black ones.

Mr. Kunz is even inspired by simple bistro dishes. He cooks a single meaty short rib of beef until it melts into a gingery, slightly spicy tomato sauce. He sets it upright on a bed of mousseline potatoes, then spikes all that softness with shreds of fried potatoes that crunch invitingly each time you take a bite.

The short rib can stand up to a full red wine, but much of Mr. Kunz's food demands a bright white. Because the flavors are always unexpected, I usually ask for recommendations about wine. The staff has never let me down.

One night I ordered a 1992 Chassagne-Montrachet La Romanée from Verget. "I'm so sorry," said the captain with an apologetic look. "I sold the last bottle five minutes ago. Can I offer you this one at the same price?" He held out a '91 Chassagne-Montrachet from Colin-Deleger, a better wine. Half an hour later when I asked to see the wine list again, it had been reprinted: the Verget was no longer on the list.

Some chefs fade at dessert, con-tenting themselves with sweet, pretty things. Not Mr. Kunz. His desserts are as vivid as all his other dishes. Chocolate-banana soufflé is accompanied by banana-topped chocolate ice cream, a collision of hot and cold. Baked apples are set on fire and served with an astonishingly alcoholic ice cream. And crème brûlée slides sexily into your mouth, its smoothness set off by the little pot of berries at its side. Even the petits fours are exotic. What is that strange yellow fruit with the twisted husk? A gooseberry.

Do these food fireworks become exhausting? Perhaps they might in a lesser restaurant. But at Lespinasse, the pyrotechnics in the kitchen are tempered by the lack of them in the dining room. As each meal comes to a close, you find you are both exhilarated and soothed.

It's quite a show.

LESPINASSE

★ ★ ★ ★

Brenda

M yron called," said Carol, rolling her eyes as she handed me the little pink slip of paper. "I think he wants to have lunch with you."

"Already?" I asked. "It can't be six months since he was boring me at our last lunch. Did he say that was what he wanted?"

"No," said Carol, "but I know a lunch voice when I hear one. After all these years I can recognize that little whine editors get when they think the restaurant critic is trying to avoid them."

"Just from the sound of their voices?" I asked.

"Try answering the phone around here for a while," she said. "The calls come like clockwork. It doesn't matter who it is—you, Craig, Mimi, Bryan . . . For some editors, getting to eat out with you guys is a significant perk."

"He has his own expense account," I said. "He doesn't need me."

"You don't get it," said Carol. "It's not about food. It's about power.

You have power over restaurants, but he has power over you. He wants to flaunt it. You've never noticed?"

"No," I said, "never."

"Well," said Carol, "open your eyes. Call him. I'll bet a million dollars he'll want you to take him to some big-deal restaurant. And that when you get there, he'll let them know he's your boss."

"He didn't do that before, at La Grenouille."

"You just didn't notice. Call him. You'll see. Offer to take him some-place small—that little Korean place we went to last week—and see what happens."

"What will?"

"You'll go someplace fancy. I don't know how he'll make it happen, but he will. And I'll bet he won't want you in disguise."

"Why not?"

"How's he going to let them know he's your boss if you aren't you?"

"Oh come on!" I said.

"I'll make you a bet," said Carol. "If I'm wrong I'll—"

"—answer my mail for a week?"

"Fine. And if I'm right, you take me and Donald to dinner."

"In disguise?" I asked.

"Oh," she said, "definitely." She stopped for a minute, thinking. "In fact, if I win I get to design the disguise."

"You're on," I said. "I hope I lose. I could use your help; I'm starting to run out of ideas."

"So what are you waiting for?" she asked. "Go call Myron."

The Weekend editor was a dumpy little man who wore his gray hair pulled into a ponytail, bit his fingernails to the quick, and dressed in varying shades of brown. Myron Rosen, one of the dull, capable people who made the paper run, could be counted on to assign the right stories and make reporters meet their deadlines (or have a contingency plan when they did not). He was pleasant enough, in his own tedious fashion, but like many of the minor editors he secretly resented the critics and reporters in his charge. He took his revenge by cultivating a personal aroma so ferocious that everyone on the third floor routinely plotted alternate routes around his desk. Those forced to spend time in his proximity doused themselves with cologne, which only made his corner of the newsroom more pungent. My own strategy involved gulping entire cloves of garlic before every encounter.

"Myron Rosen, Weekend." His telephone voice was crisp and businesslike, much more *Times*ian than his flaccid, slightly lisping real-life tone.

"It's Ruth," I said, "returning your call."

Myron wasted no time. "We need to discuss future assignments," he said, getting down to business. "We should have lunch as soon as possible." There was a pause, during which I said nothing. "Sometime next week?" he insisted.

"How's Tuesday?" I tried. "I have a reservation at a lovely little Korean restaurant not far from here. The food's vegetarian and extremely interesting—they cook like Buddhist monks."

"Sounds fascinating," he said. "Let me just take a look at my book." I listened to Myron rifle pages. "Tuesday would be perfect," he said crisply. Carol was wrong! Myron took a breath before adding, ". . . if you don't mind changing the venue. I have a doctor's appointment on the Upper East Side, and it would be so convenient if we could meet around there."

"Hmm," I said, hedging for time. "Let me see if I have any restaurants I need to check out in that neighborhood."

Myron didn't miss a beat. "What about Daniel?" he asked, naming the city's most expensive restaurant. "Isn't it time you weighed in?"

Carol was right, and I was stunned into silence. Undaunted, Myron pressed on. "Marian Burros reviewed the restaurant right before you came. She was very tough."

"I liked her review," I said. "It took courage to give Daniel two stars. People were shocked."

Marian Burros was absolutely fearless, which made her the best kind of critic. A seasoned consumer reporter who had served time as a restaurant critic, she had no desire to step into Bryan's shoes. When he quit, I'd been told, she reluctantly agreed to fill in. Then she dipped her pen in acid and wrote deliciously wicked reviews that burned through the pages of the paper. Her most controversial target was Daniel.

Le Cirque's much-admired chef had opened his own restaurant, and everybody expected that he would immediately be awarded the four stars he had left behind. Marian, however, had no interest in everybody's expectations. Unimpressed, she suggested that the food would be better if Daniel Boulud had brought his old sous-chef, Sottha Kuhn, along with him. In the clubby world of American food, the implication that Sottha had been the real talent at Le Cirque was explosive.

"It was a gutsy review," Myron conceded, "but nobody cares what Marian thinks anymore. You're the critic now. People are waiting to hear what *you* think of the food at Daniel."

"You may be right," I said, wondering how far he would take this. "But they will surely know me, so I can't go as myself. And I've promised to spend Tuesday morning at the Metropolitan Museum with my son's kindergarten class, which I can hardly do in disguise. That's why this Korean place would be so perfect."

Myron was not daunted. "They won't be looking for you at lunchtime at Daniel," he said.

"They won't?" I asked. "Why not?"

"All those ladies who lunch," he said complacently, "will make us seem like a couple of tourists. We'll just disappear."

"He wouldn't take no for an answer," I reported to Carol, "and so far you're batting a thousand. Daniel and no disguise."

"Gazing into my crystal ball," she said, "I see Myron pronouncing your name, very clearly, ten times before dessert."

.   .   .

Everything happened exactly as Carol had predicted. With one exception. "You were right on the money," I told her later. "He said my name twice before we were even seated, and then he dropped the paper's name a few times for good measure. And whenever the waiter was near he thought up another assignment. If you were within ten feet of our table, you knew I worked for him. But you never said that he was going to stop and make a reservation as we walked out the door. That was masterful; I saw the maître d' put a little star next to his name, so they'll dance around his table all night."

"I should have thought of that," she said, looking chagrined. "If he'd been one of the masthead men, I would have."

"Right," I said, remembering the way Warren Hoge rejoiced whenever a restaurant got its fourth star. He liked to reserve a table the night the review came out so he could watch the staff react to the news. "They sent someone out for the first edition," he'd tell me the next day, "and then there was pandemonium and champagne!"

"Frankly," said Carol, "I didn't think Myron could afford Daniel."

"Special occasion," I said. "His wife's birthday."

"Of course," she replied. "The perfect present. Now, enough about Myron. Have you ever thought about being a redhead?"

Shirley eased her bulk off the stool and padded heavily around the counter to greet us. "Another one?" she said.

"My friend thinks I should be a redhead," I told her.

Shirley examined me, her head to one side. "That would work." She turned to Carol. "Short or long?" she asked. "Did you have some image in mind?"

Now it was Carol's turn to study my face as if she had never seen it before. "Long," she finally decided.

"Straight or curly?" asked Shirley.

"Curly," said Carol. "I was thinking of something a little kooky."

"Kooky?" I said. "What do you mean, kooky?"

"Erase that," said Carol. "It's not the word I wanted. What I meant was bohemian. You know, aging hippie."

"Isn't that going to be weird?" I asked. "I mean, what would an aging hippie be doing at Daniel?"

"That's the point," she said. "I want you to look like you don't belong there."

"Won't I stick out like a sore thumb?"

"Yes," she said. "You will. That's my plan. Who would wear a disguise that made them conspicuous?"

"I get it," I said, "sort of. I look so out of place that everyone stares at me. But while they may think I look strange, they won't think I'm me, because if I were me I'd be trying to blend in."

"Exactly!" said Carol.

Shirley was laughing and shaking her head. "Do you know that you're both crazy?" she asked. "But I don't mind. And I'm sure we can find the wig you want."

Humming a little, she walked over to the cupboards and began pulling open the drawers. As wigs tumbled out she snatched this one and that, creating a pile of burnished hair that grew steadily larger, a haystack in shades from copper to maroon. "Might as well have some fun," she said, handing me a wig cap.

"Too big," said Carol when I put on the first one, a flaming frizz that turned me into Bozo the Clown.

"Too small," she said when I slipped on tight little curls. Glancing into the mirror, I saw that I had the forlorn look of a hennaed poodle.

"Wrong, wrong," she cried when the next one went on. Fat, strawberry-red curls hung by my cheeks, making me ludicrous, like an aging Ann-Margret.

The short straight cuts made my head look too small for my body. The preppy copper pageboy was cute and perky and plain wrong for my face. I was going quickly through the pile, slipping on one wig after another and turning to face them. Each time they shook their heads.

"Okay," said Shirley, when the pile had dwindled, "see how this one works." The wig she handed me was long and oddly scruffy, with none of the neat shininess of the others. When I slipped the hair on my head it didn't slide into place the way wigs usually do. It just sort of flopped forward and sat there, a solid mass of carrot red that hung into my eyes and fell below my shoulders.

I pushed aside the messy bangs and looked into the mirror. I looked rumpled and sleepy, as if I had just climbed out of bed. "Brenda," cried Shirley, "comb your hair!"

"Brenda?" I asked. "Brenda? Where did that come from?"

"I don't know," she said, "it just sort of came to me. Do you like it?"

"Brenda," I said, trying it on for size. "Yeah, she could be Brenda."

"It doesn't seem like a wig," said Carol. Her voice was small and strained. Looking at her, I suddenly understood Shirley's strategy, knew why she had made me try on so many wigs. She had known that the first ones wouldn't work, but she had also known that they would enhance the drama of finding the right wig.

The effect on Carol was startling. "You seem—" she was struggling for words "—like Brenda." She kept her eyes on me for a few more beats and then said, "I feel as if I know exactly who she is. I know what kind of makeup she wears. And I can see her clothes."

Looking in the mirror, I felt giddy and excited, the way I did the first time I put on my mother's high heels and suddenly saw myself as a grown-up. Afterward, studying my parents the way all children do, I began to notice that my father always looked the same but my mother was a chameleon with the ability to choose whom she wanted to be. I watched her primping for a party and saw that she became someone else when she dressed up. Once she lost weight, and for a while she dyed her hair, and both times her personality changed with her looks. Then I began to study the other girls in school and realized that making new friends could be as simple as changing the way I dressed.

Most little girls, I think, grow up with the instinctive understanding that we have the power to direct the way the world sees us. It is why fashion has such a powerful pull. But until the moment that Carol met Brenda, this had never been a conscious consideration. "And what *does* she wear?" I asked now.

"Vintage," said Carol. "Definitely vintage. Brenda likes bold, old clothing. Japanese kimonos, cocktail dresses from the twenties, those great old shoes with platforms. Bright, bright colors. And I think she wears glasses."

"Glasses?"

"Yes," said Carol firmly, "she definitely wears glasses. Big ones with colorful frames. She's not one of those people who wears rimless glasses, hoping nobody will notice that they're sitting on her nose. Dorothy Parker didn't have her in mind when she wrote the poem."

Shirley was beaming. "I wish," she said fervently, "that you were here to talk to all my customers. These poor women come in with no hair on their heads, and they have such a great opportunity to remake themselves. It's their chance to try on new personalities. But what do they want? To look as much like their old selves as possible."

"Of course they do!" cried Carol with such heat that I suddenly remembered that AIDS had claimed her daughter. "When people are ill they need to be reminded that they're no different than they used to be, just because they're sick. They need to know that they're the same people they always were."

Shirley saw that she had stepped into quicksand. "You're right," she said, hurriedly extricating herself, "of course you're right. I don't push. But I keep thinking it's a wasted opportunity." Sighing heavily, she walked around the counter, back to her own side.

"No wonder she loves working with you," said Carol when we were back on the street. "You're her dream come true, a living testimonial to the power of her product." She stared at the wig on my head and asked, "Do you ever go back to show her what you look like in full regalia?"

"No," I said.

"This whole thing embarrasses you, doesn't it?" she asked.

"A little," I admitted. "When it's just a costume and I don't get into character, I feel like such a fraud that I'm afraid someone's going to come along, pull the wig off my head, and cry, 'Aha!' But getting into character can be eerie. It makes me feel sort of schizophrenic, like my thoughts are mine, but not mine. And people react to me in a whole different way, as if I really were someone else."

"You're lucky," she said. "Most of us would love to be someone else, at least part of the time. C'mon, let's go finish Brenda. I know a terrific vintage store on Thompson Street. The owner is nuts, but she has great stuff."

Michael's Resale, where I usually shopped, was a musty upstairs store on Madison Avenue with a sad, slightly apologetic air. The clerks were older women who seemed to look down on their customers, and they always made me feel like a pitiful specimen trying to pass for rich.

But here we were assaulted by the thump of rock music the minute we walked into the store, and surrounded by a happy swirl of noise and color. A woman stood in the center of the room, so laden with costume jewelry that she looked like a Christmas tree, and when she spotted me she called out, "You're a 1264." Going to a rack, she began collecting garments. "You're in luck," she said as her arms filled. "Twelve-sixty-four just dropped off a new consignment. Take a look."

Then she squinted at Carol and said, "You might be an 823. A little conservative, but just your size with a very rich husband. The guy's a dope; he buys her clothes but doesn't give her spending money. So what does she do? She buys two of everything and brings me one to sell. That way she always has money in her pocket and I always have plenty of merch. I wish the world had more dopes like him."

She extracted an old Chinese silk coat from the rack; it was soft beige with printed flowers dancing down the front. She held out the beautifully worn silk and said, "Twelve-sixty-four. Can you see yourself in this?"

"That's exactly what I had in mind!" cried Carol as I reached to touch the coat. It was soft, and as I stroked the cloth it changed color, going from beige to mauve as it rippled in the light.

"She has a taste for the exotic," said the proprietress. "See if it fits." She looked at Carol and started pulling suits from the rack. "Eight-twenty-three, just look at these labels! Armani. Jill Sander. Dior."

"We're not here for me," said Carol.

"Suit yourself," said the proprietress. Slightly miffed, she turned to help a skinny dark-haired girl zip up a Pucci skirt. "It's dripping with character!" she whispered huskily.

The girl spun happily, twirling so that the bright turquoise cloth flew out in a circle from her waist.

"Aren't you glad," the proprietress asked her, "that you don't have to deal with shiny newness?" She seemed to mean it, to think of the original owners as garment-tamers whose main purpose in life was breaking in clothing to make her customers comfortable.

I shrugged into the coat. It was much too big, but so soft and beautiful, the color changing as I moved, that I began putting on layer after layer beneath it. Watching, the proprietress softened. "Do you wear orange?" she asked suddenly. "Some redheads don't, but I have a long orange tunic, silk, that would look fabulous with that coat. And some green silk capris. You'd be a knockout."

On anyone else the outfit would have looked brazen; on Brenda it just looked whimsical. "I knew it!" said the proprietress. "Don't you look fabulous? Do you like it? How does it feel?" She had a sudden inspiration and fumbled at her blouse, removing one of the ornaments. Handing me a huge brooch covered in rhinestones, she said, "Try this. Pin it right at the throat."

I took the thing, which was heavy in my hand, and did as I was told. It was gaudy and very silly and it looked remarkably right. The proprietress grinned. "Twelve-sixty-four called that her Sparkle Plenty Pin. Now I want you to try these shoes."

They were green suede platforms, the heels much higher than anything I'd ever worn, and they made Brenda look ten feet tall. She resembled me in no way that I could discern, but I liked this large woman with her messy hair and friendly face.

"Got any glasses?" asked Carol.

"Big bowl over there," replied the woman, pointing. Carol rummaged around. "These!" she suddenly shouted triumphantly, waving some curved green frames in the air. "Put them on." I hooked the glasses over my ears and looked in the mirror; the lenses were tinted a subtle gray, obscuring the last vestige of Ruth.

"Lipstick!" said Carol. "You need lipstick."

"I never wear it," I said. "I mean, not normally."

Carol made an annoyed little sound; she didn't either. "Here," said the proprietress, holding a tube in her outstretched hand. Carol grabbed it, turned, and painted on a generous red mouth, completely ignoring where my own lips ended.

It was just the right touch; the transformation was complete. Brenda was cozy and crumpled and she looked so warm-hearted that I wanted to get to know her. What would she be like?

"Don't forget about 823!" the proprietress shouted to Carol as we walked out the door. "She'd be perfect for you. Most of her clothes still have the original tags!"

I wore my new clothes home, wondering if anyone would recognize me. Gene would be the first test; instead of using my key, I rang the doorbell. When he pulled the heavy glass door open I waited for his great, friendly laugh.

It didn't come. He just stood staring, open-mouthed, looking at me so frankly that I tugged at my wig, thinking I must look ridiculous. Then I saw that his expression was goofy, unlike any I had ever seen him wear. He was acting as if I were a gift, a surprise package that had been unexpectedly delivered to his door. He actually bowed a little from the waist. "Come in, come in," he said, motioning me forward. I walked in and he followed so closely that he was practically stepping on my heels.

"And which of our lucky tenants have you come to visit?" he asked. I began to laugh and he said, "Am I funny?" giving me the dazed look of a love-struck kid. "All visitors here have to be announced," he continued gently. "Who shall I call? Who should I say is here?"

"Michael Singer," I said. I found that I was using my radio voice, which is lower and slower than my normal one. "Please tell him it's Brenda Rose."

"Certainly, Miss Rose," he said, going to the phone. It was nice of him to play along like this, I thought, hoping that Michael would do the same when presented with this unfamiliar name.

Apparently he did, because Gene was motioning me into the elevator. He never took his eyes off me as we ascended to the tenth floor, and I could feel him ferreting out the little bits of Ruth beneath the disguise. He jerked the elevator when it stopped, which surprised me—Gene was the smoothest driver in the building. He laughed a little, embarrassed, as the elevator rocked to a halt. And as he pulled the gate open he said, "First door to the right," in a very soft voice. And in an even softer one he added, "I'll be looking forward to the pleasure of taking you downstairs again" in tones of utter sincerity.

Disconcerted, I waited until the elevator door had closed. But when the gate had clanged shut and the elevator was chugging its way back to earth, I pushed open the door and peeked in. Michael and Nicky were standing at the end of the hallway, and when Nicky saw me he came running, joyfully calling, "Mommy, Mommy, Mommy!" as he leapt into my arms like an exuberant puppy.

"Who are you?" he asked, fingering the red wig.

"Brenda," I said. "Do you like her?"

He leaned back and gave me a critical stare. "Yes," he said solemnly. "You look like a very nice person."

"And what do you think?" I asked Michael, a little embarrassed.

"Nice," he said. He stared at me for another minute and added, "I don't think you're exactly my type, but I'd be happy to go out to eat with you."

"Can we, Mommy?" asked Nick. He put on his most pleading smile, looking from Michael to me and back again. "Daddy, can we take Brenda out to eat? Can we take her out right now?"

"Not tonight," I said. "I'm going to cook dinner."

"Please, please, please," Nicky begged. "Please can we go to the chop chop place?"

Michael cocked an amused eye at me, waiting for my reaction. "Your secret would be safe with us," he said under his breath. "No one would know it was you at the chop chop place. And Brenda looks like she might enjoy it."

"The chop chop place" was Nicky's name for his favorite restaurant, Benihana, an establishment no self-respecting restaurant critic would set foot in. It was a marketing strategy disguised as a restaurant, and while I couldn't help admiring the way the owners maximized real estate and minimized labor, it depressed me. I hated the food and its assembly-line quality, and I hated the way they rushed you through your meal.

These sensible thoughts sped through my mind, buzzing like bees. Then they had flown past, disappeared, along with the thought of the chicken I'd been intending to roast, and Brenda was smiling her big red smile and saying in her soft, warm voice, "Benihana is an excellent idea. A perfect idea. How smart of you to think of it. Let's go get dressed for dinner!"

Where's your mom?" Gene asked Nicky when we got into the elevator. I had a sudden pang; Nicky had gone along with Miriam, and now I was asking him to do it again. It seemed like a lot to ask of a kid.

But my son didn't blink. "She had to go somewhere for her job," he said, as if pretending I was someone else was the most natural thing in the world. "She can't come with us tonight," he added helpfully, and I understood that to him these costumes were nothing but a very fun game.

"Well, you're lucky to be going out with Miss Rose," said Gene, giving me the goofy look he had worn when he first saw me at the door. "I bet you like redheads as much as I do."

Nicky frowned. "Her hair's not red," he said. "It's like that metal stuff."

"Copper," said Gene. "It's called copper. You're right. But I think it's the most beautiful color hair can be. I've always been a sucker for redheads."

"Not me," said Nicky loyally. "I like brown hair like Mommy has."

Gene ruffled his hair. "You're a good kid," he said. "I'll be sure to tell your mother what you said."

I looked to see if he was serious. I couldn't tell. Nicky giggled, and looking down I saw sheer delight on his face. Why not? For once he knew more than a grown-up. When we reached the ground floor Gene leapt out of the elevator and scurried down the hall like a big, benevolent turtle. "You folks have a beautiful evening," he said, pulling the door open for us. Nicky giggled again.

People smiled at us on the street, as if we were the most adorable family, and I found myself smiling back, looking people right in the eye. My mouth felt big and loose and generous, and the shoes made me feel tall and powerful. I found that I was striding forward, leaning into the wind like one of those gaudy carved figures on the prow of a boat. It made me feel a little lightheaded and utterly optimistic.

There was a line at Benihana. Michael winced. "I know you hate lines," I heard myself saying in Brenda's low, slow voice, "so why don't you go for a walk around the block? Nicky and I don't mind waiting, do we, hon?"

Hon? Where did that come from? I looked down to see if Nicky was giving me strange looks, but he was just smiling back, saying, "No, we don't mind waiting."

The man just in front of us turned to say, "You have to wait if you want Willie." He looked down at Nicky and added, "Willie does tricks!"

"All the chefs do tricks," I said. "That's why we're here. Nicky loves the way they make the chicken go flying onto his plate."

"According to our friends," said the man, "Willie does the best tricks."

He held out his hand. "I'm Bill. This is Christopher. And we'd like to ask you a question. Where did you get that *amazing* coat?"

We were fast friends by the time we were finally seated, and it turned out that Bill had been right: Willie *was* worth waiting for. His hands flying at the speed of light, he chopped vegetables and arranged them into clown faces on the grill. He sent diced chicken flying all over the restaurant—into his hat, into his pocket, ricocheting from Michael's plate across mine and right onto Nicky's. He urged Nicky to try mushrooms (he liked them!), got him to taste shrimp (he didn't like them), and with his antics set the tone for the evening. At dessert time Bill made a little cap out of napkins and perched it on Nicky's head so we could try filling it with fruit. Nicky seemed surprised that I allowed such rowdy behavior. To be honest, I was sort of surprised myself.

"Here's our phone number," said Bill as we paid our checks. "Call the next time you're planning to come. We'll join you. It just wouldn't be the same if you weren't here."

"I like eating dinner with Brenda," confided Nicky on the way home. "She talks to people. Being with her is fun!"

"More fun than when I'm really me?" I asked, struggling to keep my voice neutral. I was surprised to find that I was hurt.

"Yes," said Nicky. "Brenda's more fun."

Michael squeezed my hand, somehow knowing what I was feeling. "What are you talking about?" he said. "She *is* really you. She's just you in a particularly good mood." Then he laughed and added, "Maybe you should be Brenda more often."

And then we were home and Gene was running to open the door, grinning at me with that ridiculously goofy grin. "I can't help it," he said, "I'm a sucker for redheads." He turned to Michael and said, "Your wife's not home yet."

"She may not be home until very late," Michael murmured. "But Brenda's going to stay and keep us company until she gets here."

He and Gene exchanged glances, and I had the oddest feeling. Can you be jealous of yourself?

. . .

Daniel?" said Michael a few days later when I pulled the red wig onto my head. "You're taking Brenda to Daniel? Do you think she'll fit in?"

"No," I said, explaining Carol's strategy, "I'm sure she won't."

"It's just crazy enough to work," he said. "It's so completely counter-intuitive. Who's coming?"

"Jules," I said. "And he's bringing some new girlfriend he says we'll like. She's a painter."

Michael looked relieved. "I don't know how the food will be," he said, "but I do know that we're going to have fun."

It was Jules who had introduced Michael to me. I had known him since college, when he'd become like an instant cousin, and we'd been moving in the same orbit ever since. Jules traveled light. Right after I moved to Berkeley, Jules came knocking on the door of the rambling Victorian house I was sharing with a group of friends. It was midnight and he had just broken up with the love of his life. "I'm only staying until I find my own place," he said, but eight years later he was still there, living out of a suitcase in the spare room. Jules moved to Los Angeles soon after Michael and I did, and for a while he parked his suitcase in our house in Laurel Canyon. Now we were in New York, and Jules and his suitcase were in a loft in SoHo, although that was liable to change on a moment's notice.

Small and thin, with a face composed entirely of angles, Jules had the peculiar elegance of William Burroughs, to whom he was distantly related. "I suppose he'll be wearing that beat-up brown leather jacket?" Michael went on.

"Probably," I said. "I don't think he has another."

"Good," said Michael. "We're going to make them crazy at that restaurant." He flung open his closet door, saying, "Now, what do you think I should wear?"

"Nothing special," I said hurriedly.

"Oh no," he said, "you wouldn't want me to look as if I didn't belong with you." He pulled out a bright blue shirt. "I think I'll wear this."

"You're rainbows," said Nicky when we went to kiss him good night. The babysitter laughed. "Nobody," she said in her Irish brogue, "would take you two for critics." She examined us for a second and said, "No worries. Everyone in the restaurant will have to put on sunglasses when you pair walk in!"

T he rest of your party is already here," said the maître d' dryly. It was only a few weeks since my lunch with Myron; was he looking at me too closely? I forced myself to give him a big smile, fighting the urge to flee as I felt the lipstick slide across my teeth.

"Follow me," he said, scurrying out from behind his little stand. "Your table is not ready." He hadn't recognized me after all! Galloping behind him, I understood that he hoped to bury us in the back of the bar, hoped we would somehow become invisible. But as he sped toward the dark corner where he had parked Jules, every head turned to stare at us. I waited for my face to tighten with self-consciousness, but instead I found myself slowing down, looking curiously around with Brenda's big lips formed into a smile. Carol's strategy was working, and it felt fine not to be hiding.

"Jules!" cried Michael when our little parade finally came to a halt. The maître d' pointed uncomfortably to the chairs and beat a very hasty retreat. "I'd like to introduce you to Brenda Rose."

Jules looked me over, his lips twitching. He was, indeed, wearing the brown leather jacket. He did not get up. "Nice," he said. "Amazing, actually." The woman with him had long black hair, and with her black skirt, black turtleneck top, black tights, and ballet shoes she looked exactly like a beatnik from the sixties. "This is Lorna," he said.

The beatnik stuck her hand out across the nuts and flowers that crowded the surface of the table. "Thanks for having me," she said. "I find it so incredible to be here. I've always wondered what these places were like."

Michael and I squeezed into the small space that had been allotted to us. Our knees touched. "I love this about New York," Lorna continued, gesturing around the warm, dark room. "An hour ago I was chasing drug dealers off my stoop so I could get out the door of my apartment. Then I walk up Avenue C, through streets reeking of urine, climb into the clatter of the subway, and fifteen minutes later I emerge into"—she pointed at a woman across the room whose low-cut black dress formed the perfect backdrop for an ostentatious diamond necklace—"all this."

As she said it, the woman got up and trudged resolutely toward us. She was a redhead too, but one of the soignée ones; she looked as if her time was evenly divided between her beautician and her personal trainer.

"I adore your coat," she said, reaching out to pet the silk. "Did you get it in China?"

"No," I said, "a thrift shop on Thompson Street."

"Oh," said the woman, taking a disappointed step back. "Too bad. I'm going to Hong Kong next week and I thought you might know someplace there that sells vintage clothing."

She turned to retreat to her seat just as a waiter arrived with a little silver tray. "These gougères," she said as she walked off, "are simply divine." With that she stretched out her arm and scooped one up as if we were all guests at a cocktail party.

"Hey!" said the waiter, startled.

"Those were ours!" said Jules.

"Do strangers always talk to you?" asked Lorna.

"They talk to Brenda," I said. And then I didn't say anything else because I had taken a bite of one of the little puffs and I was concentrating on the way they simply evaporated into hot, cheesy air when my mouth closed over them.

Gougères

1 cup water
¼ pound (8 tablespoons) unsalted butter
1½ teaspoons salt
1½ cups all-purpose flour
5 eggs
1 cup diced Gruyère cheese
Pepper to taste
½ cup grated Gruyère cheese

Preheat the oven to 375°F.

Combine the water, butter and a teaspoon of the salt in a saucepan and bring to a boil, stirring until butter melts. Remove the pan from the heat, let cool slightly, stir in the flour, and mix well. Return the pan to the heat and stir with a wooden spoon over high heat until the mixture comes away from the sides of the pan. Remove from the heat.

Stir in the eggs, one at a time until well combined. Add the diced cheese, the remaining ½ teaspoon salt, and pepper, stirring well.

Drop the dough by rounded tablespoons onto a well-buttered baking pan. Smooth the top and sides of each gougère with a knife, and sprinkle with the grated cheese.

Bake in batches for 25 minutes, or until puffed and golden. Serve immediately.

Makes 8 cocktail servings

.   .   .

We waited in the bar for a long time. We didn't mind; we were enjoying ourselves, looking at all the rich people in the room while an endless array of tidbits kept us busy. When our table was finally ready, the maître d' galloped us back across the bar, through the back door into the nether reaches of the dining room. The chatter of diners swelled at the sight of us, rising until it was a wave passing through the restaurant. Then it died, snuffed out by the overwhelming sense of well-being that hovered in the air.

One couple was frankly watching us, making no attempt to disguise their interest. The woman had thick white hair, and her patrician face, completely devoid of makeup, was soft and pretty despite the wrinkles. Her eyes moved slowly around our group and then settled on me and stayed there. Embarrassed, I picked up one of the tiny spring rolls the waiter had just set on the table and took a bite.

The crunch was so loud I jumped; it was almost supernaturally crisp. Then the crab inside came spilling out and I closed my eyes, allowing the sensuous flavors to permeate my body. When I opened them I found that the white-haired woman was still watching. I tossed my head and threw her a big smile. She colored and turned away.

"Okay," I said, keeping my voice low as I went into my spiel. This was private. "Lorna, here are the ground rules. Order as much as you can eat, the more the better. You can have anything you want so long as it's different from what other people are ordering; no duplicates. If you see something that interests you, claim it quickly. The first one who calls it gets it, and I don't negotiate food fights. Any questions?"

"Yes," she said. "What do *you* eat?"

"Whatever everyone else doesn't want. But I get to taste your food."

"So I can have the peekytoe crab salad," she said.

"All yours," I said.

"I wanted that," said Jules.

"Too late," said Lorna.

"Okay, then I claim the oyster velouté," he said.

"Lobster salad's mine," said Michael quickly.

Good, I thought, that leaves the linguine with truffles for me.

"Now what about main courses," I asked. And as I said it the white-haired woman leaned over. "Please excuse my interruption," she began. Her voice was quite high, with an English accent that sounded more pretentious than authentic. "But you should not miss the short ribs; they're exquisite!"

"Muriel!" said her husband, "please!"

"No, really," I said in my Brenda voice, "we are grateful for your help. Do you have any other suggestions?"

"Yes," she said reverently, "foie gras with quince."

"Please excuse my wife," said the man formally. His lips were tight, his face as stiff as a sheet of cardboard, and he held his hands out as if he were offering a benediction. "She can't help herself. Muriel doesn't understand that people want their privacy even in public places." He seemed genuinely embarrassed.

"It is quite obvious that these are people who appreciate food," Muriel said earnestly, "and they probably don't get to eat in places like this very often." And then, realizing what she had implied, she broke off. Her white hair made her red face even more so. "I'm so sorry," she blurted, "I didn't mean . . ."

"It's okay," I said, delighted by all this. Brenda's low voice was gentle. "You're absolutely right. This is a once in a lifetime experience for us, and we wouldn't want to blow it. Please go on."

She lifted her chin and threw her husband a small, triumphant look. "Just one teensy little suggestion. The wine-poached pear with verbena ice cream. It's very beautiful and you won't find that anyplace else!" With great dignity she lifted her goblet and saluted us with her wine.

"Brenda, Brenda, Brenda," said Jules, shaking his head. His lips twitched. "I'd like to get to know you better."

"Me too," said Michael, and once again I felt that odd little twinge. But then the first courses were there, and I was tasting the velouté of oysters, holding it in my mouth so I could savor the smooth, rich feel of the liquid as I picked out the flavors, first the oyster itself, then a hint of lemongrass. I felt the sea urchin slide beneath my tongue, as subtle and sneaky as the glow of a buttercup under your chin, and then admired the pop of the caviar as it was crushed beneath my teeth. It was wonderful soup, as if the chef were dreaming of the sea.

I tasted the linguine, fragile ribbons as delicate as butterfly wings with curls of white truffle skittering between them. "More truffle?" the waiter said, and then he was showering more of the pungent white shavings onto my plate.

"For Brenda," murmured Michael, "endless truffles. Maybe you should dye your hair."

I laughed, as if the idea was ridiculous, but I was beginning to understand that Brenda's world was a gentler place than mine: people wished her well.

When the *civet de lièvre,* hare stew with wine and onions, arrived it had a flavor so funky and complicated that I tasted it and tasted it again, wondering whether a New York chef would use the traditional blood to thicken the sauce. It had an elusive fermented flavor that I could not figure out. "Blue cheese?" I guessed, knowing that was not quite right. The waiter must have been watching, because he leaned over conspiratorially and whispered "Chocolate" in my ear.

"Chocolate?" I asked.

"*Oui,*" he said. "*Chocolat.*" He pronounced it the French way. And then he winked.

The wine contributed its own magic to the evening. The sommelier suggested the Marcassin Upper Barn, Gauer Vineyard and I said, yes, yes, anything, and the wine almost knocked me out with its richness. When he suggested that we follow it with an '88 Gazin, I knew I could trust him. And I could. The wine was plummy and delicious, perfect with the wild hare and the short ribs, which were everything that Muriel had promised.

Muriel and her husband were still there, lingering over coffee, as we left. Daniel Boulud was standing at the table, cozily talking to them in the special half French–half English language that was all his own. Muriel interrupted him to ask, "Did you have a good dinner, my dear?" as we passed.

The chef turned to look at us, and I saw how attractive he was in his chic little glasses. "Oh yes," I said, "a wonderful meal. A meal to remember. Thank you so much." And then, mischievously, I turned to Daniel and said, "You should hire this woman to oversee first-time customers. She made sure that we ordered all the best dishes. This was truly a four-star meal."

"Brenda," said Michael when we were in the taxi. He took my hand. "Eating with you is an experience."

I stroked his hand, smiling in the dark. I felt good, and I knew that it was not because of the wine or the good company or the wonderful food we'd just been served. I was experiencing the opposite of that horrid feeling you get when you know that you are behaving badly but feel helpless to stop it.

Brenda was my best self, the person I've always wanted to be. She was generous and funny, optimistic and smart. She was kind. Brenda, I imagined, would know how to be nice to Myron. But would they ever get the chance to meet? Now that I had discovered Brenda, I had a new dilemma: I hoped that finding the Brenda inside me would not always require a wig.

RESTAURANTS
by Ruth Reichl

....

A GREAT RESTAURANT is like a race-horse: it may take a while to discover its style, but once it does the ride is exhilarating.

Daniel, a year and a half into the race, has finally hit its stride.

"Four stars?" asks a friend one morning. It is 8 A.M., and he is calling to say thank you for the dinner we finished a mere seven hours earlier.

"I have never had a better dinner," he says, dreamily recalling ethereal linguine topped with slender shavings of white truffle. "If I concentrate," he adds, "I can still smell the truffles and feel those noodles dissolving in my mouth like gossamer ribbons. What a meal!"

"Can't we talk later?" I ask crossly. But he is busy remembering a velouté filled with plump caviar-topped oysters, butter-drenched leeks and sea urchin roe. The voluptuous flavors were rich and decadent, so that the hint of lemongrass in the cream soup combined with the bracing taste of caviar to deliver a gentle shock. "It was perfect!" my friend insists.

"Aren't you going to give them four stars?"

"I don't know," I say. "I have to go back a few more times."

"But was there anything wrong with the meal?" he wants to know. I pull the covers over my head and think for a moment. I hope he'll hang up. No such luck.

"They were nice to me when I walked in the door," he says, "and it was abundantly clear that I was not one of their regular customers. All my clothes put together did not cost as much as one of those custom-made shirts the other men were wearing. And although neither of us had a single piece of jewelry, the hostess could not have been more welcoming."

"Didn't you think the bar we waited in was awfully small and crowded?" I ask. "Our knees were hitting those of the people next to us. I thought it was uncomfortable."

"O.K.," he admits, "it was small. But they made up for it by bringing out that plate of lovely little cheese puffs."

"They're called gougères," I can't resist saying.

"Whatever," he says. "They were delicious. And we only had to wait seven minutes for our table. I timed it."

"But didn't you think the dining room was awfully noisy?" I persist grumpily.

He has to concede the point; the dining room was crowded, and noisier than it should have been. "On the other hand," he reminds me, "you said you thought the flowers were fabulous."

They were. The drama of the flower arrangements dominates the restaurant, transforming a bland beige room into a place with personality. There are no windows, but the flowers announce the seasons and set the stage for the food with designs so spectacular you find yourself rushing in the door to look at them.

"And you liked the service," he prods. He is right about that, too: the service that night was smooth and sweet, more like that in a stately mansion than a large restaurant. It was formal, thoughtful and not at all stuffy. The waiter passed the amuses gueules as if he were serving at a dinner party, urging us to eat the tiny crab spring rolls and mushroom toasts while they were still hot. One day at lunch, two Brazilian runners were seated at the next table. Before they had finished their meal, the waiter had not only offered tips for tourists in New York, but also convinced them that Daniel would be the perfect place to carbo-load before the marathon; the chef, he assured them, would be happy to create some special pasta dishes.

"Remember the nine-herb ravioli?" my friend asks now. Who could forget it? The floppy squares of pasta were filled with a bright green puree of herbs and painted with a vivid red coulis. Colorful leaves of herbs were scattered across the top with fragrant bits of toasted pine nuts and shavings of cheese.

"And the wild hare stew?" he asks. At that I sit up and sniff the air. I do remember the civet de lièvre. Its deep red wine sauce was thickened with blood and a touch of chocolate; it was so rich and exotic I was seduced into taking one bite and then another as I tried to chase the flavors back to their source. Served with a puree of chestnuts and the roasted loin stuffed with porcini mushrooms, the stew was a masterpiece of hearty regional cooking.

Daniel Boulud was, for 6 years, the much-acclaimed Chef at Le Cirque, but in his own restaurant he is working with a new confidence. He seems to be cooking for himself with a menu that offers both hearty French food and classic cooking so technically proficient it takes your breath away.

Chilled lobster consommé is a tour de force. The soup is as clear as crystal but so expressive of lobster that if you close your eyes and take a bite, you are surprised to find your mouth filled with liquid. The soup, decorated with rounds of lobster topped with crème fraîche and caviar, is dotted with coral cream when it is served. This is an astonishing dish worthy of a temple of haute cuisine. Still, if you want to continue with a less complicated course, you could order something as down-to-earth as tripes gratinées, hearty cuisine bourgeoise that would be at home in a great country bistro.

Mr. Boulud also offers a changing celebration of the seasons: daily specials that depend on little more than great ingredients. One might be the simple luxury of a large yellow potato mashed with lots of butter and fresh truffles, another an abundance of porcini sautéed in clarified butter, sprinkled with bits of rock salt and a small shower of herbs.

"And wasn't that foie gras fantastic?" my friend asks, reminding me of the way the unctuous liver had been balanced by the austerity of fresh quince. Fully awake at last, I begin to revel in last night's dinner as my friend and I start shouting the names of dishes, giddily recapturing a cornucopia of flavors.

"Pumpkin soup!" I say, recalling the bright orange puree anchored by a small mound of grated squash topped with black trumpet mushrooms, tiny bits of bacon and crunchy little pumpkin seeds.

"Steamed skate!" he cries, and in my mind I can see a broth the color of clover, and feel the way the corduroy texture of the fish was emphasized by the soft lobster dumplings in watercress-lobster broth.

"Quail salad!" I say, thinking about a lunch when I was served the most appealing salad I can remember. Leaves of mâche were topped with a pair of tiny fried quail eggs and laced with velvety strips of foie gras, silky pieces of grilled quail breast and rough shavings of Parmesan cheese.

"And the wine!" my friend says, reminding me of the sommelier's suggestions from that list of fabulous and fabulously expensive bottles. We had settled on a '91 Chassagne-Montrachet from Colin followed by a wonderfully plummy '89 Bon Pasteur.

"Desserts," my friend says now, almost reverently. Together we recite the sweets of the evening, like children recalling Halloween treats. I liked a fruit soup that looked like a reverse sunset, a mint green verbena ice-cream sun setting in a magenta wine-poached pear. He liked the gratin of chocolate, a slim disk of warm chocolate on a fragile sugar wafer. We both loved the crème brûlée with macerated strawberries, and were charmed by the finale, a plate of petits fours with its fanciful pulled-sugar birds and flowers.

"So?" says my friend. "Four stars?"

"It was a great meal," I concede, pushing back the covers, "but I still have to go back and see if Daniel can sustain that level of cooking."

Five meals later, it is clear that the restaurant can. I have had an occasional disappointment: a salty soup, a 15-minute wait for dinner, a lost reservation at lunch. But even on an off day, the restaurant is so exciting that you wake up the morning after a meal at Daniel eager to remember every bite.

It's quite a ride.

DANIEL
★ ★ ★ ★

Thank you for your splendid review of Restaurant Daniel," wrote Daniel Boulud after my review appeared. "We are particularly pleased that you were inspired to write in an innovative style."

Other people wrote in much the same vein. One person called it the strangest review she'd ever read. Another asked if I had been abducted by aliens. A third said that I did not quite seem myself.

Rereading the review, I saw what had happened: Ruth did not write the review. Brenda did.

Dinner with Chairman Punch

Everybody at the paper had an Abe story.

My friend Janet Maslin, the chief film critic, told me one about the time a star reporter decided to quit. He spent weeks agonizing about how he was going to tell the boss. He even had nightmares about it. Finally he took a deep breath and marched straight into Abe Rosenthal's office.

To his surprise, the executive editor was very nice. Abe looked sad. Abe wished him well. Abe even told him he would be missed. The reporter was very relieved, and he walked to the door with a spring in his step. But just as he put his hand on the doorknob, Abe called out, "Do you remember Jim, the guy who left the paper last year?"

"Sure," the man answered, "I remember him."

"Do you know where he went?"

"No," the reporter answered, "I can't remember."

"Exactly!" pounced Abe. And as the door closed, a wicked smile spread across his face.

. . .

Abe, they told me, was ruthless. Abe loved power. Abe was mean. He moved his men around the world like pawns on a chessboard, caring not one whit about their own desires. People assured me, on an almost daily basis, that I was very, very lucky I hadn't been at the paper in the days of Abe Rosenthal.

I couldn't help feeling that they were all protesting just a little too much. I sensed an undercurrent of envy running through these stories. They hated him, but they were proud of him too. And they were proud of the paper he and Arthur "Punch" Sulzberger had produced.

Now the next generation of Sulzberger had taken over the family paper. The outside world had named him "Pinch" but around the newsroom Punch's son was generally known as "Young Arthur." The new publisher was just a little too touchy-feely for the old guard, and Max Frankel, the retiring editor, didn't have a mean bone in his body.

And things were about to get worse. Joe Lelyveld was taking over at the paper, and Joe, as everyone knew, was a truly decent guy. Far too decent, my colleagues assured me, to be a great editor.

My own Abe encounter ran true to form. I first met him at one of the retirement cocktail parties given to outgoing editors as a consolation prize. These were held in the only glamorous room in the dusty old building.

To get there you took an elevator to the top floor. It spit you out into one of the grim corridors that welcomed reporters every morning. This one, however, was different from the others; it made you run a gauntlet of portraits, all the people who had won Pulitzers for the paper. Who the hell do you think you are, they seemed to shout at you, sauntering down our hall? I always found myself moving faster and faster, desperate to reach the small flight of stairs at the end. By the time I got there I was running, and then I shot up, making my escape.

It was a masterful piece of stagecraft, intended to strip you of arrogance. When you finally burst into the room at the top, your sense of self had been diminished. The room itself finished the job.

It was a luxurious two-story atrium made of glass, a smug perch in the center of Manhattan. From up here the glittering midtown lights seemed no more than a piece of jewelry designed to decorate the paper. Waiters circulated with little round trays, proffering delicate hors d'oeuvres and wine in crystal goblets. It made you feel like an insignificant but privileged participant in whatever was going on at the pinnacle of power. Each time I was invited up there I felt lucky, like Jean Arthur in a Preston Sturges film, certain that a mink coat was about to come floating from the sky and land on my head.

Abe lost no time in taking care of that.

"Oh," he said when we were introduced. He took two steps back and picked up my hand as if it were a four-day-old fish. "The restaurant critic." He said the words as if they tasted bad, as if he wanted to spit them out quickly and fill his mouth with something tastier. He did not relinquish my hand, just held it as if he were fending me off while he considered his next words.

From all the stories I had imagined a giant, and I was surprised to discover that he was a small man with a perpetually peeved air. With his glasses, his sharp, beaky nose, and his wispy hair, he looked exactly like a contentious owl. I thought of the Pogo comic character, the one who utters absurd malapropisms. Abe's words, however, were clipped and concise.

"Hiring Bryan Miller is one of the things I am most proud of," he said, biting off the syllables. "*He* was very good." And then the great Abe Rosenthal turned away, searching out his next victim.

"Bryan took him to dinner all the time," said Carol when I related the conversation the next day. "He had no choice. But you got lucky; Max had no desire to be your dinner guest." She tapped the elegant lace-up oxfords she always wore and added, "Believe me, you would have known it if he had." Her phone rang, but before she picked it up to say "The Living

Section" in her clear, cool voice, she made one more pronouncement: "Now that Joe's the editor, you're safe. Food is definitely not his thing."

I considered Joe and thought she was probably right. He was a wisp of a man, with the gray pallor of an ascetic and the anxious abstraction of an intellectual. The only outward clue that he had been anointed steward of America's finest news-gathering organization was a slight stoop in the shoulders and a heaviness of step, physical signs that this slight, sandy-haired man now felt burdened by the weight of the world. Abe had gotten taller with the job, standing up straight as he reveled in the power. Joe, the rabbi's son, seemed to shrink beneath the weight of his huge and terrible responsibility.

So I was surprised to pick up the phone one morning and hear, "Please hold for the executive editor." Joe wanted to have lunch with me after all. It was the first of the many surprises Joe had up his sleeve. The secretary said that she would make the reservation, and I wondered where we'd go: Joe was obviously not interested in lunch at Lutèce.

Joe was late, and I stood in the lobby, chatting with the guards while I waited. They were eating lunch, enormous submarine sandwiches that seemed too big for mere mortals, purchased from some place on Ninth Avenue. Nevertheless, by the time Joe rushed up with an apologetic smile the sandwiches were gone.

"I have a meeting in an hour," he said. "Would you mind if we just get a bite somewhere nearby?"

He took me to one of the hotels that were starting to open in Times Square—the vanguard, we were told, of an army of gorgeous new buildings that were about to invade the neighborhood. They were supposed to rout out sleaze and bring new life to this sad and used-up patch of Manhattan, but it was hard to imagine that Times Square would really have a renaissance. The first few hotels were anything but promising.

The table was tiny, the food forgettable, and I discovered that Joe had no small talk at all. As the conversation dragged we both looked around uneasily, longing for escape. During the excruciating silences I fished for something to say. He didn't seem to have any questions for me, so I tried throwing a few at him. "Yes," he said. "No," he said. I have never met a more uncomfortable conversationalist, and in desperation I resorted to asking about his days as a foreign correspondent.

Joe had been in Hong Kong, Johannesburg, New Delhi. He had won a Pulitzer for his book on South Africa, *Move Your Shadow*, but that was not what he wanted to talk about. He wanted to discuss the food in India and Hong Kong, and he did it with real enthusiasm. He was so animated that I understood how much he had loved all those foreign places. Suddenly the lunch was flying by, and I no longer had the sense that he would go back to the office and put a check mark by my name. "Let's have lunch again soon," he said when we parted. "Do you think you can find a good Chinese restaurant within walking distance?"

"Probably not," I said. He looked so crestfallen that I quickly asked, "How do you feel about Korean food?"

"I'd like to go to a Korean restaurant," he said with a sweet smile that made it clear he was telling the truth.

Please hold for the executive editor." It was a few days later. After the usual pleasantries—what a nice lunch it had been and so forth—Joe got to the point. "I have just learned," he said, "that the chairman has never been to Flushing. Can you imagine?"

"Shocking," I said.

"I was talking about how much it's changed, how very Chinese it's become," Joe continued. "I started telling him how much it reminded me of Hong Kong and he said he'd like to see it. So I want you to find the best Chinese restaurant out there and set up a banquet for us."

"Gladly," I said, trying to sound upbeat, efficient.

"Who's the chairman?" I asked Carol.

"The big guy," she said. "Punch Sulzberger. He's not the publisher anymore, but he's still Mr. Chairman at this company."

"Joe says he's never been to Flushing," I said.

"That's impossible!" she replied. She thought about it for a second and then reversed her decision. "I guess it's not. But why would you care?"

"Joe wants to organize a tour. And he wants it to end with a fabulous Chinese banquet. That's where I come in. You know anyplace out there? I've been to great Korean restaurants in Flushing, but every Chinese place I've tried has been terrible."

"Me too," she said. "But if it reminds him so much of Hong Kong, you ought to call the Hong Kong Tourist Board. They might have some ideas."

They did. My contact told me about a new seafood palace that had just opened. She said that once you got inside the door, you felt as if you were in Hong Kong. They'd held their own banquet there the week before, and been extremely impressed.

"She said that at lunchtime they serve all the trendy new dim sum they're now making in Hong Kong," I told Carol. "Come with me?" Carol, who loved the Number 7 train, never had to be asked twice.

We climbed into the bowels of the Times Square station, going deeper and deeper beneath the surface of the city, below all the other subway lines until it felt as if we had reached the center of the earth. It got quieter as we descended through the dank, filthy layers of the station, and as we slithered through the final strata I began to wonder whether we would ever again see the light of day. Then the train came wheezing into the station and the doors slid open in such a sinister invitation that I hesitated at the threshold.

It was an ancient train, the walls covered with interlocking graffiti, the seats torn, the floors pocked with grime. Half the lightbulbs were out and it was so dim that it was hard to see the other passengers. We sat down, balancing on the edges of our seats, trying to make ourselves as small as we could. The doors slid closed.

We traveled east, from one ghostly stop to the next. Each time the doors slid open, pale, silent people boarded the train. No one ever seemed to get off, and I felt my breathing get shallower and shallower. I started to worry that I was going to have a panic attack. And then, suddenly, the train was climbing, climbing, up into the light and we were bursting through the surface and the train was flooded with sunlight and everyone was smiling. I began to breathe again as I gazed at the city sprawled beneath us, looking clean and beautiful. The river had become a silver thread, sparkling off in the distance. Manhattan, sleek and elegant, winked from the far side of the water.

Now the train whistled through the streets of Queens, turning us into voyeurs as we stared at the dioramas in the uncurtained windows. A breakfast table flashed past, a coffee cup overturning in slow motion on the table. Then an unmade bed, an old woman in a wheelchair gazing blankly at the blue screen of a television while a young woman in a quilted housecoat vacuumed around her. Below us the colors of the children playing ball changed as we passed through staid pub-filled Irish neighborhoods and raucous Jamaican ones where the sidewalks became a riot of violent hues and the throbbing sound of metal drums wafted up to the train. And then we were in India, and the aroma of cardamom, cumin, ginger, and turmeric was so powerful that we had to resist the urge to jump off the subway and follow our noses to a restaurant. The scent changed again, and by the time we got to Flushing Main Street, the end of the line, the air was filled with garlic and soy sauce. We got off and clambered down the stairs, ravenous now.

It *was* as dense and intense as Hong Kong—little grocery stores and bakeries and restaurants crowded together in a dizzying mass. Men stood on corners spooning clouds of homemade tofu out of big silver pots and frying fragrant turnip cakes on jerry-rigged griddles balanced on cardboard boxes. Billows of anise and five-spice announced that women were cooking red-cooked oxtails on one side of the street while the competition on the other side dished up bowls of fish balls and steaming tripe. Frogs escaped from the straw baskets that held them, hopping down the streets, dodging men wheeling whole roasted pigs and racks of ducks.

After the boisterous streets, KB Garden Restaurant seemed as cold

and quiet as an icebox. Shiny philodendrons, still wrapped in congratu-
latory red ribbons, stood at attention in the front of the room. Tanks
hugged every wall, fish swimming in frantic circles as they waited to become dinner. Peering through the throng of waiting customers, we could
see that the restaurant was a vast, high-ceilinged hall, so large that the
other side of the room might have been in a different state.

Dozens of women trolled the room, swooshing down the aisles with
laden carts, stopping to hold out baskets of dumplings—har gow and siu
mai and some I'd never seen before—and plates of vegetables, roasted
meats, pastries.

A hostess in a slim silk dress handed us a number and we waited our
turn, growing hungrier and hungrier as the minutes passed. "Dim sum
with two people is so embarrassing," said Carol. "You end up ordering
more than you can eat, just for the variety, and then everyone looks at you
as if you were a great big pig."

The young woman in front of us turned to look at her and I experienced a quick moment of embarrassment; engulfed in the sing-song
sound of Cantonese, we had been talking the way tourists do, as if nobody
could understand what we were saying. "It *is* uncomfortable to be alone
when eating dim sum," she said. Her face was Chinese and very beautiful,
her accent clipped and very British. "The moment I walked through that
door I wished I had not come. " She tossed a strand of long black hair
over one shoulder and smoothed her suit. Was it Chanel or just a knock-
off? I couldn't tell, but I understood that she felt as out of place as we did.

"Would you join us?" I was taking a chance.

"I would not be *de trop*?"

"No, please, you would be doing us a favor. We're eager to try as much
as possible."

"You are certain?" she asked, her face softening. Her name was Diana,
she was from Hong Kong, and she was doing graduate work at N.Y.U.
"Sometimes I so much miss being at home. I am filled with a longing to
hear familiar sounds, smell familiar smells, be among faces that are not
white," she said. "So I come to Flushing. But once here I realize that I am

as foreign here as I am in Manhattan, and I understand that the idea was not good. This bears no resemblance to home; the people are poor, their accents unfamiliar."

"And the food?" I asked.

She smiled. "Yes," she said. "The food. That is not unfamiliar. That is why I come."

The hostess led us to a table and I began turning this way and that, searching out the good carts. Meanwhile Diana sat like a statue, calmly raising one manicured hand. "We will now order tea," she said, issuing instructions to the waiter in rapid Chinese.

"If you do not order tea," she said, "they bring you the cheapest swill they can buy. It is dreadful stuff, nothing you would want to drink. But even if you do not care about the quality of the tea, by demanding the best you make the establishment understand that you know what is good and are willing to pay for it. And then you get a better meal."

"What did you order?" I asked.

"Iron Goddess of Mercy," she said. "It is always my preference. It comes from the Wuyi Mountains in Fujian. The mountains there are very steep and in the old days monkeys were trained to climb up and pick the leaves. It is a lovely story, but the tea is even lovelier and extremely fragrant."

The tea was strong and very dark with a taste that reminded me of whiskey, of olives, of cold winter nights. "I asked the man to bring us some duck webs in oyster sauce as well; they are very good here and I will be devastated if they run out. And I also ordered some big dishes. You must not leave without tasting the shrimp."

She pointed an elegantly manicured fingernail toward a tank on the wall; the waiter was dipping a net into the water. He came up with a tangle of shrimp angrily waving their feelers at the intruder. He dumped them unceremoniously onto a tray and a waitress rushed off to weigh them. Two minutes later he was setting a plate of rosy shrimp, steaming slightly in their shells, onto our table. Their feelers were still.

"You simply pull off the shells and dip them in this sauce," said Diana, removing her rings as if she were rolling up her sleeves. With one rapid motion she slipped the shrimp from its carapace, dipped it into the soy and scallion sauce, and put it into her mouth. Her small white teeth closed around it. "Excellent," she said. "This reminds me of home."

The shrimp were plump and sweet, with a soft delicacy that was not like any shrimp I've ever tasted. For a moment I imagined that we were actually in Hong Kong . . . and then I was back, eating another shrimp, and another, the shells piling up into a small mound on my plate.

Great platters of green snow pea shoots were set on the table, and a whole sole, simply steamed in ginger. Diana was stopping carts filled with clams in black bean sauce, and tiny spareribs coated in rice flour. We ate bowls of ginger-laden congee, the thick porridge hot enough to cook the slivers of raw fish served on the side. The duck webs were all texture, gelatinous and so soft that the bones dropped from them when you put them in your mouth and all you tasted was mushrooms, soy sauce, ginger, anise, and wine reverberating down to your toes. At the end we had little dot hearts—the deep yellow tarts made of lard and filled with sweetened egg yolks—that are one of life's primal pleasures. And then, finally, those crisp little sesame balls that melt into such sensuous chewiness it seems like a trick.

We didn't talk much—just ate the food and watched the carts and listened to the activity in the big room. "I am so happy," Diana said, sighing, when the bowls were empty. "It was lovely to have your company. Please be my guests."

"That's out of the question," I replied.

"But it would give me such pleasure," she said.

Wondering how to stop this argument, I had a sudden thought. "I have a great favor to ask of you."

"Yes?" she said, raising an eyebrow.

"I want to order a banquet. I need your help."

The eyebrow went down. When I explained the purpose of the banquet, her lips curved into a small smile. "The chairman of the New York Times Corporation?" she breathed. "I would be very honored."

I had forgotten how much the Chinese respect status. When Diana summoned our waiter and asked for both the bill and the banquet manager, she looked positively regal.

The man who presented himself was not impressed. He was young and sharp, with his hair slicked back, his tuxedo pressed, his shirt starched. He doled out a supercilious smile meant to tell us how lucky we were to have his attention.

Diana took his measure, swept him with a cool look, and spoke in a commanding tone we had not heard before. He stuck his hands in his pockets and gave a deliberately careless answer.

Diana's face turned to ice and her voice became a bark. The man was startled into standing at attention. She said something in an even sterner voice and he stood up straighter. Ten minutes later, when he pulled his card out of his pocket, all the starch had left his body.

She glanced at the card and handed it to me. "Now you give him one of yours," she said in a different voice, one that said she was tired of all this and ready to depart. The man respectfully accepted my card, saying in careful English, "I can promise you, ladies, that this will be a banquet to remember." Diana nodded a curt dismissal and he shot off before she could change her mind.

"What did you say to him?" I asked Diana.

"I began by informing him that you desire to have a banquet for some very important people. A dozen, I said—is that about right?"

"I don't know," I admitted. "But it must be, more or less."

"He asked if you were willing to spend three hundred dollars."

"That's so cheap!"

"An insult," she said, flicking it away with disdainful fingers. "But merely the opening shot in the negotiation. I replied, very casually, 'Oh, we might spend more. Maybe even five or six hundred dollars.' Then I paused and said, so low that he had to ask me to repeat it, 'They might even spend eight hundred eighty-eight.' That impressed him. It's a big number and eights are lucky to us. It showed him that I was a serious customer."

"What did he say to that?" I asked, fascinated.

"Oh, he was impressed. He said, 'Well, for that I could do a lobster salad.'"

My face fell. "Lobster salad? Who wants lobster salad?"

Diana laughed. "Please do not look so sad," she said. "We were negotiating. Of course I told him that was not what we had in mind. I said"— and here her voice took on the contemptuous tone she had used with the banquet manager—"I see you don't have anyone in the kitchen who is capable of cutting vegetables. Too bad. I thought this was supposed to be a good restaurant. Oh well, there are plenty more we can try.'"

"What did he say?"

"He was very quick to contradict me. Of course, he said, of course their people could cut vegetables. And then I said that we only wanted the banquet if the head chef, the *dai si fu,* was going to cook it. I said that we needed a person who understands the way to treat important people."

"What did he say?"

"He said that he could accommodate us. He said that last night they did a banquet where they served a phoenix with five thousand feathers on its back. That's a complicated cold plate. He said that the night before they served pandas at play, with pandas made of tofu, playing with carrot balls. It sounded quite ornate; the beasts were cavorting around a gelatin lake on which daikon swans were swimming. The landscape was dotted with broccoli trees and there were paths made of cold meats and walls built of sugared walnuts."

"Wow!" I said. "Sounds impressive."

"Perhaps," she conceded, "but I think he was just talking. It's a famous dish and I don't believe that they really served it. So I yawned and said, 'Pandas at play is pleasant. But don't you ever do anything original?'"

"You didn't!"

"I did! And then he said that if we were willing to pay the men in the kitchen for their trouble he was sure they would produce something really special, something no one had ever seen before."

"Oh, good," I said. "Joe will like that."

"I asked him what he took us for, that of course we intended to pay the men in the kitchen. We hardly expected them to do extra work for free. I said that we were entertaining big shots, white people who spend much of their time in Hong Kong. I threw down a challenge. I said that all my friends say it is impossible to get good food in Flushing."

"Did that impress him?"

"Definitely." Diana's smile flashed briefly. "That is when Raymond asked for your card and gave me his. He went back into the kitchen to make up a menu. He will fax it to you this afternoon."

"What do I do then?" I asked.

"Send it back!" she replied. "Whatever he offers, you must not accept it. He'll think that you don't care, or that you don't know what you're doing. You have to tell him it's not good enough, challenge him to be better, fax him back, change the menu a few times, be demanding. That's how it's done."

"I never could have done this without you," I said.

"I know," she replied. "And now I don't feel badly about allowing you to pay for my lunch. But I must go; I want to buy some superior shark's fin and fermented tofu. They will tide me over until I come back."

We walked out of the restaurant, going in opposite directions. Not until the subway doors had closed did I realize that I had neither her last name nor her number.

"Some reporter you turned out to be," said Carol.

The menu arrived a few hours later. Carol and I stood by the fax machine as the document, half in ornate Chinese calligraphy, came rolling off the machine.

I read the first dish and rejoiced; Raymond had suggested the many-feathered phoenix surrounded by jellyfish, spicy pork kidney, beef shank, pork shank, little fried fish, jellied eels, thousand-year-old eggs, smoked fish, and squid with celery. "He took Diana at her word!" I said.

"Maybe," said Carol, "but what's this?" Her finger was pointing to the next line. "Egg rolls?"

I shuddered. It was an insult.

"And this?" she said. On the line below the white-cut chicken and the eight-treasure winter melon soup was lobster salad.

"These sound good," I said, noting the next line: fried roe shrimp and whole steamed flounder with its own fried bones.

"Yeah," she said, "but look at this! It sounds like some tired dish from Chinatown." Her finger was resting next to something called steak kue. It was followed by Peking duck and fried rice served in pineapples. The finale was sweet dim sum.

"Diana didn't get all that much respect!" I said.

"He must be testing you," said Carol. "But at least he offered the phoenix with a thousand feathers."

I crossed out the squid and substituted baby octopus. My pencil slashed through the insulting egg rolls and replaced them with steamed scallops in the shell, with XO sauce. I left the chicken, but asked for shark's fin soup instead of winter melon. I put Dungeness crab with ginger and scallions where the lobster salad was, and replaced the fried shrimp with live boiled ones.

"I sort of like the idea of the flounder," I told Carol. "Do you think my honor will be compromised if I accept it?"

"You can't change everything all at once anyway," she said. "You have to leave something for the next go-round."

"Okay, but the steak kue, whatever that is, has to go immediately. And Peking duck—does he think I'm a fool? In a Cantonese restaurant? I'm asking for red-cooked pork belly and crispy chicken."

I watched the fax slowly move through the machine and take its message off to Flushing. Ten minutes later I had my reply.

Raymond offered fried soft-shell crabs in place of the Dungeness. He didn't have any baby octopus and he wondered if my guests were going to be happy with the pork belly; perhaps I'd like to try some roast baby pig?

"You can't have the pig and the crispy chicken," Carol pointed out. "Maybe you should change the chicken to something more elaborate."

Each time a dish changed, the entire menu had to change with it. It was an oddly pleasurable process. After the first flurry of exchanges everything slowed down, and for a few days we proceeded at a languid pace, a relaxed Ping-Pong of flying faxes. When it was all over I had raised the ante (shark fins are expensive), but the chairman was going to get a spectacular meal.

I called Joe's secretary and left the message that I had found the restaurant and finalized the menu. When, I asked, did Joe want to have the banquet?

She called back to request a copy of the menu.

"He wants to see it?" I asked stupidly.

"That's what he said."

I shrugged and put the document into one of those interoffice envelopes we were always being exhorted to use to save paper.

For a few weeks there was an ominous silence from the third floor. I began to worry. When Joe finally called, he was not reassuring. KB Garden Restaurant, he said flatly, would not do.

"Why?" I asked. "The food is wonderful."

"Yes," he said, his voice dry and unfriendly. "But I went there."

"You actually ate there?" I asked, surprised.

"Yes," he said. "It is not at all what I had in mind. Were you aware that they serve their banquets right in that enormous room? The food was good enough, I suppose, but we need something better for the chairman. We need a private dining room. You'll have to find another restaurant."

"Does he think I have nothing better to do?" I fumed. "I don't have time to go running out to Flushing every day to find a restaurant just to please him!"

"Ruth," said Carol, "you have time. Or you have to make time. Unless you want to have nothing *but* time. If you know what I mean."

I did know what she meant, but I resented it. Everyone else treated me as if I were the Princess of New York and here was this guy reminding me that he was my boss, that I served at his pleasure. It made me prickle with irritation.

Each trip on the Number 7 train made things worse. I was following every lead, trekking out to Main Street every few days. But the places with good food weren't good enough for the chairman; they were too big, too cold, or too shabby. And the ones with décor worthy of such an august personage had food that was not fit to eat. I was in despair. Time was running out.

And then Ken Hom came to town.

When I first met Ken we were both living in the Berkeley flatlands on very little money, both madly in love with food. He had a reputation as both a cook and a tour guide. Poor people bragged about being invited to his house for meals. Rich people bragged about the remarkable tours he arranged for them in Hong Kong. "I always wished I had the money to go along," I told Carol, "but eating at his house was pretty wonderful."

"I've heard of him," she said. "I think Craig mentioned him. He said he was a terrific cook."

"He is, but now he seems to spend most of his time in France. He's got a fourteenth-century château he's been restoring."

"Where'd he get the money for that?"

"He's England's best-selling cookbook author. He had some cooking show on the BBC, and his books sell by the millions."

"But does he know anything about Flushing?" she asked.

I shook my head. "Probably not. But if anyone can find out, he can. After all, he was just a kid from Chicago before he became Mr. Hong Kong. Joe seems to think Flushing is just like Hong Kong, so I'm going to ask Ken to pretend that it is."

Ken's publicist thought that a food tour of Flushing was a swell idea; she assured me that her client was well acquainted with Queens. I believe the words she used were "knows everything there is to know." I doubted that, but I was certain that by the time we met, she'd make sure he did; after all, a story in the *New York Times* is every p.r. person's dream.

Ken arrived in a limousine. He jumped out, wearing what looked like a million-dollar suit set off by a long white silk scarf. "Look at you!" I said, kissing him.

"Look at *you*," he replied, and we both burst out laughing. I climbed into the cozy car and promptly forgot that I was supposed to be the *New York Times*.

"Can you believe that they pay us to do this?" I said.

"Shh," he whispered, looking more like an excited adolescent than England's hottest celebrity chef. "We can't ever let them know that we would do this for free."

Where did Ken find out so much about New York's newest China-town? I'll never know. He whirled me through Flushing as if he had grown up there, introducing me to men whose nicotine-stained fingers beckoned us into hidden rooms with tanks of improbable fish. He found fruit and vegetables I had never seen before in New York—durian, man-gosteens, galingale—and women came whispering out of the darkness to offer mysterious packages of spice. We ate Sichuan food so hot that each bite sent shock waves through my body, and funky Fujianese dishes laced with musty red wine paste.

We drank beer and whiskey, and he beckoned me down rickety stairs into restaurants where mine was the only white face. Eating a bowl of soft noodles with a mysterious crunch, I discovered that the long white strands were laced with tiny crabs. As my teeth dissected another shell, I thought, finally, that Joe was right, this really was an Asian city, once you penetrated the invisible wall.

It was very late at night when we got to the Taiwanese restaurant. Was it the fourth meal, the fifth, the sixth? I had lost count, but I had also lost all interest in food. Undaunted, Ken ordered a platter of spareribs, and when they appeared my appetite came with them; they were thin and crisp, absolutely irresistible. Great bowls of beef and noodle soup, thick with five-spice flavor, came next, and I ate that too, along with bracing platters of clams with basil.

It was past midnight and customers were still coming through the door as the air grew thick with smoke and the strangely lonesome Chi-nese music grew louder. I thought that this would be the place to bring the chairman, but I knew I was only thinking that because it was late and I was tired and happy and filled with too much Chinese whiskey.

There was no traffic going home, and the road beneath us was an unbroken ribbon stretching back to the city, the wheels turning in a comforting thrum. "Let's have another adventure soon," said Ken when I stumbled out of the car. "Come to France. Let me cook you a really fabulous meal. Just wait 'til you taste my duck!"

Nice piece," said Carol a few weeks later, when the article about my adventures with Ken appeared. "Sounds like you had fun. But wasn't the whole point to find a restaurant for the banquet?"

"How could I tell him that the places he took me weren't fancy enough?" I said. "I was embarrassed. I didn't want to insult him."

Carol wasn't fooled. "You just forgot. You were having too much fun."

I acknowledged this with a rueful smile. "Don't worry," said Carol, "I've had another idea. The last restaurant in your article made me think of it. What about Taiwan?"

"What about it?"

"Did you ever ask any of the Taiwanese officials where to eat?"

It was an excellent notion. The people from the Taiwan mission to the United Nations were very helpful. The woman with whom I spoke said that her own favorite restaurant might be just what I was looking for. It was not large. And yes, if she remembered correctly, there was a private dining room.

Carol and I were on the next train.

Flushing First Taste was small, with a kind of shabby elegance meant to convey seriousness. Cloths covered the tables and three solemn gods presided over the back of the room, which could be closed off for banquets, keeping watch over a locked case filled with expensive bottles of whiskey, Cognac, and Scotch, each carefully labeled with a customer's name.

The chopsticks were of good quality, a promising sign. And the dishes that we ordered—paper-wrapped chicken, crisp, tiny pork ribs, pea shoots cooked with eggs in chicken fat, steamed fish fillets in rice wine—were all wonderful. Carol and I looked at each other.

"Do you think?" I asked.

She nodded. "This," she said, "is definitely the place."

But I had learned my lesson; this time, I took nothing for granted. I gave Joe's secretary the address of the restaurant and waited for his call.

When it came (he approved), I moved to the next step and began planning the menu. Remembering Diana's advice, I went back to Flushing for a meal and started the negotiation. And then the faxing began.

It took three days, but at the end I had a menu that was surprisingly similar to the one I had negotiated at KB Garden Restaurant. I proudly sent the final product to the third floor.

"You aren't going to believe this," I told Carol a couple of days later.

"Let me guess," she interrupted. "Joe wants to rewrite the menu?"

"He doesn't think what I've chosen is sufficiently splendid for the chairman. He's taken charge and everything has become fancier. Now there's abalone on the cold platter. We've replaced the squab with stuffed blue crabs and the duck with baked lobster. And instead of baby pig we're having salt-baked crab."

"It sounds like it's all seafood," she said.

"It is, pretty much. They're always the most expensive ingredients. But I have to hand it to Joe; we're going all out. The pièce de résistance is going to be dancing shrimp."

"What?"

"It's a dish I've always wanted to try. They put live shrimp into rice wine and slowly heat it up. The shrimp die drunk and happy and according to everything I've read, the flavor is amazing."

"Too bad you won't get to taste it."

"Oh, I get to taste it all right. Joe expects me, and Michael, to be there."

"Really? Who else is going?"

"Oh, nobody who counts. Just the chairman, the publisher, the managing editor, and Arthur Gelb. Remind me who he is."

"That would be the great Arthur Gelb to you. He used to be the managing editor. Not to mention holding just about every other powerful job at this paper."

"Yeah, I thought he had to be somebody big. Plus assorted wives. And us."

"When will this feast take place?" she asked.

"Next Tuesday," I replied, "September eighteenth."

"Pray for a major news event," she said. "It's the one thing that will save you. If something big happens, they'll have to call it off."

On Wednesday, September 19, 1995, the *New York Times* published the Unabomber Manifesto. "You must have a direct line to Heaven," said Carol when I showed up that morning. "You got your major news event. What a relief!"

I shook my head, and Carol crossed her arms and looked at me incredulously. "Don't tell me they all went anyway?" she said. "I don't believe it!"

"At six o'clock on the button," I replied, "a small squadron of limousines pulled up on West Forty-third Street to take us to the great Flushing feast. I knew from the get-go that it was going to be bad: in the scramble for seats Michael and I got separated."

"Oh no," she said, "Donald would kill me. Who did he go with?"

When I said "Gene Roberts," Carol winced.

The managing editor was a severe and awkward person, but when I saw Michael climbing into his car, I thought he and Michael might actually get along. Gene had a national reputation as a journalist's journalist. But I caught an occasional glimpse of their car as we inched our way forward in the agonizingly dense rush-hour traffic, and I could see that

Gene was in back, Michael in front. Every time I saw them, Michael looked more miserable.

"He said Gene treated him like an imbecile," I went on. "He apparently asked Michael what he thought of the paper's Whitewater coverage and then got mad at the answer. Gene's supposed to be such a straight shooter, and Michael never minces words. I'd have thought it would be okay."

"Why would you think that?" asked Carol. "Nobody ever talks straight to those guys, and they don't like it when someone says they've made a mistake."

"Apparently."

"Great way to start the evening."

"Oh wait," I said. "It gets better. In my car everyone was second-guessing the printing of the Manifesto. The conversation went on forever; the traffic was terrible."

"So did Punch get his tour of Flushing?"

"By the time we got there, we were so late that we just got off the highway and went right to the restaurant. I thought we might take the tour as an intermission during dinner, but by then things were pretty tense. Besides, there were no cars to take us."

"The cars didn't wait?" she said. "How'd you get back?"

"We had to call more cars when we were done. I guess it's cheaper if they don't wait."

"Seems like a weird time to pinch pennies," said Carol.

"I guess. I was just so glad to finally be there. I think the manager was afraid we were going to stand him up. He bowed and smiled and showed us right into the private room."

"Was it okay?" she asked.

"It was nice," I said. "They'd closed off the back of the restaurant and the room looked pretty. Very private. The suits seemed happy for at least a minute. Then the waiter pointed to the big golden pot sitting in the center of the table and said proudly, 'That's for the dancing shrimp.'

That was when the trouble started. The chairman went pale, and young Arthur looked uncomfortable, and I thought uh-oh, we've got a p.c. problem with the shrimp."

"Ooh," she said, her voice pained, "I never thought of that."

"That wasn't the problem. You're not going to believe this: the chairman doesn't eat shellfish! He's allergic, I think."

"No!" said Carol.

"Yes," I said. "We might just as well have gone home. That pretty much put a pall over the whole event. He was very nice about it, but even the phoenix platter was mostly seafood."

"All that work!" moaned Carol. "All those meals. All those trips on the Number Seven train!"

"Yeah," I said glumly. "It was pretty much downhill from there. Everybody tried. Young Arthur gave a toast, but it was like listening to some guy from the Moose Lodge being insincere. He thanked Joe for arranging this, nodded in my direction, and said something so formal to the chairman that you'd never know he was his father."

"The truth is," said Carol, "that even though they're father and son, they barely know each other. But cut to the chase: how was the food?"

"The dancing shrimp were amazing! The waiter filled the pot with fragrant herbs so that when he lit the fire beneath it, the whole room filled up with this great piney perfume. Then he brought in the shrimp—they were wriggling around—and as the wine was poured over them they began to dance. A couple of them danced right out of the dish! The waiter added them to the broth one by one, and then snatched them out. They were incredibly good—sweet and silky soft."

"Mmm."

"Then we had little stuffed blue crabs, and baked lobster with pea shoots and salt-baked crabs."

"All seafood," she said.

"All delicious," I said. "And thank God it was Joe who made the menu."

"What did the chairman eat?"

"Chicken. And more chicken, and more chicken. He couldn't even eat the winter melon soup, which was amazing, because it had seafood in it. And then, ta da! We got a dish he could eat. It was soy sauce chicken. I've never had a better chicken; it was moist and fragrant with crisp skin and almost as much fat as a duck. But I guess by then the chairman was pretty sick of the stuff."

"What'd you talk about?" she wanted to know.

"Oh God," I said, remembering, "don't ask. It was so embarrassing. They kept making these horrible white guy jokes, as if the waiters couldn't understand what we were saying. Maybe they couldn't, but I was so embarrassed. Everyone liked the steamed grouper with ham and shiitake mushrooms, and they loved that fried rice served in a pineapple. It was familiar food. But then it was time for dessert."

"Let me guess," she said. "They weren't into hot papaya soup with white fungus?"

"You should have seen the faces."

"But they must have liked the little pastries?"

"Yeah, except that by that time everyone was remembering that the cars had been sent back and worrying about how we were going to get home."

"You had to wait?"

"It took a while. When we finally climbed into ours, Michael said, 'I bet that was the last time the chairman comes to Queens.' And then he looked at me and said, 'I would have given anything to be at home tonight, eating your Thai noodles. I sure hope that Joe has more luck with the Manifesto than he did with that dinner with Chairman Punch.'"

Betty

The woman climbed onto the M104 bus so wearily you knew that her knees ached and her ankles hurt and her swollen fingers chafed against the string handles of the shopping bag they held. She tackled each step as if it were a hurdle, slowly hauling herself up one, then another, and the next. When she had mastered the final hurdle she paused, winded by the effort. With slow deliberation she set the bag down and clicked open the worn pocketbook dangling from her arm. Some searching produced a puffy change purse, and she carefully counted out the quarters and dropped them into the fare box. As the final *ping* rang out, she bent for the shopping bag, hefted it, and headed timidly up the aisle, breathing soft "Excuse me's" as she went.

Her hair was short, gray, and chopped off at the bottom, as if she had scissored it herself. Her skin was powdery white. She wore no-color glasses. The ragged hem of the dress that strayed beneath the formless coat was a nondescript print—white squiggles on a dark blue background. The handbag was large and square. And her feet were laced into sensible shoes: high-heeled oxfords, the black leather perforated with little holes. Timeless, ageless, sexless, her anxious eyes surveyed the nonexistent seating possibilities, and by the time she reached me they were registering dismay. She set the shopping bag down. It sighed, folding wearily in upon itself. Just as it ceased moving, the driver gunned the engine and both the bag and the woman lurched forward. As she reached for my seat to keep from falling, another soft "Excuse me" escaped into the overheated air.

She smelled sweetly old-fashioned—a powdery mixture of talc and that perfume they used to sell at Woolworth's in little blue bottles—but beneath the flowers was something else. It was the musty scent of old apartments. It was the smell of peeling paint, boiled vegetables, and dirty laundry. It was the aroma of loneliness.

When I stood up, she looked utterly surprised. "For me?" she whispered, pointing to the seat.

I nodded and we switched places. As she sank down she said, "Thank you, dearie. No one ever stands up for me" in a voice so soft I had to lean down to catch it. "Sometimes," the whispery voice continued, "I feel invisible."

Invisible. The tide of people moving inexorably toward the back of the bus pulled me along, but as I traveled up the aisle, the word kept echoing in my head. Invisible. I watched her from a distance and saw that she was right. I waited for an eye to catch hers, or a smile to move in her direction, but the people on the bus moved past as if her seat were empty. I was so absorbed in this surveillance that I did not notice when the bus went sailing past my stop.

We headed up Broadway and the Gaps, the Benettons, the Circuit Cities, gave way to little bodegas and 99 Cents or Less stores. In that fall of 1995 the gentrification of the Upper West Side did not extend past Eighty-sixth Street, and as we traveled north the neighborhood grew increasingly tattered and the crowd increasingly thin. All the fur coats got off.

At Ninety-eighth Street the woman pressed the buzzer and began the difficult process of extricating herself from the seat. As she staggered down the aisle, no arm reached out to help. No one paid her the slightest attention until she was laboring slowly down the stairs, and then it was just the man behind her, frowning at the pace of her progress. When she finally reached the bottom step he pushed past in exasperation, nearly knocking her over.

I got off and followed as she navigated the streets. In the grocery store the brusque Korean woman behind the counter silently watched her slowly count out coins for a quart of skim milk, a box of Raisin Bran, and a can of dog food. Next door in the drugstore, the bored cashier filed her nails, never even lifting her head as the woman paid her for Correctol. On the sidewalk nobody stopped to nod or smile as she shuffled past. And when she reached her building, the young man walking out brushed impatiently by, letting the heavy door swing shut behind him. She caught it just before it closed, grimaced, squeezed through.

I scanned the names listed next to the buzzers on the door, wishing I knew which one was hers. She was not Clementina Suarez, I was certain of that, nor was she likely to be James Poldor. I wondered if she could be Katherine Reynolds? Probably not. Howardina Saunders? Not likely. Definitely not Samaritana Ratazzi or Bobby Lynn Nelson. June Jarvis Farley? Possible, but I thought not. And then a modest name leapt out at me, a gray cloth coat of a name: Betty Jones. My invisible woman was Betty Jones.

Becoming Betty Jones was easy; her clothes can be found in any thrift store. The dress, the coat, the square handbag, and the glasses were all waiting for me in the first Salvation Army store I tried. I even found the shoes, a pristine pair of Enna Jetticks that fit me perfectly.

"Oh my God," said Carol when I appeared at the office dressed in my latest purchases. "What did Michael say?"

"That he wouldn't be seen with me looking like this," I replied.

"Who can blame him?" She laughed. "Where'd you find her?"

"On the bus," I said. "When I got up to give her my seat, she said she felt invisible. And I realized that she was just what I've been looking for. I followed her home; her name is Betty Jones. What do you think?"

Carol examined me, her eyes running over the cheap gray wig I had bought at the crowded Chinese wig store on Fourteenth Street, and the shapeless dress. She nodded. "If you keep your mouth shut and have everyone call you Aunt Betty, nobody will know you're there. Who's your first victim?"

"Tavern on the Green."

"Please watch for Ruth!" said Carol.

"Exactly," I replied. A few months earlier, to the enormous amusement of the entire staff, an anonymous reader had sent me a memo written by the restaurant's manager, Thomas W. Monetti, asking the staff to "watch out for Ruth." He'd attached a photo, along with a list of the aliases I had been using. He told them I had very curly long hair, mentioned that it was unruly, and in what I considered a rather low blow said that I pushed my hair in front of my face so that people wouldn't recognize me. (Surely he gave me more credit than that!) For some reason he seemed to think that I liked small groups ("she only travels in parties of two or three"). He also had the idea that I had an "advance person," described as a "gentleman about thirty-eight years old, who usually comes in and checks the front desk and lobby area first and then waits for Ruth, either in the cocktail lounge or at the table."

"I'm sure Michael was thrilled by that," said Carol. "And didn't the man say that you went into the ladies' room to speak into your secret tape recorder? You don't do that, do you?"

"I haven't used a tape recorder in at least ten years," I said. "He got a lot of stuff wrong. In the next memo, which I didn't show you, the guy said I was short and always wore black."

"You do wear a lot of black," she said.

"You mean, unlike every other woman in New York?"

"Point taken."

"That's not my favorite bit," I said, scanning the memo, looking for the passage. "Here it is: 'Another thing that may help you recognize her: I have been told that she's always smiling. She smiles a lot.'"

"Well, you do," said Carol reasonably.

"What a great clue: they stop all smiling women at the door," I said. "But it doesn't matter because their system sucks. I was there in June, which is when that second memo was posted. I wasn't even in disguise, and they never made me. They were so busy looking for some short smiling woman in black with a thirty-eight-year-old advance man that they completely overlooked two grumpy couples with an excited little boy."

From a distance Tavern on the Green looks like an enchanted fairyland surrounded by a golden haze. For three years Nicky and I had passed the restaurant every day as we walked home from school, and every day he looked longingly up at the thousands of little lights they had strung through the trees. Some days he ran up and pressed his nose forlornly against the window, reminding me of the Little Princess dreaming about a better life.

For three years my desire to make my son happy did battle with my good sense. I had been at the restaurant many times over many years and the food had never been anything but dreadful. There were no credible reports of improvement until a few months ago, when the owner had, with a great deal of fanfare, finally hired a good chef. Patrick Clark was a big cheerful guy who had been in Los Angeles when I was. I had always admired his food, and I thought that if there was anyone who could save a restaurant serving 1,500 meals a day, he was it.

"Bad?" asked Carol.

"Worse than I thought it could possibly be. We got there at seven-thirty and by a quarter of nine we had eaten our way through the bread basket and were begging for food. I kept getting up to take Nicky on walks, trying to entertain him. We went to the gift shop; we examined all the different dining rooms; we even went outside to look at the topiary gorilla. But when we came back, still nothing."

"Did you ever eat?"

"Yeah, and when the food finally came I have to admit it was okay. But by then Nicky was asleep on my lap. Now when we pass the place he doesn't even glance at the lights."

"So I guess you're not taking him," said Carol. "Who *are* you taking?"

"You remember my mother's friend Claudia? The acting coach? She's bringing some friend of hers. She won't tell me a thing about her, but she says that as soon as I meet Helen I'll understand why we need to have her with us."

"So you'll be three old ladies?" said Carol. Her eyes crinkled with laughter. "I can't wait to hear about it!"

Michael and Nicky watched me dress.

"I think she looks like a very nice person," said Nicky loyally. "She looks like Matt's grandma."

"See," I said, turning to Michael, "you could come along and call me Mom."

"Thanks anyway," he said.

"What's your name?" asked Nicky.

"Betty," I said. "Betty Jones."

"How old are you?" he asked.

"Sixty-eight."

"You look older," he replied.

"I've had a hard life," I said.

"Don't you have any children?" he asked. Like all beloved children, he felt very sorry for childless grown-ups.

"No," I said, "I'm a spinster."

"Oh, too bad." And then, "What's a spinster?"

"A woman who's never been married."

"Poor you," he said. "No children. No husband. You must be lonely."

"Yes," I said.

"Are you poor too?"

"Pretty poor," I said. "At least not rich. Tonight Claudia is taking me out to dinner."

"Did you warn her?" asked Michael. "Does she know she has to pay the bill?"

"Yes," I said. "I told her to bring a credit card and I'd pay her back. And I told her whom to expect. She's never met Chloe or Brenda, and I think she's sort of eager to see who I've managed to concoct without her help."

"Good luck," he said.

"'Night Mom," said Nicky. He examined Betty for a moment and added, "I'm glad you have someone to be nice to you."

I put on the shapeless black coat I had bought for Betty and threw a shawl over the gray wig. I pulled on sensible black wool gloves and picked up the square black pocketbook. Glancing in the mirror, I realized that only a few inches of the real me were visible, just below the glasses.

Still, I was not prepared for Gene's reaction. When the elevator door swung open, he didn't smile or say hello. He just stood there as I got on, waiting to close the door, and then allowed the car to descend. As we fell toward the ground he stared straight ahead, and when I exited, the "Good evening" he murmured was a mechanical response to my "Thank you." I couldn't help feeling that if I had remained silent, he would not have acknowledged me at all.

As I walked up Riverside Drive, not one of the many people walking dogs, wheeling strollers, or carrying briefcases glanced my way. No doorman tipped his hat as I went by. By the time I got to the corner, I felt as insubstantial as the wind; when people looked my way they saw only the buildings at my back. When I waved my hand the taxis hurtled past as if I were not there. I finally resorted to stepping into the middle of the street.

"Where to?" asked the driver, who had stopped to avoid hitting me.

"Tavern on the Green, please," I said, practicing my softest voice.

"Speak up," he said, and when I repeated myself he stepped on the gas so hard I was thrown back and pinned against the seat. The cabbie stared straight ahead, racing madly through the avenues as if he were piloting a bumper car in a small-town carnival ride. He shot through every light just as it turned, passed to the right of cars, swerved through intersections cutting off pedestrians. "Slow down!" I pleaded. In answer he stepped on the gas, narrowly averting a baby carriage that was nosing into a crosswalk.

"Please!" I shouted, but he did not acknowledge my alarm. Perhaps it was how he always drove, but it made me feel like an old boot, a piece of junk that he was desperate to deposit at its destination.

When we swerved into the driveway and shuddered to a halt in front of Tavern on the Green, I was very grateful. I pulled the door open and staggered onto the pavement. I was so shaken that my hands trembled as I counted out the money and pushed it through the window, feeling every minute as old as I looked.

Claudia was standing beneath the awning, her diminutive body dwarfed by a handsome hawk-faced woman with short blond hair who was clad entirely in cashmere and furs. As each taxi pulled up, Claudia studied its occupants. She stared at me for a moment, and I should have felt triumphant when her gaze moved on. Perversely I felt only sadness.

I limped morosely up to tap her on the arm; my shoes were too tight and my feet hurt. She turned toward me, considered my face, and asked, "Betty?"

As I nodded and bent to kiss her, she said, "I want you to meet my friend Helen. But come inside; it is frigid out here. You must be cold too." She took my arm and we walked into the fantasyland that is Tavern on the Green. Looking up at the lights twinkling in the foyer, I remembered how thrilled Nicky had once been by the tacky theatricality of the place.

"Oh," I whispered, trying for the reverent tone of a tourist walking into Chartres cathedral for the first time, "isn't this lovely?" My voice was filled with wonder as I scrutinized the overdone room. "It looks just like Christmas."

"Lovely," said the tall friend, casting a suspicious glance at Claudia, as if asking what on earth she meant by foisting such a peculiar person upon her. An elegant specimen, she made no attempt to disguise her disdain for this tawdry room—or for me for liking it. "It's a museum of things that should never have been made," she said fiercely, plowing through the crowd to initiate the process of checking us in. All around us heads swiveled to watch her progress, and I saw that she was an attention magnet. Had Claudia brought her along as a decoy?

"My compliments," Claudia whispered when she was gone. "You look quite remarkable."

"I know," I said in my most pathetic voice. "At the moment I am not feeling at all like myself. Oh, not in the least." And I threw back my head and opened my mouth, gazing up at the dangling ornaments with what I hoped looked like innocent awe.

The dining room was heaving with candles, balloons, plants, paintings, and chandeliers, but even their combined forces were not enough to combat the chill of a big glass edifice on a windy winter day. To my dismay the young hostess insisted that we check our coats and then led us inexorably through the urban greenhouse to a table right against a window. "Prime seating!" She smiled.

When I asked, "Do you think we might be able to sit somewhere a little warmer?" she did not trouble herself with an answer. Turning on her heel she left us to shiver on our narrow chairs.

"You have to be more forceful!" cried Helen. "You made it sound as if she'd be doing us a favor to give us another table. We're paying for this meal; it's her *job* to make us happy." The intensity of Helen's irritation made me realize that the Betty Joneses of the world are a particular trial to elegant older people. "A cup of tea," she announced now, waving her hand imperiously at the nearest waiter, "I must have a cup of tea." He ignored her.

Undaunted, Helen lifted her beringed fingers to the next passing person, who happened to be a busboy. He ignored her as well. At that Helen simply stood up and marched toward a waiter unwise enough to be standing idly, but visibly, nearby. He looked unhappy, but he moved off in the direction of the kitchen.

"Helen," Claudia told me, "is quite an expert on tea." She thought for a moment and added, "Actually, I think she considers herself an expert on everything."

"How do you know her?" I asked.

"She was an aspiring actress," Claudia replied, "who came to me for lessons. As an actress she was quite hopeless, but over the years I have found her to be a rather entertaining friend. Although"—she cast a dubious eye over me—"had I known that this was the role you had planned, I doubt that I would have chosen her as our dinner companion. The wealthy, I find, can be quite obtuse and they often permit themselves to behave very badly."

"Our tea," said Helen, strolling back and seating herself with the smile of a Cheshire cat, "will be here directly."

The tea arrived but there was nothing in its wake. "Have you ever seen such terrible service?" cried Claudia. "You could be wearing a sign that said, 'I am the restaurant critic of the *New York Times*,' and nobody here would give a fig."

"Oh, I doubt that," said Helen knowingly. "If that Ruth Reichl were here, I imagine things would be quite different."

"Do you?" asked Claudia. I peered at her face, which was alive with mischief, and realized that she had not let her friend in on my secret. All at once I began to understand why Helen was here. And in that moment I began to enjoy myself.

When the captain finally came to take our order, I gave it to him in my most timid tones. "I can't hear you," he shouted. "Speak up."

"It's so loud in here!" I repeated. To be honest, I could hardly hear myself.

"Please, lady," said the captain, "talk louder. I'm not deaf, but you talk so soft."

"It's too loud!" I said again.

"You say you want the salad?" he asked.

"NO," I said, raising my voice a bit, "the dumplings."

"Caesar, or beet and walnut?" he asked.

Helen watched in exasperation and then extracted a sterling silver pen from her pocketbook. "I," she announced to the waiter, "will write the order down for you." She glared at me.

"Thanks, lady," he said gratefully. "Makes my job easier." He pocketed the paper and moved off.

All around us people were videotaping each other, celebrating anniversaries and birthdays, so enchanted with Warner LeRoy's antic room that they didn't seem to mind the tardiness of the food.

At our table things were considerably less cheerful. The service was so slow that after a great deal of small talk and five pots of tea, I felt compelled to apologize. "I always seem to get bad service," I told Helen. "I don't know why."

"Well, I do," she snapped. "You look like an old lady. And waiters consider old ladies their natural enemies. They think that they will complain constantly, order the cheapest dishes on the menu, and leave a six percent tip. I have found that it is essential to appear prosperous when going out to eat."

"I didn't know that," I said demurely. I was about to add that appearing prosperous was no problem for her, but fortunately the waiter chose that moment to arrive and ask, "Who gets the crab cakes?"

Helen took her irritation out on him. "Oh, do your job!" she snapped.

He looked at the order in his hand and plunked the crab ungraciously at her place.

"Those look good," I said. "And my dumplings are delicious. Would you like to try them?"

"I do not care for Chinese food," she said, waving it away.

"Taste it," I insisted, thrusting the plate under her nose. "It's not Chinese. It just looks it."

"No, thank you," she said firmly, pushing my arm away. I got the distinct feeling that she was reluctant to let her lips touch anything that had touched mine.

I took a bite of the dumpling and a robustly beefy flavor filled my mouth, quickly followed by the insistent prickle of horseradish. The two flavors grew stronger as I ate and before long the heat and richness were radiating down my throat and through my body.

"The crab cake *is* excellent," Helen conceded. And then, even more reluctantly, she added, "Would you like to try one?"

"Yes, please," I replied. It was a fine crab cake—generous lumps of fresh meat bound together with a bit of egg and a lot of faith.

"Do taste mine, too," said Claudia, cutting off a chunk of foie gras and topping it with a slice of poached pear. "So lovely. But is this goose or duck liver?"

"Duck," I replied, unthinking.

"How can you tell?" she asked.

"The taste," I said, "and the color. Goose liver is richer and smoother. The livers are bigger, which makes them easier to devein, and they have about thirty percent more fat, which gives them a smoother character. They're paler too."

Helen looked at me with grudging respect. "You're a cook?" she asked.

"Not exactly," I said. "You know there's a difference between French and domestic foie gras as well. I'm pretty sure this is domestic."

A series of emotions flitted across her face, and I saw that she was wondering if she might have misjudged me. For a moment I felt a slight softening of her attitude. But then the hostess led a distinguished gentleman with silver hair to a nearby table. He was accompanied by a beautiful young woman, his granddaughter most likely, because when he sat down he did nothing to hide the small appreciative nod he gave Helen. His eyes openly assessed the beige cashmere and good jewelry before moving on to Claudia. He quickly dismissed her, and then his gaze wandered in my direction. Instantly his face changed and he jerked backward, as if he would like to retract the nod. Helen caught that too, and immediately edged her chair away, trying to disown me.

The busboy cleared the table; the waiter brought our main courses. Helen took a bite of her fish and nodded thoughtfully. "I adore Chilean sea bass," she said in a voice meant to carry to the next table, "such a rich and elegant fish."

"Actually," I said, "that's not Chilean sea bass."

"Thank you very much," she replied indignantly, "I am quite aware of what I ordered."

"I know you ordered Chilean sea bass," I insisted, trying to reclaim a little dignity for poor Betty, "but there is no such thing. You are eating Patagonian toothfish."

"I couldn't be," she said.

"You are. I'm sure you won't be surprised to learn that it didn't sell very well under its own name. So they changed it."

"Really?" There was grudging respect in her voice. I thought I'd see if I could keep it. "May I taste those prosciutto-stuffed mashed potatoes?" I asked. She passed me a bite and I tasted, thoughtfully. "Good-quality pro-sciutto," I said.

"How do you know?" she asked.

"I can taste it. Real prosciutto, the kind they make in Parma, has a sweetness and a softness that others lack. Lesser prosciutto has a waxy quality, and it's often over-salted. The color's different too."

"How odd that someone like you should know so much," said Helen, giving me a long slow look.

"Yes," I said sweetly, "isn't it?" And I turned back to my food. Meanwhile Helen and the man at the next table kept exchanging glances, and Claudia sat there like a director admiring the scene she had created.

"Dessert, ladies?" asked the waiter.

"Oh no," said Helen, "I never eat sweets." She glanced briefly at the next table. The silver-haired man smiled. Claudia ordered gingerbread, and I pointed at a waiter walking cautiously across the room.

"Young man," I said, pointing at the drink the waiter was carrying with such care. It looked like a captive rainbow. "What is that beautiful con-coction?"

"A pousse café, madam," he replied.

"A who?" I asked.

"It's a kind of cocktail."

"All those layers? How do they make it?"

"Carefully," he said, "very carefully. You see, different liqueurs weigh different amounts. So if you start with the heaviest, and then keep pouring a lighter liqueur on top, you can keep them from mixing. At least, a good bartender can."

"Isn't it difficult?" I asked.

"Oh yes, madam," he said, "very."

"What if you trip while you're carrying it?"

"The bartender kills you," he said solemnly. "And the court rules it justifiable homicide." This was clearly a joke he had made before.

"I'll have one," I decided.

As he walked away I murmured, "Grenadine, crème de cacao, maraschino, curaçao, crème de menthe, parfait amour, cognac."

"What's that?" asked Helen.

"The order of a pousse café. Red on the bottom, followed by brown, white, orange, green, violet, and finally the cognac on the top. They have to be made very, very slowly. Bartenders usually pour them over the back of a spoon to spread out the liquid. They're difficult to make correctly."

"I thought you didn't know what it was," she said, giving me another long look.

"I was just testing him." I peeked at Claudia and saw that she was enjoying herself hugely.

When the drink came, I held it out to Helen. "Would you care to taste it?"

"Oh no," she said. The silver-haired man was looking at her again and she smiled—a little coyly I thought—and said, "Well, maybe just a sip."

She grimaced—the thing truly was horrid—and then there was a small awkward silence. Helen was looking at me, clearly weighing whether or not to say what was on her mind. Finally she decided. "May I speak frankly?"

"Certainly," I said.

"I don't know what to make of you, but you seem like a good enough person. Why don't you take better care of yourself? A good haircut—and perhaps a silver rinse—would do wonders. I have a facialist who could improve your skin tone. And I could point you to a shop where a few chic outfits would not cost much money. I just can't understand why anyone would go through life looking so . . . pitiful." She looked at my face and added, "I hope I have not offended you?"

"Not at all," I said. "That's very kind. I'd be very grateful for your help." Claudia made a little choking sound.

"What, may I ask, is so funny?" asked Helen.

"Later, my darling," gasped Claudia, attempting to control her mirth. "I will tell you later."

Helen looked miffed and Claudia abruptly changed the subject. "Have I told you," she asked, "that I am moving to Los Angeles for a few months?"

"You didn't tell me that!" I said, so shocked that I used my own voice. Helen's eyes narrowed. I lowered it to ask, "Why?"

"One of my old students has been given an excellent role in a big new film, and he insists that I must come coach him. I thought it might be fun. And I cannot deny that the notion of leaving New York for the duration of the winter has enormous appeal."

"I'm going to miss you," I said.

"Don't worry, my darling," she said, patting my hand. "I will come hurrying back. I could not bear to miss seeing the transformation Helen has planned. I suspect you'll be an entirely different person. In fact, I'm sure of it." She tried to catch Helen's eye but Helen was, once again, looking at the man at the next table. I wondered if anything would come of it.

RESTAURANTS
by Ruth Reichl

....

PATRICK CLARK is a terrific chef. Unfortunately, he is only human, and it would take a magician to make food good enough to overcome the service at Tavern on the Green.

Consider the meal I had in the spring, soon after Mr. Clark took over the kitchen of America's largest-grossing restaurant. We were seated at 7:30 P.M. By 8:30 we had eaten our way through the entire bread basket, visited the gift shop twice, taken a stroll through the gardens, admired the lanterns and the topiary. We begged for food. When we could find someone to beg. Once I looked across that vast windowed room, past the balloons, flowers and chandeliers, and counted only four service people. They were all studiously avoiding our waving hands.

Finally our first courses came. I relaxed as I tasted a fine shrimp cocktail with a jazzy smoked tomato rémoulade and a parsley-lemon salad. Crab cakes were impressively served with a spicy pumpkin seed sauce. I admired roasted chunks of lobster meat in a spicy red Thai curry sauce. Even plain old Caesar salad was dressed up with sheets of crisped Parmesan. There was just one problem: my asparagus soup was nowhere to be seen.

It took a while to attract someone's attention and point out that I had not been served. Ten minutes later, the soup showed up. No apology, but after the waiter had painstakingly poured it into my bowl, he proudly announced, "Not a drop!"

Then our entrées came so quickly that the appetizer plates were still on the table. "Hold that please," said the waiter, indicating that I was to pick up my soup bowl so he could put my entrée down. Meanwhile, my companions were clearing off the extra plates and stacking them on the floor.

For all that, the food was impressive. Mr. Clark is serving more than 1,500 meals a day, and he has carefully constructed his menu within the limits of quantity cooking. He builds each plate around a sturdy centerpiece, starting with food that can take a little abuse and using imaginative accompaniments to perk it up. His grilled pork porterhouse, a robust portion, was served with a glorious mush of potatoes, bacon and cabbage. On the side, standing in for applesauce, was a zesty rhubarb-apple chutney.

Grilled swordfish steak was accented with sautéed pea greens and wild mushroom dumplings. He made salmon special by giving it a Moroccan glaze, setting it on a buttery bed of savoy cabbage and a cake of couscous. But he also knows when to leave well enough alone; his rotisserie chicken was sensibly plain, served with haricots verts and potatoes mashed with just a hint of green chilies.

Should we chance dessert? Anticipating another endless wait, we quit while we were ahead. There was, however, one bright point. As one friend noted, "They certainly didn't rush us."

Every restaurant has its off nights, but in my experience they are standard at Tavern on the Green. One recent night, we waited 40 minutes after placing our order before any food arrived. The captain acted as if he were bestowing a favor each time he honored us with his presence, and the waiters hardly deigned to glance our way. A request to take dessert home was met with this response: "We don't do that." But the worst thing was that after being requested to surrender our coats ($1 each), we found ourselves seated next to the window, freezing. We spent a small fortune on tea trying to get warm.

Still, the dinner was delicious. Short-rib-and-horseradish dumplings were a sly take on a Chinese dish. Soups were thick, a little too sweet, but satisfying. Crab cakes were filled with chunks of sweet crabmeat. And foie gras sautéed with pears was completely luxurious.

Grilled Chilean sea bass was nicely cooked; it's a very forgiving fish. A fine loin of venison was paired with a puree of squash and cranberry sauce. And a double rack of pork, another huge portion, came with irresistible cheese-filled mashed potatoes and braised red cabbage.

Desserts were good, too. I liked the cheesecake and the crème brûlée. But the dessert that seemed most appropriate to this gaudy, glitzy, enchantingly over-the-top room was the banana split, an exercise in American excess that is almost good enough to make you forget how shabbily you have been treated.

Looking around at that fairyland of lights, I felt a surge of rage. To thousands of visitors, Tavern on the Green is New York. They are so happy to be here that you see them all around the room, videotaping one another as they eat their meals. This is an expensive restaurant; does it really have to be such a blatant example of our famous rudeness?

No, it does not. I discovered that on my last visit when waiters and captains were suddenly hovering attentively over my table. The food came in a flash. It was warm in that inner circle of the Garden Room in more ways than one. Forgive me for thinking that I must have been recognized.

The evening seemed enchanted. I looked out over that splendidly silly space as I ate beautifully arranged poached shrimp in a lime, soy and ginger sauce. Orecchiette were beautifully cooked and tossed with broccoli rabe and sausage. And if the thick fillet of smoked salmon on truffle mashed potatoes seemed more appropriate as an entrée than an appetizer, who's to quibble with generosity?

Then there was moist turkey with stuffing, sweet potatoes, brussels sprouts and cranberry sauce: a holiday on a plate. Pork, one of Mr. Clark's best dishes, was as satisfying as it always is.

As I sat there, basking in the attention and enjoying the Christmas decorations, I looked around at the people seated on the edges of the room. I hoped they were having as nice a time as I was. I suspected they were not.

TAVERN ON THE GREEN

★

......

Betty never got her makeover. Helen was furious when Claudia told her the truth, and when I called to apologize, she hung up on me. But in the ensuing months Betty slipped unobtrusively in and out of Felidia, Aquavit, Lutèce, and Gramercy Tavern. My most useful disguise, she usually went with a group, sitting silently at the table like somebody's poor old aunt, the charity case, brought along out of duty or as an act of kindness. Betty never looked at a wine list and when confronted with the menu tended to say, "You order for me, dear. You know much more about food" in a voice so soft it was barely audible. Since she never paid a bill she had no need for credit cards, and she continued to be as anonymous as a shadow.

Even so, I knew I was pressing my luck the day she dined alone at La Côte Basque. I had been to the restaurant four times in total anonymity, but my most recent visit had been with a couple who had bought me at a charity benefit, and I had gone as myself.

Charity dinners seemed to be part of my job. I don't know which charity first realized the secret yearning of many people to watch the critic at work, but once they discovered that they could auction this opportunity off for thousands of dollars, the requests came pouring in. How do you say no to worthy causes when so much money is at stake? How do you say no to your child's school, your doctor, the American Heart Association, the public library, the James Beard Foundation . . . Although these dinners with strangers were a terrible nuisance, I rarely had the heart to turn them down. Every once in a while I'd end up eating with someone so offensive that I'd swear off charity dinners, but that never lasted very long.

The Côte Basque couple had in fact been lovely people. And everything was fine until, halfway through the appetizers, Mr. Stewart inadvertently blurted out how much he had paid for the chance to dine with me. It was such an embarrassing amount of money that I summoned the sommelier and ordered an insanely expensive wine. I shouldn't have done that: the sommelier, who had ignored me up to that point, looked at me long and hard and then went running off to the maître d'. Suddenly the hoverage increased. Could I really expect to get away with being Betty now?

But I had to go back. As I wrote the review, rhapsodizing about the duck, I realized I had tried it only once, and that it had been with the Stewarts. What if the chef had cooked me something special? I imagined angry readers looking down at their duck and saying, "That woman liked *this*?" Once was not enough. I put on the wig, the too-tight shoes, and the frumpy blue dress and headed for the subway. Nobody paid me the slightest attention.

But when I walked into La Côte Basque, every eye in the room turned. And then, of course, politely looked away. I walked slowly toward the maître d'—the shoes were really uncomfortable—and said hesitantly, "Excuse me?"

The man gave me a kind but slightly pitying look. "Yes?" he said. "May I help you?"

"I don't have a reservation . . ." I began. He surveyed me quite openly, not disguising the fact that he was trying to make up his mind. He didn't know me, I was sure of that; I could almost see him wishing that I were a man so he could wrap me in a borrowed jacket and tie.

"Just yourself?" he asked. I nodded. It was still early, and the restaurant was not full, which may have been why the decision went in my favor. "Right this way, please," he said, and I wondered where he would put me. He wouldn't want to parade me through the dining room, but he wouldn't want me in one of the high-visibility seats up front either. I wondered how he would solve the dilemma. In the end, he tucked me off to the side, handed me a menu, and scurried quickly away. This was not exactly celebrity treatment, but it could not be faulted.

The captain who took care of me was entirely correct; he neither fawned nor ignored me. The food was just as I'd remembered. Better, actually. I had finished my first course, a caviar-studded seafood salad, and was halfway through the delicious duck when a flutter of energy swept through the room. I looked up to see a female of a certain age moving in my direction. Swathed in red satin, she looked like Peter Ustinov in drag, and she was moving so slowly that she resembled a carnival float propelled by hidden wheels.

She came nearer and nearer, and then the maître d' was pulling out the table to seat her on the banquette next to mine. The woman shot me a look of undisguised horror and turned to the maître d'hôtel. "Don't you have anything else?" she asked, waving a fat paw in my direction. I thought how much she resembled one of those ugly Chinese lap dogs. "I don't like this table," she blared. The maître d' hastily pushed the table back toward the banquette, smoothed the cloth, and turned on his heel. "But of course, madame," he said, leading her away.

I had had enough. I asked the waiter if he would pack the remains of my duck in a doggie bag and bring me the bill. He hesitated for half a beat, began to say something, changed his mind, and said, "Certainly."

I paid the bill in cash, counting out the change, dollar by dollar. I added the tip; then, thinking of old ladies everywhere, added some more. Clutching my doggie bag, I scurried out of the restaurant, convinced that the diners in their fancy finery were watching my departure with both relief and disdain.

I boarded the uptown subway, thinking how happy I was going to be to get the wig off my head and the Enna Jetticks off my feet. I was thinking up ways to describe the duck when a homeless man came shuffling through the car. His pants were torn and his army jacket was layered with the filth of too many nights on the sidewalk. A sad woolen cap was pulled down over his reddened ears and a moth-eaten gray scarf twisted around his wattled neck. He looked so ragged that people tucked their feet beneath them as he passed, hoping to avoid his touch. When he got to the end of the car he turned, took a breath, and began to speak.

"I'm hungry," he said, his voice rusty from disuse. "I'll take anything. If you have half a sandwich you didn't eat at lunch, or the core of an apple, I'd be happy to have it. Maybe you've got a few crumbs of potato chips left in the bottom of the bag. That would do too."

I noticed that as he walked down the aisle the other passengers looked down or buried themselves in their papers. Hunger is embarrassing. When he reached my seat, I handed him the bag from La Côte Basque and he stared in disbelief. Grabbing it, he walked to the end of the car and sat down in the seat that says it is reserved for the handicapped. I expected him to tear into the food and stuff it into his mouth, but he did not. With great dignity he spread the scarf on his lap as if it were a napkin, then pulled the container from the bag and set it on the scarf. Removing the wrapping, he examined his windfall. "Roasted duckling!" he croaked. And then, very delicately, he picked the leg up in his fingers and ate it slowly, savoring every morsel.

I did not take a shower when I got home. I did not remove the wig. I sat down and began writing a piece called "Why I Disapprove of What I Do."

WHY I DISAPPROVE OF WHAT I DO
It's indecent to glamorize a $100 meal. Or is it?
by Ruth Reichl

"You can't be a restaurant critic," M.F.K. Fisher once said to me, "unless you are one of those ambitious sorts, willing to walk on your grandmother's grave." I nodded meekly and agreed.

It was the early 1970s. In Berkeley, Calif., where I lived, the view was extreme: food, like so many things, had become intensely political. Frances Moore Lappé had just written *Diet for a Small Planet,* which had convinced me, and everyone I knew, that eating meat was greedy and irresponsible. We thought the only moral response was to become vegetarians, which we did briefly, but with a vengeance.

Shopping for millet at the Co-Op, we would stand in the checkout line extolling the pleasures of tofu.

Those of us who didn't really consider tofu *pure* pleasure were in trouble. I found myself sneaking extra cheese into Ms. Lappé's recipe for con queso rice and substituting cocoa for carob in her spice cake. Couldn't food be good and good for you?

Pondering this problem, I became a cook. I was not alone. All over Berkeley, overeducated people were opening restaurants. Our parents were horrified: It was long before the era of celebrity chefs, and there was nothing glamorous about the work. Saying that your daughter was a cook was about as attractive as confessing that she had decided to dig ditches for a living.

But I found restaurant work deeply satisfying. I loved the hard physical labor. I loved working with food, feeling peaches slip from their skins to reveal the fruit's hidden color, sniffing the air as onions caramelized. But what I liked best was watching people eat the food I had cooked, leaning in to listen to one another. Good food, I saw, was about more than merely eating.

And then a small alternative arts magazine asked me to write a restaurant column. I did it for free; I even paid for my own meals without getting reimbursed. I climbed up on a soapbox.

I wrote about the China Cup Café, where a woman named Della Hardmon served inspiration with her food. "Anything you want very bad, and work very hard for, you can have," she said as she made salmon croquettes and collard greens. I wrote of the nutritional advantages of the Indian diet as I introduced my readers to the joys of dosa and idli sambar. One review

made a case for the collective ownership of restaurants, another extolled the virtues of the northern Chinese breakfast of soy milk. I even managed to get in a dig at imperialism when I reviewed a Guamanian restaurant.

If you had asked me then if I would accept a job as a restaurant critic for the *New York Times*, or any establishment publication, I would have replied, without a second thought, "Of course not!" And not just because I did not want to think of myself as an ambitious sort, walking on my grandmother's grave. Working in restaurants was honest labor; anyone could see that. Writing about them for the mainstream press was not; it felt like joining the enemy.

But reviewing was fun; so much fun that when mainstream publishers started paying me for my opinions, I didn't do the decent thing and refuse. Before I knew it, I had stopped cooking professionally. Then I stopped cooking altogether. "She's joined the leisure class," my friends said.

I disarmed my critics by inviting them along; nobody I knew could afford to eat out, and nobody refused. We went with equal amounts of guilt and pleasure, with a feeling that we were trespassing in the playgrounds of the rich.

Which, in fact, we were. We didn't belong in those starchy restaurants. We knew it, and when we climbed out of my rent-a-wreck, resplendent in vintage from the Salvation Army, everybody knew it too. We always got the worst table. And then, because I didn't own a credit card, I had to pay in cash. The year turned into two, and three, and more. I got a credit card. I got good clothes. I was writing for increasingly prestigious publications. Meanwhile, a voice inside me kept whispering, "How *could* you?"

The voice is still there, yakking away. When I receive weekly letters from people who think it is indecent to write about $100 meals while half the world is hungry, the voice yaks right along. "They're absolutely right, you elitist pig," it hisses. And when it asks, "When are you going to grow up and get a real job?" it sounds a lot like my mother.

And just about then is when I tell the voice to shut up. Because when

my mother starts telling me that all I'm doing with my life is telling rich people where to eat, I realize how much the world has changed.

Yes, there are still restaurants where rich people get to remind themselves that they are different from you and me. But there are fewer and fewer of them. As American food has come of age, American restaurants have changed. Going out to eat used to be like going to the opera; today, it is more like going to the movies.

And so everyone has become a critic. I couldn't be happier. The more people pay attention to what and how they eat, the more attuned they become to their own senses and the world around them.

When I remember that conversation with M.F.K. Fisher, I wish I had not been quite so meek. When I re-run the loop in my mind, I turn to her and say this: "No, you're wrong. A. J. Liebling had it right. All it really takes to be a restaurant critic is a good appetite."

In March, when the article was published, people who had never spoken to me before made a point of telling me how much they liked it. I was happy about the response, but remembering what it felt like to be Betty, I understood that my piece was actually a cop-out. In my mind's eye I saw the woman in red at La Côte Basque, and the man on the train waving his duck leg, and deep down I knew that there was something basically dishonest about what I had written. The feel-good ending nagged at me; I was making excuses, and the Betty inside me knew it.

A FRUGAL REPAST
FOR BETTY

When I trailed Betty home, she bought cereal and dog food, but I like to think that she is the kind of person who makes herself a nice meal every once in a while and savors it slowly, over the course of a few days. This is the meal I imagine her making at the beginning of spring, when she wants to celebrate having survived yet another New York winter. It is a perfect little repast that provides wonderful leftovers that are good hot or cold.

Roast Chicken with Potatoes, Onions, and Garlic

Everyone makes a big to-do about roasting chicken, and as a food professional I know I ought to believe that one way to tell a great cook is by his or her roasted chicken. But you know what? I think that's all a lot of nonsense. Nothing is easier than roasting a chicken. As in most cooking, it's all about the shopping. The main point is to begin with a good farm-raised chicken that has some flavor. Once you've got your bird, all you really have to do is throw it in the oven and try not to overcook it. It's hard to ruin this, but here's my method:

1 farm-raised chicken, about 3½ pounds
1 lemon

Olive oil

3 or 4 smallish Yukon Gold potatoes (or any other variety except
russet), each peeled and cut into 8 pieces

1 large onion, cut into 6 pieces

3 or 4 cloves garlic, unpeeled

Salt and pepper

Preheat the oven to 400°F.

Wash the chicken under running water and pat it dry. Remove and reserve the extra fat from the inside of the chicken. Very gently run your fingers between the breast and the skin, beginning from the neck end, loosening the skin from the breast on both sides. Being careful not to puncture the skin, place the excess fat beneath the skin (the chicken will then baste itself).

Puncture the lemon a few times with a fork, and place it inside the chicken.

Pour enough olive oil into a roasting pan to make a thin film over the bottom. Toss the potatoes, onion, and garlic into the pan and turn until they are covered with olive oil.

If you have a rack, put the chicken on it, breast side up, and place it in the roasting pan (you may have to jiggle things a little to fit it over the potatoes and onions). If you don't, just put the chicken right into the pan. Pour a little olive oil over the chicken, and salt and pepper everything in the pan.

Roast for about 1 hour, or until an instant-read thermometer inserted into a thigh reads 170°F. Remove the pan from the oven and let the chicken rest for 10 minutes.

Carve the chicken into serving pieces, surround them with the potatoes, onions, and garlic, and squeeze the lemon over the top.

Serves 4

Pureed Watercress

This is one of my very favorite vegetables. Cooked like this, watercress resembles creamed spinach, but it is both easier (watercress is a snap to wash) and more flavorful (watercress has such an interestingly spicy bite).

Salt
1 medium potato, peeled and cut into 12 pieces
4 bunches watercress (1 to 1½ pounds total) washed
½ stick (4 tablespoons) unsalted butter
Pepper

Bring a large pot of water to a boil. Add a tablespoon of salt and the potato, and cook for 20 minutes.

Add the watercress to the boiling water, and when it has come back to a boil, cook for 1 minute. Drain in a colander, pressing on the vegetables to extract as much water as possible.

Put the watercress and potato into a food processor, and whirl until it forms a smooth puree. Add the butter and whirl again until it has been incorporated.

Add salt and pepper to taste, and serve.

Serves 4

Roasted Rhubarb

Rhubarb is America's most underappreciated vegetable. I love its color, its bittersweet flavor, its ease of preparation. And I love the way it appears in the early spring, a harbinger of good things to come.

You can throw this in the oven while the chicken is roasting, and then eat it warm or cold, as it is or topped with a drizzle of cream, sour cream, or vanilla ice cream. In the morning, mixed with yogurt and some strawberries, it makes a great breakfast. And all by itself, it makes a fine accompaniment to any pork dish.

2 pounds rhubarb, sliced into 1-inch pieces
½ cup sugar

Mix the rhubarb and sugar together, put into an ovenproof dish, and roast in a hot oven (anywhere from 325° to 425°F will do fine) for about 30 minutes.

Serve hot, warm, or at room temperature.

Serves 3

Food Warrior

First there was the phone call. I was sitting on the floor, playing a math game Nicky had brought home from school, so relaxed that when the aggressive voice blared, I was surprised into holding the receiver away from my ear.

"Page Six?" I shouted back, bewildered. "The *New York Post*? Who?"

"Bryan Miller," said the voice. It was a woman. "Are you aware that he has been sending scathing letters about you to your bosses?"

"Excuse me?" I shook myself, trying to get into the right frame of mind. "Letters?"

"Yes," said the voice, "he's been writing them for years. Have you seen them?"

"No."

"Have you heard about them?"

"No," I said again. I thought of a question of my own: "How did you get my number?"

"We're Page Six," said the woman, as if the answer were obvious. "So you don't know anything about these letters?"

"No," I said, "I don't."

"Let me read one to you," she said. "I'd like to get your comments."

"No thank you." I had finally come to my senses. "I don't want to hear it. And please don't call again." Then I did what I should have done the instant I heard that New York's best-read gossip column was on the line. I hung up.

I immediately called Carol. "Do you know anything about Bryan's letters?" I asked. The awkward pause was so eloquent that, even through the phone, I could sense the blood draining from her face. "How long has this been going on?" I asked. "Why didn't you tell me?"

"A long time," she said in a whisper. "They're really nasty. What good would telling you have done? Would you have wanted to know?"

Would I? I wasn't sure. "Anyway," Carol continued, "I tried to warn you. Don't you remember?"

I had a vague memory of Carol, before I really knew her, telling me to watch out for Bryan. Thinking hard, I was able to conjure up Carol saying that the former critic was bitter about giving up the job. "Watch your back," I remembered her saying, but I had thought she was speaking in a general way. Not once had it occurred to me that the warning was concrete. "Are there a lot of letters?" I asked now.

"A few." She was clearly uncomfortable.

"What do they say?"

"I'm sure you can figure that out. Basically that you've destroyed all his wonderful work and they should do something about it."

"What?" I asked.

"I think," she said dryly, "the implication is that the something they should do is get rid of you."

"And bring him back?"

"He never said that. At least not in any letter I saw. But I haven't seen them all. I've just seen the ones they sent upstairs. There are probably more. Why don't you ask Warren?"

"He's in London," I said, reminding her that Warren Hoge was now London bureau chief. Depending on how much you liked him, Warren had been moved either because he was a good writer or because he was a bad manager, but whatever the reason, he was now on the far side of the ocean.

"They have phones in England," she said.

I looked at my watch. It was late afternoon. "What's the time difference?" I said.

"*Call* him," she said.

Warren picked up on the first ring. In a voice hoarse with fatigue, he said he'd just filed a story about six IRA terrorists who had been captured with ten tons of explosives. One of the Irishmen was dead.

Compared to Semtex my own concerns seemed silly, and I was sorry that I'd called. I hedged, asking about the bombing, reluctant to say that I wanted to ask about Bryan's letters. But he already knew.

"Page Six called me too," he said. "You have nothing to worry about."

"But why didn't you tell me about them?" I cried.

"You were new to the job," he said. "When the letters first came, we discussed whether to tell you or not. In the end we decided that it would not be useful knowledge."

"Were there others?" I asked. "From other people?"

"Of course there were," he said. "That happens when we get new critics. We expected it. But I didn't think you needed that kind of pressure. We all thought you were doing a good job, and that's what I told the people who wrote."

"Thank you." And then, because I didn't know what else to say, I said weakly, "Good night. Stay safe."

I put down the phone and sat down on the floor. "Are you okay, Mommy?" asked Nicky, stroking my hand.

"Yes, sweetie," I said, "I'm fine."

"Are you going out to dinner tonight?" he asked.

"No," I said, suddenly making up my mind. "No, I'm not going out to dinner tonight. I'm going to cancel my plans and have dinner with you."

"Yay!" he shouted. And then, "Can we have whatever I want?"

I nodded, knowing what was coming next. At the age of two my son had developed a passion for matzo brei, and for at least a year he ate it every night. He could not pronounce the words, so he gave it his own name. In our house "manna" was the ubiquitous comfort food, and now, with the unerring instinct of a child, he had zeroed in on exactly what I wanted. If ever there was a "manna" moment, this was it.

We went into the kitchen, and Nicky dragged a chair to the counter and climbed up. I got out the colander and handed him the box of matzos. With ceremonial solemnity, my son slowly broke the cracker into little pieces. With equal seriousness he ran water over them until they were damp, drained them, and put them into a bowl. Then, very carefully, he broke a couple of eggs into the matzos and gently mixed them with a fork. "See," he said, "each matzo has some of the egg." He held out the bowl for me to inspect.

I threw a lump of butter into a pan, and then threw in a little more. This was no time for restraint. Nicky slid over until he was next to the stove and picked up a long wooden spoon. "I can smell when it's time to put in the matzos," he said, sniffing the air. "Now!" I picked up the bowl and upended it over the pan. As Nicky stirred, the fine smell of butter and eggs slowly filled the kitchen.

Michael was still at the office, working on one of his more cheerful pieces; he had found an obscure rabbi in Brooklyn who seemed to be raising money for the man who assassinated Yitzhak Rabin. It was just as well, I thought, that he wasn't home; his conversation was now peppered with references to the Yigal Amir defense fund, which was not exactly soothing. I set the table for two and got out the good silver and my Aunt Birdie's gold-rimmed plates. I put candles into my grandmother's silver candlesticks, and together Nicky and I lit them. I poured myself a glass of wine and filled Nicky's glass with orange juice. Solemnly we clinked them together.

"I wish," said Nicky wistfully as we ate our manna, "that we could have dinner together every night."

"Me too, sweetie."

Matzo Brei

2 matzo crackers
2 eggs
Salt
3 tablespoons unsalted butter

Set a colander inside a bowl (to catch the crumbs) and break the matzos into little pieces, dropping them into the colander.

Remove the colander from the bowl and hold it beneath running water until the matzos are damp. Allow them to drain; then put the damp matzos into a bowl.

Break the eggs into the bowl and stir with a fork just until mixed. Add salt to taste.

Melt the butter in a small skillet over medium heat. When the foam subsides, add the matzo-egg mixture and cook, stirring constantly, for about 4 minutes, or until the egg is cooked and there are a few crispy little bits.

Put on plates and serve at once.

Serves 2

The next morning I read Warren's story. It was straight out of the movies—a sleeper IRA cell building bombs in a sleepy West London neighborhood. It was a good story, and Warren had written it well. Still, after I dropped Nicky at school I couldn't keep myself from stopping at a newsstand to buy the *Post*. Opening it up I read, blazoned across the top of Page Six in giant type, "War of the Times' Dining Divas."

It was juicy stuff. Bryan said that I had "destroyed the system that Craig, Mimi and I upheld." He claimed that people came up to him every day to tell him that they didn't read the restaurant reviews anymore because they were "irrelevant and trite." He claimed that, thanks to me, the *Times* was losing its clout, and that "it gets worse every day."

"It's just a lot of blah blah blah," I told Carol when I got to the office.

"Maybe," she said, "but people are eating it up. Good thing you didn't comment; anything you said would have sounded defensive. They'll call again, but no matter what dirt they throw at you, keep your mouth shut. Anything you say, they'll twist."

"Bryan talked to them," I pointed out. "When they called him he actually had the balls to admit that he'd written the letters. I sort of admire him for that."

"Who do you think sent them the letters?" she asked.

"It could have been anyone," I said. "What difference does it make who it was? At least Warren stood up for me." Warren, the *Post* reported, had said that Bryan was "dead wrong."

"I guess you'll find out how sincere that is," said Carol.

"Meaning?" I asked.

"Weren't you supposed to have lunch with Montorio today?"

"Yeah," I said.

"If he cancels, you'll know you're in trouble."

"And if he doesn't?"

"Where are you going?"

"La Caravelle," I said.

"If he's still willing to go," she said, "you're fine. It's so public, and he's so political. He'd never be seen there with someone who was about to lose their job."

All morning I waited for the call saying that John was canceling lunch, but it never came. In fact, as we made our way to the restaurant he never even mentioned Page Six. But I could feel his muscles tighten when we walked in and every eye looked up to survey us. The proprietor, a sweet-faced little man who always reminded me of a Shetland pony, came trotting forward to welcome John, and the room went still as he led us down the lane of pink banquettes to our table. In that adorable jewel box of a room, I had a sudden vision of the scene in the movie when Gigi walks into Maxim's and the frame freezes. Then she smiles and moves forward and the action continues. Monsieur Jammet pulled out the table, John and I sat down, and the noise in the restaurant rose again until we were all snugly wrapped in a cozy cocoon of sound.

Notes: La Caravelle, 9/24/1996, lunch with John Montorio

It's a great place to talk, simultaneously public and private. Sitting side by side on the banquettes is like being on stage; everyone eyes everyone else, avid for drama. It's exciting. On the other hand, I have to crane my neck to see him, and by the end of the meal I feel like a crippled goose.

The prix fixe lunch, $36, turns out to be a good deal if you don't drink. We don't. With plain water the meal ends up costing about $100 for the two of us, with tip.

John starts with the foie gras and apples. It's fabulous. (Try to find out where Renaud gets his foie gras. It seems creamier, richer than the Hudson Valley stuff.) He's crisped it so that the outside becomes a crust and when you bite through it the interior comes rushing into your mouth with the silky urgency of marrow. The apples are a great contrast, both sweet and acid, but unlike the foie they resist the teeth. Lovely!

I start with the quenelles de brochet, because I feel like being self-indulgent and I love them so. Very few restaurants still make these ethereal dumplings, a marriage of air and ocean, and even fewer do them right. But as far as I can tell they've been floating out of Caravelle's kitchen since Joe Kennedy used to come here with his cronies, and they never seem to change. They're a ridiculous first course—so big, so rich, so sure to make the next dish a disappointment—but I can never resist them. Imagine how magical they must have seemed before the invention of the food processor. I take a bite and the softness surrounds my mouth with the taste of lobster, of fish, of butter and then it just dissolves, disappears, leaving nothing but the memory in my mouth. And I take another bite, and another, and suddenly I'm floating on the flavor, and the world has vanished.

"You look different," John says after the third bite, and I realize that the magic has kicked in, and I am peacefully suspended on clouds of quenelle. It is such a lovely sensation.

Unfortunately I come thudding back to earth with the vegetable ravioli. When I order the dish the captain makes it clear that this is not a good idea. It is brilliantly done; he doesn't utter a sound, but his face goes oddly grim and his shoulders slump and all the smiling enthusiasm John got when he ordered the leg of veal disappears. I choose to ignore the warning and he's so unhappy that he finally says, his French accent very strong, "It's all vegetables, unh?" in a tone that makes his low opinion of vegetables very clear. And I say, stupidly, "But I like vegetables." He shrugs with the air of a man who has done his best.

Still, he can't help himself, and when I order the tomate confite for dessert he cries, "Wouldn't you like a nice soufflé instead?" Once again I stupidly ignore this, so I guess I deserve the dreadful gingered tomato thing on a bed of fennel, with a tasteless quince sorbet on top, decorated with julienne of basil. It tastes so remarkably like the vegetable ravioli that if they had switched dishes I probably wouldn't have noticed. John, wisely, sticks to sorbets: cassis (refreshing), coconut (too sweet), and pear (perfect).

Do they know me? Probably; the service is too good. I suddenly remember Joe Baum telling me, years ago when I interviewed him as he was opening the Rainbow Room, that he always gave his staff instructions on how to behave when a critic was in the restaurant. The main point, he said, was to make sure that the service on either side was perfect. I look right, and sure enough the captain is hovering over a white-haired woman wearing pink Chanel and wreathed in clouds of gardenia, saying, "Yes, madame, the duck is very crisp. And yes, madame, of course we'd be happy to cook a duck and serve you just a half of it. I'll eat the other half myself." (Here he laughs heartily and her rubies twinkle with gratitude.) On my left he interrupts the two gentlemen of a certain age, engrossed in fifty-year-old tales of the publishing business, to suggest that they might prefer a plate of cold asparagus to a plain green salad. They do. The asparagus is beautiful—very fat, very green. The man sighs as he eats it, and says something about his grandfather's gardener. As far as I can tell, a swell time is being had by all.

Even us. At our table John is going out of his way to make me feel appreciated. He never mentions the Bryan thing, but he's very sweet and personal, clearly trying to make me feel I'm part of the *Times* family. As he forks up slices of veal—rosy, tender—and spaghetti squash mixed with zucchini—nice, but what's it doing here?—he even tells me that he dreamt about Michael last night. The two of them were riding around on giant bumblebees shooting at their enemies with machine guns. "Rat-a-tat-tat, boom!" he says, aiming straight at the Chanel gardenia woman. She jumps. He couldn't possibly have made that up. Or could he? The implications are so obvious.

Outside John asks, "Do you think they knew you?" And I say that I think they might have, and that Brenda is going to have to take over from here. He says, very wistfully, that he'd love to come along sometime when I'm in disguise. I say sure. I'm lying; there's no way he's ever going to meet Brenda.

As I finished writing the notes Page Six called again, saying that Mimi Sheraton wanted no part of Bryan's fight. Did I want to comment about *that*. I was tempted. But I remembered what Carol had said. As soon as I put the phone down it rang again. I picked it up and shouted, "I told you I don't want to talk to you."

"You haven't told me anything," said a whiny male voice. "We've never spoken before."

"Who is this?" I asked.

"David Shapiro," said the whiner, "and you belong to me."

"Excuse me?" I said.

"You're mine," he said. He laughed loudly, a big horsey *ha ha*, to show that he was joking. "Last night I outbid everyone else at the hospital fund-raiser and won dinner with the restaurant critic of the *New York Times*."

"I see you didn't lose any time in making your claim," I said. It was usually months before I heard from the people who bought dinner with me; often I never heard from them at all.

"Why wait?" he replied, "I'd like to make some plans with you."

I suggested dinner at Ici. He said he'd never heard of it.

"It's good," I assured him. "I've been three times. The name's a play on the initials of Eric Clapton, who's one of the owners. They've got a talented young French chef, and I've been impressed with his cooking."

"I paid an awful lot for this dinner," he said morosely. When I did not answer, he continued, "I intend to get my money's worth."

"I see," I said.

"The terms of this deal," he said, "were that the dinner was to be in a restaurant that was mutually agreeable. And to that I don't agree."

"How about Candela?" I suggested.

"Never heard of that either," he said.

"Of course you haven't," I replied. "It's new."

"I paid thousands," he said. "I think I deserve a restaurant I've heard of. Maybe Daniel?"

"I'm not working on Daniel," I said.

In the next five minutes he listed the most expensive restaurants in New York in descending order. Disappointed that none of them had a place on my agenda, he suddenly recalled an appointment. I would, he said, be hearing from him again. Of that I had no doubt.

In less than twenty-four hours Mr. Shapiro was back on the line. I groaned inwardly when I heard his voice; I hadn't even met the man and already he irked me beyond all sensibility. I wondered if I had the same effect on him? From his tone it seemed likely. In an aggrieved voice he told me that he had now done due diligence and was prepared to offer me a list of restaurants that he considered acceptable.

"Look," I said, exasperated, "you did not buy a night on the town at the restaurant of your choice. You bought a research dinner with the *New York Times*. Most people are happy to go anywhere I choose."

"Most people," said Mr. Shapiro, "don't know much about food and wine. I, however, am a food warrior. I have spent years studying gastronomy. And oenology; my cellar is excellent. I'd bet it's better than yours."

I refrained from telling him how easily he would win that bet.

"And," he continued, "I'll want to drink some very good wines. After all, I paid plenty for this dinner."

"Oh please!" I cried. "You didn't pay a penny! You're going to claim it as a gift to charity and get a big fat tax deduction. The hospital gets your money. And what do I get out of this deal? Dinner with you." I put my hand to my mouth, terrified that the words had actually escaped from my mouth. But all Mr. Shapiro heard was, "I think you've mentioned that before."

If I had an ounce of sense I would take Mr. Shapiro to Daniel or Lespinasse or Le Cirque and get the dinner behind me. But if I was doomed to loathe every minute of this meal, I was damned if the food warrior was going to enjoy it.

So we spent weeks in negotiations. He suggested Les Célébrités, I countered with Circa. He suggested Chanterelle, I offered Solera. When he brought up La Caravelle, I was happy to tell him he was too late: the review would appear the following day.

"Would you like to go to Michael's?" I asked, thinking that might please him.

"No," he replied, "I would not."

"Well, how about Windows on the World?" Brenda had been there five times, sliding in and out utterly undetected, but I needed to make one last visit. According to my notes the whole foie gras, served for three, was too sweet, too rich, and came with leaden potato pancakes. I had tried the squab cooked in salt ("in the manner of Barcelona") and found it salty, and the duck with kumquats was tough and lacking in flavor. I wanted to give them each another chance, and on this last visit it wouldn't matter if I went as myself. To my surprise Mr. Shapiro said yes. "I didn't think Windows on the World would be up to your standards," I said.

"It's not," he replied, "but they have an excellent wine list."

This is going to be the most miserable evening we've ever spent in a restaurant," I told Michael as our taxi barreled down the West Side Highway toward the World Trade Center. "That jerk is going to spend the entire meal trying to prove that he knows more than I do. And please, do me a favor: don't mention Yigal Amir, okay?"

"I won't talk at all," said Michael. "Will that make you happy?"

"No," I said. "Just try to be bland."

"Kiddo," he said, "I think you married the wrong guy."

"Try," I said. "Please. Because Mr. Shapiro's going to *hate* Windows. It used to have a certain dignity, but the new design makes it feel like an airport lounge. You'll see; when you get off the elevator you're facing a tacky beaded curtain, and when you get past that you find a shop selling teddy bears. The plates are shaped like the stars and the moon, and the waiters wear light green suits. You keep expecting to look up and find Bill Murray breaking into song. Poor Mr. Shapiro."

"I bet he'll want to leave early," said Michael.

"I'm counting on it," I replied.

How badly we had misjudged him.

The lobby at One World Trade Center was bright and cold, and after we had walked through the double doors, a uniformed man directed us to a desk where we were told, politely but firmly, to leave our coats.

"They want to make sure we aren't carrying explosives," said Michael, shrugging out of his coat. "After the bombing, they're taking no chances."

"Really?" I asked.

"It's a lot less offensive than frisking you," he said. "Watch. I bet they won't let anyone carry a briefcase onto the elevator."

He was right. The ride up, always a shock, seemed even longer than usual, and as usual, somewhere around the eightieth floor, my ears popped, leaving me slightly deaf. Then the doors slid open.

"Uh-oh," said Michael in a low, flat voice. I stepped out and looked around. Standing in front of the elevator were two small people who, even in the dim light of the hallway, reminded me of angry ferrets.

"Mr. Shapiro?" I asked, holding out my hand.

He ignored it and looked pointedly at his Rolex. "Six and a half minutes past seven," he said. He tugged at the little woman, then pushed her toward me. Her blond pageboy did not waver. "Meet Sherry," he said, "my wife." With that he spun around and marched toward the dining room. The acrid, slightly sweet hotel smell of Sterno, of burning alcohol and too many meals being cooked at the same time, grew stronger as we approached our goal.

At the end of the corridor, just before you reached the dining room, a full-length window opened up to the view. In the dozens of visits I made to Windows on the World over the years, I never grew accustomed to that particular vantage point, and I always found myself standing for a few seconds, pressed against the window, staring down. Higher than a skyscraper, lower than an airplane, it made New York seem unreal, an imaginary city spread at your feet.

Mr. Shapiro was unimpressed. He marched on, eager for the eating portion of the evening to begin. I'd asked him to make the reservation in his own name, and he intoned "Shapiro, party of four," in a masterful voice. But as the maître d' led us west, toward the Hudson River, still shining in the fading light, Mr. Shapiro began shaking his head. He pointed across the dining room. "There," he said, "is where we want to sit." The maître d' obligingly executed an about-face and began leading us in the other direction. The East River came into view, but Mr. Shapiro was not satisfied. He shook his head again. "Window seat," he said, thumping one fist against the other. "We must have a seat at the window. We want to be smack up against the view."

"Let me see what I can do," said the maître d', escaping to his desk. "Tables," Mr. Shapiro explained as we waited, "are like hotel rooms; never take the first one that they offer. They always try to find some dummy willing to accept the worst seat. Someone's got to sit at the bad tables, and I don't care who it is so long as it's not me. It's very important to demand the best from the outset."

The rest of us were silent.

"But of course you knew that," he added.

I did not bother to point out that in my continuing effort to avoid detection I always took the first table I was offered. We were led from table to table and Mr. Shapiro rejected them all. When he was finally satisfied, he gave a cursory glance out the window, grunted, "Restaurants with views are never very good," and disappeared into the wine list. He fumbled in his pocket and extracted a small calculator.

"My wine computer," he said proudly. "I never travel without it. I find it indispensable for sniffing out the best bargains."

"Sounds time-consuming," I said.

"Oh," he said breezily, "we're in no hurry. I make it my practice to always be the last person to leave a restaurant."

"But that could be hours!" I protested, looking at my watch.

"No problem," he said complacently. "At least not for me." And then he dove back into the wine list.

The waiter arrived wearing a small, worried frown; he had obviously been warned about us. "Is this a special occasion?" he asked cheerily. His deep Georgia accent drew out the word "special," twisting and turning it until it sounded like a sentence all its own. "Can we sing to you? Happy birthday, happy anniversary, anything?"

Mr. Shapiro did not lower the wine list. But through it he growled, "No songs!" And then, "Sommelier!"

"Pardon me?" said the waiter.

"Sommelier," said Mr. Shapiro. "The sommelier. The wine man. I'd like you to get him."

"First," said the waiter, standing his ground, "you'll want to hear our specials." Once again the word did pirouettes. He began a recitation of the restaurant's proudest dishes: the entire foie gras, served for two (did I sense Mr. Shapiro's ears pricking up behind that list?), scallops speared with sugarcane, a lobster salad that was really special (the word again). He recommended the "elegant and sumptuous seafood fiesta." Mr. Shapiro remained submerged in the world of wine. When the waiter finally wound down, he surfaced and repeated "Sommelier!" in urgent tones.

I looked up at the waiter. "Why don't you give us a chance to think about the menu?" I suggested. "We'll have to coordinate the wine with the food."

"Yes ma'am. Thank you, ma'am," he said gratefully. "I'll just go get your *ahmusey* while you decide."

"That would be our *amuse*," intoned Mr. Shapiro, from inside the list. "Short for *amusebouche,* which means to entertain the mouth." He did not lower the wine list, so he had no way of knowing that our waiter was no longer there to be edified by this information.

"Do you like wine too?" Michael asked Mrs. Shapiro in what seemed like a kindly manner. She had yet to utter anything other than hello.

"Oh, no," she said. "I just drink what Davey tells me to."

"Do you eat on command too?" he asked. I kicked him under the table.

"To be honest," she said, "I'm almost always on a diet, so I just taste. It's the boys who take after Davey."

"Boys?" asked Michael. "You have children?"

"Two," said Mr. Shapiro, finally lowering the list. "When they turn eighteen I give them a three-star tour of France. A whole month, just the two of us, eating in at least one three-star restaurant every day. Bobby and I went this summer."

"What a treat that must have been for him!" said Michael. I kicked him again under the table, struggling to keep my face straight, wondering if there was an eighteen-year-old on earth who could enjoy being cooped up with his father for a month of fancy meals.

"Bobby said it was the best trip he'd ever taken!" Mrs. Shapiro assured us solemnly. She sounded sincere. "We feel it's an excellent education."

"I want my boys to be cultivated," said Mr. Shapiro, taking over. "I want to pass on my knowledge. It's taken me years to become a true food warrior."

Beneath the table Michael's leg connected with mine and I understood that this was a plea not to ask Mr. Shapiro to elucidate the wisdom of the food warrior. But it was too tempting, and I was about to risk it when Mr. Shapiro's happy voice cried, "Here's the sommelier!" And then, in a less joyful tone, "And he's so young!"

And, I thought, so cute. He could not have been more than twenty-five, with a shock of shiny black hair falling into his eyes, very red lips, and very long lashes. His face was full of fun and his lanky body seemed to be half rubber. A taste-vin hung around his neck.

"Have you seen something that interests you?" he asked, fingering the chain.

"I was thinking of starting with this Stony Hill Chardonnay," said Mr. Shapiro.

"Ah, a connoisseur," said the sommelier. "You zeroed right in on one of our treasures. So few people know those great Stony Hills."

"I'm a bit worried about its age," said Mr. Shapiro. "An '85 seems rather old for an American Chardonnay."

"Those Stony Hills don't begin to come into their own for at least ten years," murmured the sommelier. "I don't think you'll be disappointed." It was not lost on me that Mr. Shapiro had zeroed right in on one of the list's pricier whites. "And after that?" queried the sommelier.

"A Burgundy, I think. Which ones do you favor at the moment?"

The favored wine, it seemed, was the '89 Clos de Vougeot. This was fine with Mr. Shapiro, who began quizzing the sommelier about the vineyard, clearly trying to trip him up. Failing to do this, he began holding forth about his own recent visit to the Clos and some of the astute purchases he had made on that occasion. The sommelier put on a face as admiring as that of a southern belle charming a man on their first date.

They progressed to Bordeaux. When they had agreed on an '82 Léoville Poyferré, Mr. Shapiro asked, "Will you decant it?"

"Of course," said the sommelier reverently. "The '82s are magnificent, but still a little young."

"I'm glad you don't buy the argument that wines get all the air they need in the glass."

"Ridiculous notion!" said the sommelier. I looked up, caught his eye, and realized that if Mr. Shapiro had fallen into the do-not-decant school of wine, our young man would have agreed with equal alacrity.

By now they were discussing sweet wines, and Michael's leg was jiggling beneath the table with furious impatience. Unfortunately, as soon as the sommelier moved off the waiter moved in, and the food warrior leaped into the next negotiation. By the time the ordering was over, we had been at the table for more than an hour. No bread had arrived, but we had been served the *ahmusey*: rillettes of pork on a little piece of toast, with bell pepper oil on top. Mr. Shapiro took one bite and instantly set it aside.

"Delicious," said Michael, demolishing the tidbit.

Mrs. Shapiro eyed her rillettes longingly. The toast began moving toward her mouth. Across the table Mr. Shapiro vigorously began shaking his head and did not stop until his wife's hand stopped in midair and then reversed its motion. She replaced the toast on her plate and held it out to Michael. "Want mine?" she asked sadly.

Michael picked it up. "Thanks," he said. Mrs. Shapiro's eyes never left his mouth as he swallowed the tidbit in a single gulp. An awkward silence fell over the table.

"So," said Michael cheerfully, doing his part, "David, what business are you in?"

"Education," Mr. Shapiro said shortly.

"Oh, a teacher."

"Not exactly," said Mr. Shapiro. "I'm a businessman. I manufacture educational equipment. Desks, blackboards, that kind of stuff. Most people have no idea how much profit there can be in schools."

I winced. We were heading for a cliff, and it was up to me to change the topic, quickly, before Michael gleefully elicited all the sordid details. "I guess," I said, trying to turn the wheel of this conversational vehicle, "those blackboards must buy you a lot of wonderful meals."

"Exactly!" said David Shapiro. "All those blackboards allow me to live the life of a food warrior."

We were still in dangerous territory. "What was the best meal you had on the trip with Bobby?" I asked, desperately trying again.

That did it. Mr. Shapiro now offered detailed descriptions of dinners devoured in the far corners of France. One by one the stars came out, and he polished each one in his collection.

"Robuchon," he said, "you've been there?"

"Amazing," I replied. "My friend Patricia Wells, who wrote his cookbook, made our reservation, so of course we had exceptional food. It was the only time in my life that I have eaten food of such technical complexity that I could not figure out how it had been made."

"Exactly!" he said.

Michael and Sherry were both silent.

"And Ducasse?" he asked.

"Oh, I love his food," I said. "I spent a few days interviewing him when he was in Los Angeles. Such an interesting man! It was a long time ago, and he was very concerned that the Japanese were stealing everything from the French. He thought there should be a quota on Japanese cooks in French kitchens. But I imagine he's changed his tune."

"He's a master," said Mr. Shapiro. "But did you ever meet Alain Chapel?" I told him about translating for the great chef, years ago, when he was cooking at Mondavi, and how we had scoured the countryside for the cock's combs he needed for his meal. Mr. Shapiro seemed impressed. He mentioned the Auberge de l'Ill and I told about the time I'd gone there with Paula Wolfert and Jim Villas. Next he described the great meal he had eaten at L'Espérance, and I described the way Marc Meneau had fed me and my friend David everything on the menu in one glorious and terrible five-hour meal. "Some people think Meneau is no longer as great as he once was," said Mr. Shapiro.

"Some people," I said, "are wrong."

He agreed and we continued on our journey, working our way south. Before long he was regretting the downhill trajectory of Roger Verge, and I was bragging about the time I'd spent in his kitchen.

"Are you in pain?" Mr. Shapiro asked suddenly.

I turned to look at Michael, who was holding the side of his face. "Wouldn't you be if you were dining with you?" he muttered under his breath.

"I beg your pardon?" said Mr. Shapiro.

"Yes," said Michael, "my teeth hurt. I had oral surgery this morning and I guess the painkillers are wearing off."

This was a complete fabrication. "Traitor!" I whispered. Michael did not even flinch.

"If you don't mind," he said softly, "I think I had better go home now."

"Warm water and salt," said Mr. Shapiro. "That's what you need."

"Yes," said Michael. "And, I think, a couple of sleeping pills."

And with that he escaped into the night.

Mr. Shapiro had not exaggerated when he said that he made it his practice to close restaurants. We worked our way through the whole foie gras, which was still too rich, and the pancakes, which were still too heavy. Mr. Shapiro gamely ate the squab cooked in salt. His wife and I shared the duck with kumquats, and then we went on to dessert. By then Mr. Shapiro and the sommelier were on a first-name basis. We had an '83 Rieussec, which was maderized, so we went on to an '85 followed by a Sémillon from Chalk Hill gloriously infected with noble rot. It was past 1 A.M. when the last guests departed, and Mr. Shapiro refused to even consider leaving before they did. When we finally rose from the table, we had been sitting for six hours and I was so stiff I could barely walk.

"The night is still young," said Mr. Shapiro.

"Not for me," I said, wondering what else the Food Warrior could possibly want.

We rode the elevator down in stomach-tumbling silence, and when the doors opened I fled into the echoing lobby, heading for the coat check.

"Ruth!" cried a voice behind me. Turning, I found Daniel Johnnes, author, winemaker, and wine director of restaurants like Montrachet and Nobu, waving wildly at me.

"Daniel!" said Mr. Shapiro, moving in front of me and holding out his hand.

"Yes?" said Daniel with a distantly polite do-I-know-you look. He accepted Mr. Shapiro's hand, but he did so gingerly.

"I met you at Montrachet," brayed Mr. Shapiro. "Don't you remember? I brought a seventies vertical of La Tâche?"

"Oh, sure," said Daniel, in such a noncommittal tone that I could not tell if his memory of Mr. Shapiro was negative or nonexistent.

"What are you doing here at this time of night?" I asked.

"We're having a party for Nobu up in one of the private rooms," he said. "Why don't you join us?"

"You know I wouldn't do that," I said. "I don't go to parties with chefs."

"We do!" said Mr. Shapiro. He grabbed Daniel's arm and walked him back into the elevator, pulling his wife along. As they stepped in, Mr. Shapiro waved and shouted, "Good night. Good night. Thanks for dinner. Good night." I caught a brief glimpse of Daniel's face. He looked like a man caught in a nightmare. And then the doors closed.

How could you abandon me like that?" I raged at Michael the next day. "How could you go off and leave me with those people? Were they really so unbearable?"

"It wasn't them," he said quietly.

"What are you talking about?" I asked.

Michael touched my arm. "I don't want to hurt your feelings," he said, "but they weren't the ones I couldn't stand. It was you."

"Me?" I said. "Me?"

"You," he said. "I couldn't stay and watch what you were doing. I hate it when you pretend to be that person."

"What person?" I asked.

"The Restaurant Critic of the *New York Times*. The Princess of New York. Ms.-I-know-I-am-right-about-food-and-don't-argue-with-me. Take your pick."

"Was I that bad?" I whispered. My cheeks burned and I could feel the sweat prickling against my skin.

"Worse," he said. "You were the person you used to make fun of."

I felt sick. But Michael wasn't finished. "You really enjoy food, and you're able to translate that pleasure for others. But if you turn into a . . . what did Mr. Shapiro call it?"

"A food warrior," I said.

"Yeah," he said. "If you let yourself become that. . . ." He paused for a minute and then started again. "Last night this line from T. S. Eliot kept running through my head. It's from the *Four Quartets*. 'Garlic and sapphires in the mud . . .' I remembered that when you got into this it was almost a spiritual thing with you. You love to eat, you love to write, you love the generosity of cooks and what happens around the table when a great meal is served. Nothing that went on last night had anything to do with that."

"But I did it for charity," I protested.

"There must be better ways to give," he replied. "Don't give yourself away."

RESTAURANTS
by Ruth Reichl

....

"IS THIS A SPECIAL occasion?" our waiter asks. "Can we sing to you? Happy birthday? Happy anniversary? Anything?"

The new Windows on the World is as eager to please as a puppy dog. Smiling stewards in colorful costumes welcome passengers as they disembark from their vertical voyage by murmuring, "Will you be joining us for dinner?" Hostesses greet guests joyfully, as if they were long lost friends, and waiters describe the food with enormous enthusiasm. "Look, there's Yankee Stadium!" says one, pointing proprietarily out the window, as if the city—107 stories down—existed just to please his patrons. So much energy goes into all this niceness that quibbling about the food feels churlish.

Most people in New York know the story: Windows on the World was in decline when a bomb struck the World Trade Center in 1993. The Port Authority of New York and New Jersey, the building's owner, decided to close the restaurant and find someone new to run it. More than 30 restaurateurs wanted the job, among them David Bouley (Bouley), Alan Stillman (Smith & Wollensky and others) and Warner LeRoy (Tavern on the Green). Ultimately the honors went back to Joseph Baum, who developed the original Windows on the World, and his partners, Michael Whiteman and David Emil.

Many of us were thrilled when Mr. Baum was chosen. When I was growing up, he was busily reinventing the restaurants of New York, turning eating out into an adventure. His mark was everywhere, from high-end establishments like the Four Seasons and the Rainbow Room to inexpensive fast-food chains like Zum Zum. For this project, the partners brought in some high-powered talent: Georges Masraff, the culinary director, has worked just about everywhere, and Philippe Feret, the chef, did a wonderful job at Cafe Centro. Expectations were high.

But when the restaurant opened in July my first sensation was disappointment. The architect, Hugh Hardy, and the designer, Milton Glaser, did their best to inject personality into a sterile space, but they made the room look remarkably like

an airline lounge. Still, once I was seated, the comfortable chairs and pleasantly muted twilight colors combined with the view to create the illusion of being in an airliner hovering magically over Manhattan.

And the menu had the old Baum pizazz. Windows played it safe, serving an international menu that was little more than retooled Continental cuisine, but it was done with flair. The foie gras was a "celebration dish"; the squab was cooked in a crust of salt, "a flamboyant cooking method popular among chefs in Barcelona," and vegetables "support local farmers." The first meals were shaky, but I was sure things would improve.

They have, but only a little. Consider the shellfish extravaganza that the menu calls "a world view of seafood." It arrives dripping with ice and loaded with clams, oysters, mussels and crabs. Shrimp hang over every edge. The service for two is so spectacularly enormous that I can't imagine what arrives when you order for four. And yet we sent half the platter back to the kitchen: from the flat oysters to the tired shrimp and overmarinated tough scallops, everything was dreary.

The foie gras for three is also enormous, a whole lobe of cholesterol sweetly glazed in Sauternes and served with leaden potato pancakes. Most of that went back, too. Ravioli stuffed with asparagus and fresh morels were heavy and drenched in a brown sauce so gluey I had to look at the menu again to know what I was eating.

Scallops skewered with sugarcane and served in a curry sauce were far too salty. And a grilled lobster sausage one night, surrounded by fava beans and tomato, was so watery it drooped.

A few appetizers are respectable. I liked the marinated mahi-mahi with its seaweed salad very much, and the lobster chowder is delicious. Asian seafood broth with crab dumplings is nice too, when the kitchen manages to serve it warm. And foie gras "french toast," sautéed foie gras on crisply toasted brioche, is delicious.

Salt has been a major problem. One night the whole squab (of the flamboyant cooking method) was too salty. Other nights, the mashed potatoes, spinach or risotto were too salty to eat. Spicing, on the other hand, can be timid; the lovely whole veal shank wrapped in parchment and rubbed with cumin, garlic and other spices could use more punch. I like the generous serving of seafood in ginger broth, too, and the rack of lamb. Grilled shrimp, in an aquavit-laced cream sauce topped with caviar, is unexciting but unobjectionable.

Venison is mild and pleasant, and the duck (served for two) is crisp if somewhat fatty. But almost everything else I've tried—a lobster grilled to dust, sadly overcooked vegetables, flavorless roasted fish—has been a disappointment.

Desserts aren't much better. They keep changing, but the restaurant can't seem to get them right. On my final visit, the giant plate of raspberries was the definite favorite.

But there are consolations. The wine list is extraordinary and very reasonably priced, and the sommelier, Ralph Hersom, is affable and enthusiastic, the sort of person who could make a wine lover out of anyone. And just this week the talented Hervé Poussot, who worked at Le Bernardin, arrived to take over the pastry department.

Still, if you want wine and dessert, you would be better off saving your money for a blowout meal at Cellar in the Sky, which opened two weeks ago and looks extremely promising. (It is also part of Windows on the World.) And if it is the view you're after, you can get it for a lot less money in the bar, along with sushi, shabu shabu, raw seafood and live music.

WINDOWS ON THE WORLD

★

The Missionary of the Delicious

The moment the waiter appears with the chef's standard offering, a little plate of toast topped with dull whipped pâté, it becomes clear that the meal is not going to be brilliant. And from the cottony bread to the dreary dessert, the kitchen rarely exceeds these expectations."

That was Capsouto Frères.

At Palio, I reported, the gnocchetti were gummy, the lobster drowned in an excruciating sauce. Il Postino's kichen door, I said, "bangs against the wall with such force and regularity it feels like an earthquake." I complained about the restaurant's prices, savaged the food, and ended the review like this: "It's hard to smile when you feel like a sucker."

"You're certainly in a foul mood," said Carol. "I can't remember the last time you wrote something that made me want to go out to eat. Is it you or the restaurants? Suddenly you seem to hate everything."

"I don't know what's wrong with me," I said.

But it was not true. During the winter of 1997, as I ate my way through one forgettable restaurant after another, the woman in the mirror Michael had held up was very much on my mind. For the past few years I had been staring at the images of Molly, Brenda, Betty, and Chloe, but it had been a long time since I had taken a good look at myself. Now I began to wonder if the disguises had turned into more than merely part of my job. Was I pretending to be other people because I no longer liked the person I had become?

"I read you religiously," strangers often said when I told them my name, and I'd smile modestly and murmur something polite. But when people flatter you constantly it is very tempting to think that you deserve it. I had started my career at the *Times* by insisting that there was no right or wrong in matters of taste. Did I still believe that, or had I turned into a fatuous food snob, one of those people who thought my own opinion was the truth?

Self-doubt may be healthy, but it is hell on critics. The more I thought these things, the more difficult my work became. I went to the office every day and sat at my computer, staring at the keyboard, willing the words to come. Stubbornly they stayed away. You could read it in my reviews: those that weren't mean were dull.

Going home didn't help. Michael had started working on a piece about the Rocky Flats weapons plant, and every night he came home with new information about nuclear nightmares. What if a suicide terrorist managed to enter the facility, barricade himself inside, and build a bomb? "It could take out a few states," Michael said grimly. Three worried whistle blowers had called him, so concerned about security that they wanted someone to *do something* about the situation. I eavesdropped as Michael huddled over the phone late into the night, listening to doomsday scenarios. And then I listened some more as he practiced the dark art of the investigative reporter, convincing these men to act against their own best interests. They wanted to be anonymous, and Michael had to persuade them to go on national television and tell their story; if they wouldn't do it, he said, the situation would continue unchecked. Night after night I listened as Michael slowly drew them into his confidence, talking them into doing the right thing.

"Will they lose their jobs when this airs?" I asked.

"Most likely," he replied.

On the phone he sounded completely confident, but he tossed and turned in bed, waking us both up with his nightmares. Awake or asleep, at home or in the office, nothing seemed to be going right. If Jean-Georges Vongerichten had not chosen to open his restaurant at that precise moment, I don't know what I would have done.

Vongerichten was a media darling. At Lafayette he had become famous for replacing butter and cream with concentrated fruit and vegetable juices. His Vong was New York's first experiment in upscale Asian fusion, and his bistro Jo Jo, despite being too small, too expensive, and incredibly uncomfortable, was constantly packed. For my taste his newest venture had already garnered far too much advance press. Long before it opened, all of New York knew that he had employed a private forager to root out unusual wild herbs, and every aspect of Adam Tihany's design had been written about in agonizing detail. Jean-Georges also had the misfortune to be located in the appalling Trump building, a peacock unashamedly spreading its flamboyant tail across the foot of Central Park. To say I did not expect to like the place would be an understatement.

"My first visit's today at lunch," I told Carol in late spring. "Want to come?"

"Some other time," she said, "My stomach's sort of bothering me."

"You?" I said. "You're never sick."

"I don't think it's anything serious," she replied. "But I'm going to the doctor. I'd feel so foolish if I had something and I'd ignored it." She peered at my face and added, "Stop looking like that. It's probably nothing. But if we learned nothing else from AIDS, it's that when your body talks it's wise to listen."

"Oh well," I said, going off to the ladies' room to make a half-hearted attempt at disguising myself, "I doubt that you're missing much."

In the bathroom I pulled a nondescript ash-colored wig and a pair of glasses out of my briefcase. I put on a plain gray dress. "You don't actually think you're going to fool anyone in that getup?" said Carol when I emerged. "Any idiot can tell that you're wearing a wig."

"I know," I said, "but I don't have the energy for this. I haven't even given this one a name."

"What credit card are you using?" she asked.

"Toni Newman," I said. "I just got it. Toni's short for Antoinette."

"Well, *be* Toni," she said. "Make an effort. At least go put some lipstick on."

I went reluctantly back to the bathroom and worked on my face. I put a little wisp of a hat over the wig. "Better," said Carol when I reemerged, "but far from fabulous."

Walking to the subway, I tried to imagine who this Toni might be. An unmarried woman who worked in advertising? That would do. I considered her life and decided that she was in the throes of a middle-aged midcareer crisis, trying to figure out whether it was time to quit her job and move on.

As the subway came roaring into the station it occurred to me that any sane person would want to live somewhere quieter, prettier, less stressful. Maybe Toni was going to use her life savings to open a bakery in some clean little New England town, or someplace warm and friendly like Berkeley.

I was still lost in this dream as I climbed out of the subway, up from the subterranean noise and grime into the open space of Columbus Circle. The sky was blue and as I mounted the steps to the restaurant, Trump's gaudy brass doors flashed in the sunlight. They glided silently open and I walked in. Two pairs of eyes looked up simultaneously, surveying me from behind a desk. The skinny young woman examined me dubiously, swinging her long black hair suspiciously back from her shoulder as my hand went to the wig in an involuntary, self-conscious motion. I said Toni's name and the woman hesitated, searching in her book, reluctant to allow me access to the restaurant. But while she was considering her next move the glamorous black man came gliding around the desk and started to lead me into the dining room. She made a motion, as if to protest, but he stilled her. "Right this way," he said, executing a little bow.

The dining room opened into a whoosh of cool light that had a clean, severe purity. It was so churchlike that I found myself sniffing, half expecting the smell of old stones and melting wax. But this was a different aroma—wild leaves and red wine with hints of hazelnuts, and somewhere, deep in the background, peppered caramel. There were tropical notes too, as if a gentle rain had wafted through the room, leaving behind the promise of coconut palms and mango trees. As I followed the maître d' I inhaled so deeply that by the time I sank into my seat I was intoxicated and the deep purple anemones in the vase seemed to stretch toward me, nodding their velvet heads in welcome.

I ordered the tasting menu, and when the sommelier offered to bring appropriate wines for each course, I thought, Why not? The first wine arrived and I took a sip, holding the cool pale liquid in my mouth until I could feel the weight of the sugar on my tongue. I let it run down the back of my throat, appreciating its smoothness, and wriggled into my chair.

"A little *amuse bouche* as a gift from the chef," murmured the waiter, setting down a minuscule porcini tart framed by a delicate salad of tiny herbs. I ate slowly, first the lacy licorice-flavored chervil, then sturdy, spicy wild parsley, and finally the aggressive little fronds of dill. Poring through them I discovered a single leaf of lamb's quarter, bits of sorrel, dandelion, chickweed. I followed the flavors in my mind until the walls vanished and I emerged into a deep glade that grew more distinct with each bite.

It was disappointing to come out of the woods, and for a moment I resented the luxurious modern room and the city visible beyond the windows. Then the waiter set a bowl of tiny lavender blossoms at my place and once again I forgot where I was. He dipped a ladle into a tureen and spilled the contents into the bowl, releasing a torrent of garlic that cascaded, a waterfall of scent, just beneath my nose. I closed my eyes and breathed deeply, taking in the round sweetness of the garlic, the sharp mintiness of chives, and then, something else. What? I opened my eyes to find that the waiter had set a little plate of sautéed frog's legs on the table.

The soup was not like anything I'd tried before—garlic gone green, racy, oddly elegant. The chive blossoms rang out sharply when you took the first bite and then began to fade, teasing, until you took another.

I inhaled the soup, ate the frog's legs with my fingers, dreamily tearing them with my teeth and dabbling my fingers in the lemon-laden bowl of luxuriously warm water.

All around me waiters were carving ducks fragrant with five-spice powder and drizzling caramel sauce over slices of poached foie gras. They were spooning creamed morels over asparagus the color of newly sprouted grass and dolloping roasted apricot tarts with just-churned ice cream. The smells swirled around me; in this symphony of scent I felt as if I were smelling with my skin. My body began to tingle, as if I had been frozen and was now, slowly, starting to thaw.

The sommelier offered glasses of icy Gewürztraminer that smelled like perfumed blossoms until you took a sip and discovered the elegantly astringent flavor. In front of me the waiter was covering a plate with a pristine square of halibut, blinding in its whiteness, and strewing pure red tomato confit on one side, pale green ribbons of zucchini on the other. The sauce, with its nutlike aroma, was the color of faded golden taffeta. "Château-Chalon," he whispered and I thought yes, only the Jura wine, dried on beds of straw, could have this jeweled fragrance.

Dessert was a shower of treats descending slowly on the table. First a chocolate napoleon of such restrained sweetness that it formed a bridge to the warm raspberries and vanilla cream that followed. Next a dense confit of apples, laden with orange peel. Then homemade marshmallows, great rolls of them cut with scissors, and candied shiso, and little macaroons in a box.

I had fooled no one in that disguise, but it was worth it; after that, everything tasted better to me. The following week I stumbled into a sweet little Neapolitan restaurant, Da Rosa, where the owner's mother stood in the kitchen turning out hand-made ribbons of pasta and fluffy little gnocchi while he lovingly poured one local wine after another, extolling the virtues of ancient grapes like Aglianico. I went to Canal House and rediscovered the joy of macaroni and cheese when it has enough crust. Maya opened, and I was suddenly excited about the possibility of great Mexican food. Then came Molyvos, where I ate dolmades and tyropites and grilled fish, remembering what it was like to sit on a hillside in Crete with the oregano-scented breezes blowing across your face as you looked at the wine-dark sea down below. It was a wonderful few months.

"You're on a roll," said Carol. "You're fun to read again."

"Everything's better," I said. "Michael's in a great mood. He and Rita Braver went out to Rocky Flats and got some great video. The whistle blowers are going on air and Dan Rather loves the piece. It's going to be important. And I'm about to review a new restaurant opened by an incredibly talented young chef."

"Who?" she asked.

"Rocco DiSpirito," I said. "The food he served at his last place, Dava, was amazing. The new one's Union Pacific; you have to come with me."

"Maybe after the operation," she replied.

"Operation?" I cried. "What operation?"

"It's nothing," she said. "But you know these stomach problems I've been having?"

"Yes?" I said.

"They've decided it's probably endometriosis. They're going to take a look. I'll only be out a couple of days. Really, it's nothing."

"Okay," I said. "When you get back we'll celebrate at Union Pacific."

The celebration had to be postponed: Carol had ovarian cancer. She refused to be gloomy about it. "I'm going to beat this," she said as she started on the first round of chemotherapy. "My doctor thinks my chances are excellent. And I've been researching this new treatment they've been doing in California. I'm going to be fine."

She was so convincing that I stopped worrying. But I missed her deeply. In the office or out, Carol was fun. She was also the only person I knew willing to go out on the spur of the moment, the only one who didn't care if I took her to a big-deal meal or some little dump around the corner. After she left the paper, everything changed.

The lovable, capable Trish Hall, editor of the Living Section, designed the new Dining In/Dining Out section and then deserted us to become the editor of *Martha Stewart Living*. Eric Asimov was still writing the $25 or Under column, but after a brief stint editing an early incarnation of Sunday Styles, he'd been reassigned and was now downstairs in Metro. Molly O'Neill had moved on to start her own dot-com business and Marian Burros was spending most of her time working out of the Washington bureau, despite the fact that she and the bureau chief, Johnny Apple, didn't get along very well. Faced with all their empty desks, it was hard to sit at my own and feel jolly.

I tried to get to know the replacements, but the new editor of the Dining section, Rick Flaste, was nothing like Trish. He was a gruff man and the least politic person on earth. Tall, gangly, and strangely ascetic looking for someone who loves to eat, he displayed an utter contempt for fashion. He had the air of some biblical prophet intent on predicting doom. His clothes looked as if he slept in them, and his long face and large forehead were framed by lanky strands of hair. His ideas were smart and original, but he was either too busy or too brusque to bother with charm. Even when he asked nicely, it felt as if he was barking commands. The new young reporter, on the other hand, was just the opposite; Amanda Hesser was terrifyingly sweet. She was pale, pretty, and petite, but she seemed so frighteningly ambitious that we all kept our distance. Before long I stopped going into the office. I was supposed to be sitting at my computer, writing from home, but the truth is that I had disappeared into the kitchen.

Every kitchen is filled with flames and shards, fire and glass, boiling liquids and sharp objects eager to attack you. Cooking is too dangerous to permit distraction. If you step into that arena without the proper respect, you will certainly get hurt.

"Blood!" screamed a sign over the stove in my first professional kitchen. Beneath, spelled out in large letters, were the appropriate steps to be taken in case of severed appendages, injured limbs, or major burns. Peril pounces on the careless cook, and for me this lurking menace is part of the attraction. I have found that meditation at the edge of the knife makes everything seem better.

But while cooking demands your entire attention, it also rewards you with endlessly sensual pleasures. The sound of water skittering across leaves of lettuce. The thump of the knife against watermelon, and the cool summer scent the fruit releases as it falls open to reveal its deep red heart. The seductive softness of chocolate beginning to melt from solid to liquid. The tug of sauce against the spoon when it thickens in the pan, and the lovely lightness of Parmesan drifting from the grater in gossamer flakes. Time slows down in the kitchen, offering up an entire universe of small satisfactions.

That fall, worried about Carol and wondering about my work, I spent weeks standing at the counter, chopping onions, peeling apples, and rolling dough. I made complicated soups and stews, and I began baking bread every day, as I had done when Michael and I first lived together.

In the end I came to realize that a restaurant critic's job is more about eating than writing, and every time I cancelled a reservation I grew more seriously behind. I was having a secret affair with cooking, and I knew it could not continue. But every morning, after walking Nicky to school, I'd go home and sit in the kitchen, sifting through my recipes. A jumble of handwritten pages, they were gathered into an ancient, torn manila folder filled with memories. Tomorrow, I'd think, tomorrow I'll go out to eat, tomorrow I'll go back to the restaurants. And then I'd turn over another page and a long-gone meal would come tumbling out, more evocative than any photograph could ever be.

Here was apricot upside-down cake, written in my mother-in-law's neat, careful script. Here was Aunt Birdie's potato salad, scratched in her feathery penmanship and signed with her funny little bird. My own recipes for six different pie crusts were carefully printed for the students at my cooking classes. Serafina's scrawled instructions for coconut cake were almost illegible, as if she had not quite wanted to part with the recipe. My mother's thick, bold writing danced exuberantly across a page torn from the *New York Times* in the mid-sixties. "Sounds like you!" she'd written across a recipe called "Minetry's Miracle." I looked it over; it required a pound of butter, a dozen eggs, a pint of cream, and a cup of bourbon (not to mention chocolate, pecans, ladyfingers, and macaroons). Indeed.

Then a recipe written on blue-lined paper leapt into my hand. The writing was not familiar. "Aushak," I whispered, and suddenly it came to me. An Afghan exchange student had given it to me when I was an undergraduate with a reputation as a cook. At the time these scallion dumplings had seemed too strange, too exotic, too time-consuming, and I had never attempted them. Now, studying the ingredients, I was curious. The dumplings sounded delicious. Yes, I thought, writing out a grocery list, this is my recipe for today.

Aushak

MEAT SAUCE

   3 tablespoons vegetable oil

   1 medium onion, finely chopped

   ½ pound ground beef

   1 clove garlic, minced

   1 teaspoon ground coriander

½ teaspoon diced or grated fresh ginger
½ cup water
2 tablespoons tomato paste
½ teaspoon salt
¼ teaspoon pepper

YOGURT SAUCE

1 cup full-fat yogurt
1 tablespoon minced garlic
½ teaspoon salt

DUMPLINGS

2 bunches scallions, white part discarded, green tops finely
    chopped (about 2 cups)
½ teaspoon salt
½ teaspoon pepper
1 teaspoon red pepper flakes
1 teaspoon minced garlic
25 to 30 wonton or Gyoza wrappers, preferably round

GARNISH

2 teaspoons chopped fresh mint

Make the meat sauce: Heat the oil in a small skillet. Add the onion and cook for 5 minutes, until golden. Add the beef, garlic, coriander, and ginger, and cook, stirring, until the meat is no longer red, about 3 minutes.

Add the water and cook, stirring often, until it is reduced by half, about 5 minutes. Add the tomato paste and cook, stirring, for about 5 minutes. Season with the salt and pepper, and set aside.

Make the yogurt sauce: Blend the yogurt, garlic, and salt in a bowl, and set it aside.

Make the dumplings: Combine the chopped scallion tops, salt, pepper, red pepper flakes, and garlic in a bowl. Toss to mix.

Lay a wonton wrapper on a flat surface and brush the edges with water. Spoon 1 teaspoon of the scallion mixture onto the center, fold the wrapper in half, and press the edges to make a semi-circle. Repeat with the remaining wrappers. (If you do not have round wrappers, fold them into triangles.)

Heat 3 quarts salted water in a 6- or 8-quart pot. When it is boiling, add the filled dumplings and cook for 5 minutes. Drain in a colander.

Assemble the dish: Spoon ¼ cup yogurt sauce into a serving dish, and cover it with the dumplings. Spoon the remaining yogurt sauce on top, and sprinkle with the mint. Spoon the meat sauce all around, and serve at once.

Serves 4

I walked to the market, strolling past Citarella, where the man who decorates the windows with fish was contemplating his latest creation. He added a few oysters to the design, stood back to observe the effect, and waved at me. Next door at Fairway the bins were filled with six kinds of local apples, the last of the deep-blue prune plums, the first of the pumpkins. There was some sad-looking corn and some fine-looking tomatoes. I grabbed a basket and walked in. People were sliding through the sawdust, pushing, tugging, shoving past the raucous dairy counter and the shiny dried fruits, eager to get to the deli counter and jockey for position in the smoked salmon line.

I gathered mint, scallions, and fresh garlic into my cart and went off to find the wonton wrappers. As I passed the bread a baguette called to me, and as I reached for it a voice said, "Not that one."

Looking up, I found a man with a boyish face staring at me. His warm brown eyes and mischievous grin seemed surprised to find themselves attached to such an oversized and awkward body. With one hand the man dangled a baguette before me; with the other he stopped my reaching arm. "Take this," he said. "It's baked later and delivered earlier."

"Hi Ed," I said.

I barely knew Ed Levine, but he had a reputation as the ultimate connoisseur of New York food. For years well-intentioned friends had been telling me that I should cultivate his friendship. Nobody, they assured me, knew more about the city's edible landscape. There was apparently not a pizzeria in the city that Ed hadn't sampled. If I wanted to meet the jerk chicken king of Brooklyn or the tofu man of Flushing, Ed could introduce me, and he was one of the few people who knew where to find the last women in the city still stretching strudel dough by hand. The best fried chicken in Harlem? Ed could lead me to it. SoHo's finest sandwiches? Ed was on to that as well. But although we had been introduced any number of times, neither of us had pursued the acquaintance.

"Have you tried the donuts they've been getting from Georgie's?" Ed asked now, drawing me over to the bakery counter. "Well, you should."

Ed was full of opinions: I should be buying this olive oil instead of that, my coffee should come from next door, and he did not approve my choice of smoked salmon. But his enthusiasm was so infectious that I couldn't be annoyed. When he said that my Afghan dumplings would surely be better with yogurt from the Middle Eastern store in Bay Ridge, I suspected he was right.

"I could take you there," he offered. He stopped himself, eyes gleaming. "In fact, why don't you let me take you on a food tour of Brooklyn?" He ran his fingers through his short red-blond hair and added, "You'll meet some amazing people. Bakers and butchers are undervalued in our culture, and they're so happy when you recognize what they do. We'll have a great time. Please come."

How could I possibly refuse?

You were right," I said a few days later as I climbed into his car. "Those dumplings were great, but they would be better with homemade yogurt."

"The Middle Eastern place is going to be one of our last stops," he said. "I want to take you to Carroll Gardens first. But we're going to make an unscheduled stop before we go to Brooklyn. I want you to meet Jim Leahy at the Sullivan Street Bakery. Okay?" Ed was looking straight at me as he talked. "He's an amazing guy," he continued, still looking my way. "When Jim talks about bread it's like he's speaking in tongues. Besides, we might as well pick up a little snack to tide us over."

"Okay," I said, thinking that if I didn't argue he might look back at the road.

But Ed, it soon became clear, was a trusting driver who relied on his car to take care of itself when he was otherwise occupied. For long stretches he looked at me, at the itinerary, at the passing scenery. "I haven't seen that bakery before!" he'd cry, swerving across three lanes to get a closer look, convinced that any cars foolish enough to be in our path would move before we reached them.

I was relieved when we got to Sullivan Street and Ed maneuvered the car into a conveniently vacant loading zone and turned off the engine.

It was warm inside the bakery, and hushed. Flour swirled through the air, so much like snow that when a woman came to throw her arms around Ed the two looked exactly like figures in one of those little paperweights you shake. "Ed!" she said. "Jim's going to be so disappointed that he missed you!" The air smelled of yeast and heat, and if you listened carefully you could hear, above the whirr of the ovens, the faint burble of rising dough.

Great mounds of crusty loaves surrounded us like soft mountains, and

Ed stroked one fondly, saying, "Jim is obsessed with getting the right textures." As he moved through this soft white world, flour settled on his jacket and frosted his hair. He stretched a hand to a long swath of *pizza bianca* stretching across the counter like a languid cat and broke off a corner. "Have some," he said, handing me a piece. The flatbread was crisp and slightly oily, dotted with rosemary, and so delicious that each bite enticed you into another.

"This is perfect!" said Ed, sounding surprised. He took another bite and shook his head. "When Jim first made pizzas they were cardboardy. Then they got soggy. But now he's really nailed it. What happened?"

The woman pointed an affectionately accusing finger at Ed. "This guy," she said, "can really drive you crazy. He won't accept just any old thing. He keeps nagging at you, nagging at you, nagging at you until you make it better." She smiled at Ed and added, "Your complaints were heard."

Ed nodded his head. "I wish everyone was so obedient." As far as I could tell, there was not a whiff of irony in the statement. "Tell Jim I approve."

We left and went from one small shop to another, gathering food as we traveled. By the time we walked back to the car we were laden with warm little pear tarts, turnovers, jars of jam, loaves of bread, goat cheese, and zucchini wrapped in flaky dough.

"You see why I love these people?" Ed asked. He looked longingly at the shops we were passing, loath to leave any off the tour. Suddenly he ducked; ahead of us a large man loomed in a doorway and he was pointing a finger at Ed. "You!" he commanded, coming towards us. "You! Come in here right now!"

Ed speeded up. "Sorry," he whispered out of the side of his mouth, almost running now, "but we have to get away." To the man he said, "Tomorrow, I'll come back tomorrow." And then, in another whisper, "Keep moving. If we stop and go into the store he'll start feeding us and he won't stop. He'll never let us go; we'll be here all day."

The shopkeeper was now trotting at Ed's side, trying to stay with us. "You promise?" he asked.

"Yes, yes, I promise," said Ed.

"I'll be waiting." The shopkeeper, reluctantly, gave up the race. "I have some new eggplant dishes you *need* to taste."

"See you tomorrow," said Ed, diving into the car.

Winded by the race, neither of us said anything for a few minutes. But when we were safely in the tunnel, halfway to Brooklyn, I asked, "Will you really go back?"

Ed stared at me incredulously. "Of course," he said. "I promised." He raised his hands to the sky. "I love all these people; they have so much passion. They're a little bit crazy, but they use their craziness for their business. They live right."

"Uh, sure," I said, wishing he would reconnect with the steering wheel. "You're right. Yes. Passion. Watch that car!"

"Oh, don't worry," he said, patting my leg as if I were a fussy old lady, "I've never had an accident. Really."

We came out of the tunnel and nosed deep into Carroll Gardens. Ed gestured around and said happily, "Isn't this neighborhood wonderful?" He parked, setting off a couple of car alarms in the process. They were howling as we walked into Esposito's Pork Store, but Ed paid them no mind.

It was comfortable in there, rich with spice and personality, a throwback to a vanishing New York. Housewives with loud nasal voices demanded this piece of veal breast, that slice of *bracciole*, and a little salami, not too thick, are you listening to me? They examined the heap of softly steaming stuffed peppers, asking when they were made, and wanted to know if this was yesterday's sausage and where the hell was today's? Firemen from the around the corner stood shouldering their axes and arguing over their order, scooping up mountains of chopped meats and cold cuts.

"Isn't this great?" asked Ed, as if he had personally conjured the scene. "Isn't this amazing? Doesn't it make you happy that places like this exist?" His enthusiasm was irresistible. "Meet George," he said, offering up a handsome man with tattooed arms and a thick gold chain around his neck as if he were Exhibit A. "His grandfather started this place. And you know, they still make all their own dried sausage, even their own pancetta."

"Dad's in back now," said George, "making sausage."

"See?" said Ed, as if I had doubted him.

In the darkened kitchen an old man stood quietly tying sausages with string. The air was deliciously funky, filled with the scent of pepper seeds and the fine aroma of aging meat. The man pressed a dried sausage with a weathered thumb, rejected it, tried another. He nodded to himself, sliced off a few hunks, and handed them over. The sausage was sharp, spicy, and very fine. "That's my *sopressata*," said Dad, emphasizing the possessive. "It's good."

Ed's next gift was a tiny shop filled with bakers mixing dough, melting chocolate, pulling pastries from industrial ovens. When Ed stepped through the door they all stopped to welcome him, and there was something in the gesture that made me think of those sweet moving figures department stores put in their windows at Christmas. If the bakers had broken into song, I would not have been surprised. "What they make here," said Ed, grabbing a small pastry from one of the pans, "is the most amazing rugellach I've ever found."

He popped one buttery little morsel into his mouth, and then another. By his eighth he was shaking his head sadly and saying, "It makes you realize how much bad rugellach there is in the world. Oh, okay, I'll have just one more."

The car alarms had finally subsided when we climbed back into the car, but as Ed pulled out of the parking space they started up again, sending us off with a flourish we could hear for blocks. The sound faded into the distance as the car plowed through the Brooklyn traffic, heading for Bay Ridge.

"Look," said Ed, suddenly slowing to a crawl. He pointed out the window, simultaneously lifting his foot from the gas. "Look at that collision of cultures!" As Ed indicated a Mexican grocery store, an Asian emporium, a Scandinavian shop, the car slowly drifted to a standstill. He gazed beatifically out the window as a cacophony of angry honking started up. "Don't you just love New York?" asked Ed, setting the car back in motion.

The Family Store greeted us with a virtual onslaught of sensations. A riotous mixture of caraway, cumin, cardamom, and sumac perfumed the air while bins of seeds and spices spilled onto the wooden floors. Behind them a rainbow of olives and pickles created a colorful backdrop. The refrigerated cases were filled with vivid jewels of food: pale spheres of stuffed cabbage, billowing mounds of beige hummus, bright pink muhammara, and deep emerald zucchini fritters.

"We've come for your yogurt," Ed told the smiling man behind the counter.

"Ah, my friend," he replied, running out to greet Ed, "first you must taste this." In an instant he was spooning up soft white curds with the consistency of double cream and plopping it into our mouths. It was smooth and tangy, incredibly good. He looked delightedly at our faces. "This," he cried, "is no ordinary yogurt. This is *goat milk* yogurt. I have to go to the Amish to get the milk. It is very good for you. So much calcium." He was a large man, but light on his feet as he danced through the store, insisting we try his homemade cheese ("One customer comes all the way from England in his private jet just to get this"), his pomegranate molasses, his baba gannouj. As he spoke he was taking foods from the cases and feeding us with his fingers. "Wonderful, wonderful" he crooned as we ate.

"Save your appetite if you can," whispered Ed.

We left, the yogurt cradled in my arms, and I held my breath as Ed banged the car out of the parking space and headed toward Coney Island. We nosed down streets with names like Neptune and Surf toward the looming Cyclone, a great construction of white boards and twisted metal. "There's Totonno's," said Ed in a mournful and reverent voice and the car began to slow of its own volition. "Their pizza is really great." He stared longingly out the window and then said, "Stop! Oh my God, Gerace's is gone." His foot stomped on the brake and he came to a complete halt in the middle of traffic. The honking started up. Ed, filled with lamentation, paid it no mind.

"Oh my God. The sign said 'For rent,' did you see that? This drives me crazy. They taught me how to make prosciutto bread. That place had been there forever. Oh my God, this is a tragedy." He took his foot off the brake and started forward, keeping up a keening wail for Gerace's as we drove.

Near the crumbling roller-coaster we pulled up at the original Nathan's hot dog stand, which presided over the litter-strewn sidewalk with the proud air of an ancient relic. We got out, and as we approached Phillip's, a battered candy shop, a toothless man began begging for money. With the instinctive gesture of the easy touch, Ed reached into his pocket and handed him a dollar.

He was not even aware that he had done it, for he was standing, rapt, in front of the candy shop window. "Look at that!" he said reverently. "Charlotte Russe, a classic Brooklyn confection! You can't get these anywhere else anymore." He dug another dollar out of his pocket, plunked it onto the outside counter, and burrowed his face into one of the little white cups. When he looked up his chin was covered with whipped cream and he looked like an overgrown ten-year-old.

"Hey, big guy!" A gray-haired leprechaun of a man emerged from a side door. His face ablaze with a grin, he stared up at Ed as if the sun had just come out and swung the door wide, inviting us in. In the tiny shop lollipops dangled from the ceiling, a wild swirl of colors, their sizes ranging from a few inches to a few feet in diameter. Candy apples marched along the counters, and bags of cotton candy hung from the walls like a soft rainbow. In one corner a huge, battered copper candy kettle filled with bright red sugar syrup balanced precariously atop a hot plate. Next to it apples, sticks raised like so many exuberant tails, waited to be dipped. "John makes everything you see," said Ed. And then, shaking his head as if this fact were both incredible and undeniable, he reiterated, "I swear he does!"

I reached for the largest lollipop. "How much do you charge for the big ones?" I asked, staggering as the candy fell onto my shoulder. It was as tall as I am and stunningly heavy.

"Ten bucks," he said.

"That's all?" I asked, reaching into my pocket for a bill. "I've wanted one of these since I was a little kid," I admitted, slinging the giant confection over my shoulder, "but I thought they cost a fortune."

"Other places," said Ed, heading for the door, "they do. John's the last of the old-time candy men."

"I don't know for how long," said John. "This is a dying way of life. Nobody wants to do this anymore." And then, as if talking to himself, he added, "Who can blame them? The kettle alone weighs thirty-five pounds, you get burned all the time, and you should see me when I'm finished." Then, as if shaking off the gloomy burden of his thoughts, he hugged Ed and opened the door, and as we navigated the broken sidewalk, he called out, "Don't be a stranger!"

"Isn't he amazing?" asked Ed, unlocking the car door. "People like that just make me glad I'm alive." As I settled the lollipop in the car I realized that for the first time in months I was feeling the same way. We drove past the sign in Gerace's window, which caused Ed to retreat once again into the keening wail of loss, heading for Flatbush and what he assured me was the best jerk chicken on the planet.

It was late afternoon as we drove back to Manhattan, accompanied by the ever-present music of the cars. My yogurt was nestled into a bag, waiting to turn into aushak, and all around us were sausages and pastry, lollipops and spices, chicken and cheese. Any world that contained all this, I thought surveying our loot, was a very fine place. I felt reinvigorated, alive, optimistic. The thought of getting back to work suddenly seemed like fun.

"Oh Mommy," said Nicky when he saw the lollipop, "this must be the most beautiful thing on earth." He gazed at it, dazzled by the gorgeous object that had just entered his life. "Can I really eat it?"

"Yes," I said, "but it might take a couple of years."

He stood back and examined it. "I don't think I will," he decided, petting the giant candy. "This isn't one of those foods that you eat. It's one of the ones that's only supposed to make you happy."

Emily

D o you have a reservation?" The woman's voice was so cold it
sent shivers down my back.

"Yes," I said.

"And the name is?" Her eyes, above the horn-rimmed glasses, were
hostile.

"Newman," I said. "Toni Newman."

She peered at the book, pushed her glasses higher up on her nose,
and looked again. "Ah!" she said at last, as if she had been searching desperately for clues, "here it is. And your guest?"

"She doesn't seem to be here yet," I replied, looking pointedly around
the eerily empty room.

She frowned. A handsome woman with a trim body clad entirely in
brown tweed, she had an unforgiving face framed by short, glossy silver-
streaked black hair. "Over there," she said, one twiglike finger pointing at
a carved wooden chair beside the cold fireplace. "Sit." As I folded myself

into the chair's uncompromising lines she turned back to the reservation book she had been studying when I entered the Box Tree.

I looked around the small parlor, trying to figure out why this restaurant was voted "most romantic" year after year in the restaurant polls. The Zagat guide had this to say: "exquisite," "a jewel box," "ideal for Rodgers and Hart romance."

It certainly wasn't the warmth of the welcome. It must be the stained-glass windows, I thought, the profusion of fireplaces, the walls covered with old portraits. The room I was in resembled one of those Ralph Lauren ads, the ones designed to look as if the lord of the manor might come striding in at any moment, dogs capering about his boots as he peels off leather gloves and calls for a beaker of ale. But as the minutes stretched on, the door remained resolutely closed, and when it finally opened it was to admit a tall blonde woman wearing a short black skirt and a black leather jacket. She had three miles of leg, a Polish accent, and a need for a job.

The woman at the desk surveyed her with narrowed eyes. "Are you legal?" she asked.

The blonde hesitated for a moment, looking uncomfortable. "No," she finally admitted.

This did not seem to faze the tweed woman. "Leave a resume," she said, holding out her hand. "We'll call." The blonde handed her a sheet of paper and stood, uncertainly shifting her weight from one long leg to the other. Tweed twisted her lips and made a little shooing motion with one hand while reaching for the ringing phone with the other.

"This Saturday?" she said. "Impossible!" She hung up and glared at the blonde standing before her. "Why are you still here?" she asked.

"Ven vill you call?" asked the blonde, the *w*'s all *v*'s.

The woman shrugged. "How should I know when we'll need help?" She reached once again for the phone. "No, nothing for Friday at eight," she said, "although I might be able to squeeze you in at nine forty-five. Suit yourself." She slammed the receiver into the cradle and glared at the blonde.

"Go away," she said sharply. And then she turned to the phone, which was ringing again. The blonde glanced at me, gave a defeated little shrug, and left.

A minute later a waiter appeared, his head poking comically out of a jacket so large the shoulders were at his elbows, the pockets at his knees. Tweed looked at him, her nose twitching as if some horrid odor had wafted into the room. "What do you mean by coming to work looking like that?" she barked.

"It was the damn cleanuhs," he whined in a pronounced New York accent. "They lost my jacket. I mean they switched it or somethin'. I sent mine and got this back."

"A Chinese laundry?" she asked.

"Yeah," he said, his voice rising as if she had said something clever. "How'd ya know?"

She did not deign to reply. "They either find your jacket," she said acidly, "or they replace it. You can work today, but if you show up tomorrow looking like that I'm going to send you home." With that she walked rapidly out of the room. Shoulders slumped, the waiter followed.

Carol had warned me that she would be coming from the doctor, so I was not worried by her lateness. I looked around the empty room, memorizing the details for the review. Then the shouting started.

"I told you to get ready for a private party tonight!" It was a voice that I did not recognize in the next room. And then another voice, unmistakably Tweed's, started in. "You know we don't use the benches for that. Chairs, chairs, chairs. Do you know what chairs are?" Her harsh voice was followed by the crash of furniture being moved, the grating scrape of wood being dragged across the floor. "Oh," she moaned dramatically, and the chairs screeched, "don't you understand English? I can't believe how stupid you immigrants are!" The chairs yowled and shrieked as her voice went on and on, berating the men who were, I gathered, Mexican. By the time Carol arrived, my appetite was gone.

"The hostess here," I said, standing to kiss her, "is a nightmare. Let's go someplace else." She had lost an alarming amount of weight, and when I hugged her I had the feeling that her bones might break.

"No, please," she said. Her breathing was ragged. "I'm so sorry, but I need to sit down."

Feeling like a thoughtless fool, I went off to find the hostess, following the angry sound of her voice.

"This way," she said, all saccharine smile as she led us out of the parlor. I was relieved that we were moving away from the still-protesting furniture.

The Box Tree was composed of small dining rooms, and every one was empty. The one where Tweed deposited us was chilly, with rose-topped tables waiting hopefully to welcome absent diners and a forlorn fireplace waiting for a match. Tossing us a pair of menus, she departed. "So lively!" said Carol. "So crowded!" Her thin face crumpled into a smile. "What a perfect place for a celebration!"

"You don't find this cheerful?" I asked. "All it needs is one beautiful woman."

"What are you talking about?" she asked.

"Yesterday a waiter elucidated what he called the 'Cipriani theory.' He said they build their restaurants small so that a single beautiful woman can walk in and make everyone instantly feel they're in the right place. If Julia Roberts came waltzing in here, wouldn't you think this was swell?"

"Not really," she said, pointing to the waiter, who had entered the room and now stood fidgeting in his oversized jacket, "not with him hovering over me."

The man must have seen me sitting in the parlor and must have known that I had already heard him speak, but when he opened his mouth he had acquired an English accent. Without a hint of embarrassment he described the bisque aux morilles in rounded English vowels. He went on to talk of "consommé of whole cow," throwing himself into the description until we could almost see the chef, wreathed in clouds of steam, distilling the soup to its very essence. He went through the entire menu—well, what else did he have to do?—telling us about a two-pound lobster who was, at this very moment, strolling through the refrigerator waiting to become a fabulous fricassée. The chef would steam the beast, remove the meat, and fold it into a freshly made beurre blanc. Truffled liver, he assured us, was a specialty, carved into gossamer slices and seared so quickly it acquired the texture of velvet before being bathed in a sauce fit for angels. And no sane person, he declared, would leave the premises without tasting the raspberry crème brûlée. He pronounced it "rawsberry," taking the better part of a minute to eject the word from his mouth.

"I promise," he said, when the ordering was over, "that you will have an entirely memorable meal." He was so convincing that I forgot the tweed woman, forgot the invented accent and the empty rooms behind us, and decided to believe him. "This is going to be great!" I said to Carol. Then I looked at her more closely and said, "Are you okay?"

"I'm fine," she said.

"Fine?" I asked.

"I'm tired," she said. "It's only been a couple of days since the last treatment. It takes a while to recover. But the chemo's not so bad. I've gotten to know a lot of people at the clinic. Most of them are much worse off; I'm tolerating this pretty well. The doctors are hopeful. We'll know more in a couple of months, and if it doesn't work I'll do another round. I'm going to be fine. And I'm looking forward to this meal."

I understood that she was telling me that she didn't want to talk about her illness, that she needed a vacation from the land of the sick. So we talked about the office, falling into the comforting culture of complaint shared by all employees. We told each other stories about all the bosses and their foibles, the things that they were constantly doing wrong. It was familiar. It was soothing.

The waiter came back a little too quickly, but he said "Bisque aux morilles!" with such conviction that when he set the bowl before me, I looked hopefully down into its depths. It was thick and creamy, and it gave off puffs of steam. I dipped my spoon below the surface and raised it to my mouth.

I took a taste. And then another. Still unable to believe it, I took one more. "What?" asked Carol.

It was a bowl of pure hot cream. A drop of cooking sherry might lurk somewhere in its depths, but that was all. There was not even a whisper of mushroom. Not a hint.

"You look like a cat touching a mirror," said Carol, watching me. "You know the way they look at themselves and then reach out a paw as if they can't believe it's glass and not another cat? That's how you look." She picked up her spoon and filled it with consommé. A quizzical look crossed her face. She took another taste. "I guess," she said at last, "that I must look the same."

With each new course the meal became more comical. The lobster was a scrawny thing, and it had been a long time since he had walked around a refrigerator or anything else. The desiccated meat was drenched in a gritty sauce made of flour and milk, with a bit of dill and a lot of cooking sherry. My liver was tough stuff that tasted like . . . cooking sherry.

"This is the worst food I've ever been served in a restaurant!" said Carol. "If you weren't here, I'd be positive that the chemo had robbed me of the ability to taste. Imagine being someone without a lot of money who's saved up for the most romantic restaurant in town . . ."

Or, I was thinking, imagine another scenario. Imagine being a restaurant critic with a sick friend who can only enjoy food a few days out of every month. You could have taken her to any restaurant in town, but oh no, you had to bring her here.

"You have to do something," said Carol.

"Don't worry," I said, "I will."

The shrieking of the tweed woman's voice kept echoing in my head as I sat at my computer, writing notes about the tasteless food. I tried to imagine what could make someone behave that way. And then, just like that, I made up a life for her. She had married young, and the guy had turned out to be an abusive jerk. She had stuck it out for—how many years—five, six?—and then finally left him. No children. And now she settled for a little life, all alone, living on the edges of other people's happiness, hugging her hatred close to keep her warm.

I gave her a name—Emily—and an address in that sad, shapeless neighborhood around the restaurant. It was shabby respectable, and when people asked where she lived, Emily exaggerated and said, "On the Upper East Side," with an air she hoped conjured up a Park Avenue duplex. She walked to work. When she took a taxi—which was rare—she tipped ten cents. She ate the same thing every day—what would it be? A four-minute egg, a liverwurst sandwich? At night she went home, made herself a pot of tea, hung her clothes carefully in the closet, and spent the evening watching television. She had trouble sleeping. She worried about her weight. She was anxious about the rest of her life. And given the chance, she entertained herself by humiliating the less fortunate.

How would she like eating in her own restaurant, I wondered. And then I saw that I was going to find out.

Michael was away that week, investigating an underground group that preyed on children. The disturbing story about pedophilia made me want to spend every possible second with Nicky, so on Saturday I took him and two friends to the science museum in New Jersey. As we drove I listened to them talking in the backseat, soothed by their chatter. They were discussing the existence of God and the shape of the universe.

They wanted to go through the tunnel of absolute darkness, but once we were inside, on our knees, groping our way through the pitch black, they grew terrified and clung to me. We inched blindly forward, gasping and laughing, and I just let myself be, enjoying the moment. Afterward we played virtual basketball, which was surprisingly difficult. But to this group of eight-year-olds, the most fascinating exhibit was the physics demonstration, which made science a wonderful game. The explainer blew up a small rubber balloon, squeezed it into a can of liquid nitrogen, and hurled the solid, frozen object toward the boys. They squealed and scrambled as it fell to the floor, shattering into smithereens.

Nicky's friend Matthew picked up one of the icy shards. "Ruth," he said, "couldn't you cook with that nitrogen stuff?"

"What would you make?" I asked.

"Ice cream!" all three boys shouted simultaneously.

"Interesting idea," I said. "Let's do a little research when we get home."

And that is how I came to discover Mrs. Agnes B. Marshall, an English food writer who had suggested using liquid gas to make ice cream in 1901. "Gee," said Nicky as we read about the contraption that Mrs. Marshall had invented, "cooking can be very interesting."

"You bet it can," I said, ruffling his hair. "Why don't we bake a cake?"

"Vanilla cake!" he shouted. "Let's make vanilla cake."

The boys crowded into the kitchen, where they made a wonderful mess as they creamed the sugar into the butter, pounding fiercely with wooden spoons until they had achieved a perfectly smooth emulsion. They each broke one egg into the bowl, stirring with such vigor I was glad I hadn't given them a bowl made of glass. They measured flour and baking soda with enormous concentration, and buttered the pan so carefully that not a millimeter remained bare. Then they dusted it with clouds of flour. As I surveyed my ruined kitchen, it occurred to me that life really couldn't get any better than this.

Nicky's Vanilla Cake

2 sticks (1 cup) unsalted butter, at room temperature
1 cup sugar
3 large eggs
2 cups all-purpose flour
1 teaspoon baking soda
2 teaspoons baking powder
1 teaspoon salt
1 cup sour cream
2 tablespoons vanilla extract

Preheat the oven to 350°F. Butter and flour an angel food cake or a bundt cake pan.

Cream the butter and sugar together until light and fluffy. Add the eggs, one at a time, blending well after each addition.

Mix the flour, baking soda, baking powder, and salt together, and add this to the butter mixture, mixing well. Add the sour cream and mix well; then mix in the vanilla. (The batter will be thick.)

Pour the batter into the prepared cake pan and bake for 40 to 45 minutes, or until golden. Let the pan cool on a wire rack for 5 minutes. Then turn the cake out of the pan, and leave it on the rack until cool.

Makes 1 cake, 10 servings

When I woke up the next morning, Nicky was nestled at my side, curled around the purring cats. I watched him sleep, taking in the smell of vanilla and burnt sugar that still clung to his hair. When he opened his eyes we stayed there for a while, whispering beneath the quilts, making plans for the day ahead.

"Could we go to the Rainbow Room?" he asked. We had gone there to celebrate Michael's birthday, and Nicky had fallen in love with the place. For months afterward he begged to go back. I had resisted—there's something so obnoxious about little kids in big-deal restaurants—but now I relented. One brunch at the Rainbow Room was not going to turn my child into a miniature food snob.

The elevator door opened at the sixty-fifth floor, spilling us into a hall-way lined with glowing black and white lights. Nicky skipped ahead of me into the dining room and came running back, shouting, "Mommy, wait until you see it!" and taking my hand as if he had personally designed the gorgeous Art Deco room at the top of Rockefeller Center. "Look!" he said, swinging his arm wide, "this is the view!"

He led me to a window and we looked out across the island to the Empire State Building and the river beyond it. "I think I can even see the Science Center over in New Jersey," he said. "Now look at this." He tugged me over to the buffet, which was set up in the middle of the room. "The food's *moving*," he said. "If you stand here everything you want will come to you. Isn't that amazing?"

Is it unbearably hokey to set the food in the middle of a revolving dance floor? Not from the eight-year-old perspective. My son watched for five revolutions, picking out the stations he liked best. The oysters and shrimps were not for him, but he dreamed up impossible omelets for the egg chefs and then moved on to meat, standing dreamily before the carvers as slices of beef and turkey fell from their forks. And after demolishing a hot fudge sundae he piled so many cakes and cookies onto a plate that I had to intervene. He tucked his hand into mine and looked up. "I'm having such a good time," he said. Waiters smiled indulgently down on us, and we felt charmed and lucky, as if we were momentary royalty in a marvelous castle.

"Would you like to eat here every day?" I asked.

"Oh no, Mommy," he replied, "not here. That would spoil it. This has to be special." I smiled at him, happy that he understood the true purpose of a restaurant like the Rainbow Room. But then he added, "But you know what I do wish?" His grave brown eyes looked up at me. "What I wish is that you didn't always have to go out. I wish we could eat at home, together, every night."

I'd heard that before. But I was finally starting to get the message.

Becoming Emily was distressingly easy. I started, of course, by visiting Shirley.

"How's Carol?" she asked.

"Hasn't she been in?" I asked. Shirley looked hurt, and her expression did not change when I added, "I guess she didn't want any of us to see her bald."

"But that's my job!" cried Shirley. "It's what I do." She was so miffed that she simply pawed through her pile, extracted a short black wig with bangs, and handed it over. It fit so well that I understood that all the other times she had been playing with me, making a game of discovering the perfect wig. "I bet you could have given me the right blond wig on the first shot too," I said.

Shirley shrugged.

Emily's clothes were equally easy to find: every thrift shop on the Upper East Side was rich in tweeds. I even unearthed a deep leather pocketbook with a functioning lock, and a pair of horn-rimmed glasses.

Looking at the dried-up prune I had made myself into, I saw that dining companions were going to present a problem. Michael was still out of town, but he would, in any case, make a suspiciously incongruous partner for the person in the mirror. Claudia, who would have been ideal, was still in Los Angeles. Her three-week trip had now lasted six months and I was beginning to wonder if she would ever return. And all the "How come you never take me to a good place?" people were obviously out of the question.

I called Myron, who was always agitating for a fancy free meal, but when I told him we were going to the Box Tree I felt obliged to admit that my first meal had not been stellar. He was suddenly very busy.

And then, just when I most needed her, Marion Cunningham came gamely to the rescue. She was in New York to discuss her latest book, *Learning to Cook,* with her editor, and when I told her that dinner was going to be dreadful, she just laughed.

"As if I cared!" she'd said. "I'm so happy to have the chance to spend time with you, I'd gladly eat at McDonald's."

"McDonald's might be better," I said.

"If all I wanted was something to eat," she said, "I'd stay home. Just tell me where we're going and who you'll be."

What's your name?" asked Nicky when I appeared in yet another costume.

"Emily Stone," I told him.

"And what do you do?" he asked.

"I'm the manager of a restaurant. I am a very punctual person."

"What does that mean?"

"That I'm never late. And I never make mistakes. And I'm very strict. You wouldn't like me very much; I'm a real meanie."

"Oh no, Mommy," said Nicky, "you could never be a meanie."

He was wrong.

What are you staring at?" I snapped at Gene when I got onto the elevator. Long past fooling, he had a new role: Gene had appointed himself final inspector. He liked to examine me for stray hair sticking out from under the wig, for gloves and purses that might give me away, for a necklace I'd worn before or some familiar scarf. Usually I enjoyed his scrutiny.

But tonight when he said, "You look fine," I did not reply. When he pressed on with "This is a good one. Sometimes I'm afraid you're overdoing it, but not tonight," I twisted my lips and still said nothing.

"What do you call her?" he insisted.

"Emily," I said. "That would be Miss Stone to you."

"Yes ma'am Miss Stone," he said, doffing an imaginary hat. He parked the elevator and opened the door. "Allow me to say, Miss Stone," he murmured as I brushed past him, "that you don't look like much fun."

"Mind your manners," I snarled and swept out the door.

I marched up the sidewalk, daring anyone to step into my path. Nobody did. When I reached the corner I found a young woman ineffectually waving her arms in hopes of attracting a taxi. As a yellow cab hurtled toward us, I stuck my hand commandingly into the air and it screeched obediently to a halt. The other woman made a feeble move in its direction, but I pushed her aside and dove through the door, thinking that such people did not belong in New York. If she didn't know how to get her own cab, she certainly wasn't entitled to mine. "But, but, but . . ." she was sputtering as the door slammed in her face.

"Forty-ninth and Second," I told the driver. "And step on it. Go uptown and through the park at Seventy-ninth; it will be quicker. Take Fifth to Fiftieth so you don't hit bridge traffic. And see that you make all the lights."

"Mumph," said the driver, but he did as he was told.

I sat, stiff-legged and silent in the back of the taxi, glowering at the meter as it clicked upward. When it was time to pay the fare I counted out the change, added a parsimonious tip, and snapped my handbag shut, twisting the key in the lock. I could feel the driver glaring at my back as I walked toward the restaurant.

A young couple was just ahead of me, swinging their hands as they dreamily approached the door. The man looked scrubbed, and even from behind I could see the excited pink tips of his ears through his shiny blue-black, slicked back hair. He wore no coat, and I could tell that his double-breasted black suit was well pressed and well worn, most likely rented along with the patent leather shoes on his feet. The woman was even younger; she could not have been much more than twenty, and the face beneath the feathery black hair was round and trusting, with full lips stained the color of strawberries. A beige chiffon dress foamed beneath her coat, bubbling down to her knees and up to a strapless bodice pinned with a large purple orchid. They looked young and callow, poor and hopeful. "They don't belong here," I thought, marching grimly behind them. If they had hesitated for even a moment I'd have shoved past and through the door.

But there was no halt in their dreamy progress, and I followed them in. Marion looked up as we entered. She seemed perfectly at ease in the uncomfortable chair by the fireplace, wearing her usual uniform: black pants, black jacket, crisp white blouse. Her silver hair was pulled back around her naked, gorgeously wrinkled face, and the turquoise eyes staring at me with such intensity seemed enormous. The young couple turned in unison to see who was behind them.

"Is it Emily?" asked Marion. When I nodded she got up in one smooth move and came forward to gravely shake my hand. "I'm very happy to know you," she said.

Tweed ignored the young couple, walking around them as if they were not there. "Ladies," she said, reaching for our coats, "right this way."

"They were ahead of us," said Marion softly.

"They'll wait," said Tweed curtly. Her tone made it abundantly clear that she hoped that they would not.

She led us into the dining room where Carol and I had eaten lunch. Tonight the fire was lit and the tables were filled with wistful couples in search of romance. The roses had been pushed off the plates and, for the most part, lay gasping for water on the cloths. The brassy blonde to our

left, however, had stuck hers into her décolletage, and it peeped out between her breasts, accentuating the low cut of her dress. Her portly, bald
date was having a hard time keeping his eyes off the flower. "Hooker!" I
thought acidly and edged my seat away.

Tweed returned with the young couple I had followed into the restaurant and seated them to our right. With a short happy cry the woman
picked up her rose and pushed the stem behind her ear. I grunted; between the rose and the orchid she looked like a walking florist's ad.
Tweed shot me an apologetic glance and the word "pathetic" reverber-
ated in the air between us.

"I'm going to ask the hostess to give us a different table," I whispered
to Marion. "I don't feel we belong in this dining room."

Marion's face took on the strangest look. Thinking that she didn't understand, I lowered my voice to explain. "Just study the room!" I said,
pointing left. "He's undoubtedly paying for the pleasure of her company.
And they," nodding right, "look as if they've been saving up for this meal.
We ought to have a better table."

"We're fine right where we are," said Marion. She squared her shoulders and planted herself firmly in the seat.

The waiter shook out the napkins and spread them across our laps.
His jacket now fit him perfectly, and the English accent was intact. Told
that only water was required, he made no attempt to hide his disappointment.

"Mineral, I presume?" he asked, and when he learned that New York
water would be fine, his smile lost a little more of its luster. "Is there a host
or hostess in this party?" he asked, soldiering on.

"Do you see any men here?" I snapped.

The man colored. "I beg your pardon," he corrected himself. "Which
one of you is the hostess?"

"I am."

"Ah," he smiled down at me, "good." He began to shuffle the menus,
and I put out my hand. "If," I said, "you are looking for one of those
menus with no prices, don't bother. I have brought my guest to New

York's most expensive restaurant, and I think she should know precisely what this is costing me."

"I understand perfectly," he said with what sounded like actual admiration.

"Uh," interjected the man to our right, "uh, could we get a drink?"

The waiter ignored him and went sailing off in search of fresh menus. The young man looked both crushed and embarrassed.

Marion was staring at me as if she had never seen me before, and I felt an explanation was in order. "I know that the menu with no prices is intended as a gracious gesture," I said in Emily's clipped voice. "I know it's a way of allowing your guests to have no concern for the cost. But let me tell you this; dinner here costs eighty-six dollars a person, and I see no reason why that should be a secret."

"Of course," said Marion. "It's a great deal of money. Who could blame you for wanting your largesse to be a matter of record?" There was no sarcasm in her voice, but I felt it was there, skulking in the background, and it made me squirm. I wished she had not given up alcohol; I yearned for a glass of wine.

"Are you certain a little wine would not appeal?" asked the waiter and I smiled, thinking he must have read my mind. But before I could answer, Marion did.

"We don't want a thing," she said. "But these young people on our right are getting thirsty."

"Oh," he said carelessly, "I'll get to them eventually."

"Why don't you get to them now," said Marion, her voice edged with steel. "They've waited long enough."

The waiter took a step backward. He looked defiant. She stared him down, and at last he turned to take their order. "Is that really our business?" I murmured. Marion did not reply.

On our left the blonde had downed two martinis in rapid succession and was now waving her glass about, saying querulously "'Nother, wanna 'nother." Meanwhile the young man on our right was saying proudly, "We will have champagne!"

"Certainly, sir," said the waiter, bowing in such an exaggerated manner that the effect was more sneering than respectful.

When he brought the bottle in its metal bucket, he made a great display of pulling it out and ostentatiously presenting the label. Everything he did was correct but he somehow managed to convey contempt with every line in his body. Slowly he extracted the cork, making it pop loudly. He poured an inch into the young man's glass and stood waiting, a bored expression on his face. When the young man made no move to pick up the glass, the waiter began to tap his foot, raising an eyebrow in my direction.

Marion watched for a moment, and then she leaned across the table and said, very gently, "He wants you to taste it." The young man gave her a small grateful smile, picked up his glass, sipped. "It's fine," he said. Without looking down the waiter splashed the wine into the glasses, filling them a little too full so that the liquid fizzed onto the table.

The young woman waited until he was gone and then picked up her glass and took a sip. Her eyes went very wide and then she sneezed. When I laughed—just a little—she colored deeply.

Marion gave me a look I could not fathom and picked up her menu. "I think I'll have the lobster bisque," she said more loudly than was absolutely necessary, "and then the scallops topped with that puree of hazelnuts and butternut squash. Raspberry chutney sounds wrong in that dish, but who knows, maybe it works. After that I suppose I'll have the tenderloin. It's the only dish that doesn't sound overly fussy."

We placed our orders and then the young couple placed theirs. The young woman gave Marion an apologetic look, turned to the waiter, and said, "Bring me what she's having, please."

"Oh, why can't they mind their own business?" I cried.

"The way you're minding yours?" Marion retorted.

It occurred to me that age was not sitting well with her, and I suddenly found myself at a loss for words. There was an awkward moment of silence while I tried to think of something to say, and then the food arrived to provide conversational fodder. My appetizer, cumin-rubbed shrimp, was good for at least five minutes.

"That's quite a trick," said Marion when she tasted it. "A kitchen miracle: they've made those shrimp mealy and tough at the same time, and that's not easy. If you were *trying* to achieve that effect, you probably couldn't. What I imagine they did was buy head-on shrimp, let them sit too long, and then overcook them. Shrimp have an enzyme at the back of the head that makes them mushy after death. That's why they're usually sold headless." She took another minuscule taste and nodded. "Yes, if you followed that recipe, you might end up with something this sorry. On the other hand, they're no worse than my scallops—if that's what these little white discs really are."

At the next table the young woman was taking a timid forkful of her appetizer. Her face lighted up. "I never had scallops before," she confided to her date. "I thought they'd be fishy or something. But these are okay; they don't taste like nothing at all."

"Did you hear that?" I asked Marion, mimicking the woman. "'They don't taste like nothing.'" I kept my voice very low. "That might be because they're pollack or some other cheap whitefish cut to look like scallops. It's a classic food cheat. No wonder the chef created that strange goop of a dish: the nuts, the squash, and the chutney are all there to disguise the fish and fool the suckers." I nodded right. "Like them."

"This makes me so angry!" said Marion.

"I know," I replied. "It's outrageous the way they cheat their customers!"

"Not that." Marion's blue eyes were appraising me, and I was chilled by their icy coldness. "You," she said. "You're what's making me angry. These disguises have gone too far. I hate the person you've become."

It was as if she had thrown her glass of water at my face. I could feel the makeup that covered it—the greasy foundation, the thick coat of powder, the lipstick with the chalky taste of cold cream. The wig felt so tight I could barely breathe, and I sensed the hair coiled beneath it, yearning to be released. The glasses balanced on my nose felt suddenly heavy and I snatched them off. And then I started to laugh, and the laugh went on and on until I was afraid I was going to choke.

"Oh, hon," said Marion, when I had finally wound down, "I almost forgot that you were you. How can you stand it?"

I looked down at the terrible tweed suit, and suddenly I couldn't. I had wanted to know what it felt like to be Emily, and now I knew: not good. I didn't want to be her, didn't want her clothes or her values or anything else to do with her life. It was extremely unpleasant to find how easily I had been able to summon this mean, petty person who was waiting inside me. Because if Brenda was my best self, Emily was my worst.

Marion was watching my struggle. "I keep remembering the first time I met you," she said. "It was in San Francisco, at that party for James Beard. Your hair was wild and curly and your clothes were so colorful that you stood out in the crowd. The next time we met you were wearing two different socks—and you told me it was on purpose! We went back to that commune you were living in and you started cooking dinner. I think it was for a dozen people, but more kept showing up and every time the door opened you just smiled and threw a little more water into the soup. I kept looking for that person, but all I could see was—" She went silent and pointed across the table.

"Enough," I said, "let's forget about Emily, okay? She's going to go away now, and we're going to try to enjoy ourselves as much as possible in this ridiculous restaurant."

After that, everything was fine. Marion told me about the cooking classes she'd been giving. "I put up signs all over the neighborhood saying that I was looking for people who had never cooked before, that I'd teach them for free. It's fascinating. Do you have any idea what a recipe looks like to someone reading it for the first time?"

"None," I said.

"It's a foreign language! I told one of my students to toss the salad and he put the bowl on the counter, walked to the other side of the kitchen, and started throwing the lettuce into it."

"You're kidding."

"No," she said, "it happened. And if you think about it, why wouldn't that make sense? My students want to know why the recipe says to cream the butter when there's no cream in it, why bone and debone mean the same thing. If you don't know the language, it's just jibberish."

For my part I talked about Carol, and for the first time I allowed my-self to voice what I had been thinking deep inside: that she was not going to get better. And then, somehow, I found myself telling Marion what Nicky had said after our meal at the Rainbow Room.

"Do you want to know what I think?" she asked. She didn't wait for an answer. "I think it's time for you to do something else."

My heart lurched. "What would I do?" I asked.

She studied me for a moment and said, "I don't know. But I have an idea. I know this astrologer . . ."

"I don't believe in that stuff!" I said. "You know that."

"I don't either," she replied. "But it doesn't matter. This man is very wise, and he always helps me in a crisis. I'm going to buy a session for you. When you think you're ready, give Alex a call. Believe me, it will be worth your time." She wrote a phone number on a piece of paper and handed it to me. And then, as if she had not just tossed a bomb onto the table, she took a bite of beef tenderloin and changed the subject. "This restaurant," she said, "should be ashamed to be serving this meat."

As the evening progressed the bald and the blonde, who were far more interested in liquor than in food, grew more raucous. Meanwhile, the young couple on our right were growing quieter and quieter, as if they understood that they were being cheated but were not quite sure how. Marion looked at their woebegone faces and I could see her strug-gling with herself. Finally she could no longer contain it. Leaning toward them, she said, "Forgive me if I'm speaking out of turn. But I don't imag-ine that you come to restaurants like this very often." As she spoke I was reminded of the woman at Daniel, Muriel, who had said something so similar. And then, of course, I thought of Brenda.

"No ma'am," said the young man, pulling his shoulders back as if standing to attention. "I have been saving up for this evening. It's the first time we've been to such a fancy restaurant."

"You don't look as if you're enjoying it," she pressed on.

"We are!" said the young woman. "We're enjoying it very much. Aren't we, Richie?" Her eyes entreated her date to support her position.

But he gave her an apologetic shrug and turned to Marion. "No," he admitted, "we are not enjoying this."

"Neither are we," said Marion. "This is a very poor restaurant."

"But the books!" he said, looking very young, very earnest. "I read all the books and they said that this was the best place. The most romantic."

"Unfortunately," said Marion gently, "the books are not always right."

And then Emily vanished forever, even though I was still wearing her black hair, and Brenda was speaking. "Let me pick up your check," she was saying. "Take the money you were going to spend here and go to another restaurant. A good one."

He was shaking his head. "Oh no," he said, "I couldn't let you do that."

"Yes you could," said Marion, and her smile was bright and encouraging. "Of course you could."

"I'll even tell you where to go," I said. "I could make the reservation for you."

"Where?" asked Marion, beaming at me.

"The Rainbow Room," I said.

"I couldn't let you do that," he repeated.

"Yes you can," I said. "It's sort of part of my job."

"What are you talking about?" he said, in a voice that conveyed all the things he was too polite to utter. He glanced under the table as if he expected to find a camera hiding down there. "What do you do?"

"What I'm *supposed* to do is make sure that people don't waste their money in places like this," I said.

"I don't get it."

"I'm a restaurant critic."

He was wavering. I could feel it. "How do I know that's true?" he asked.

In response I did something I had never done before. Right there in the middle of the dining room, I pulled Emily's wig off my head.

The young woman gasped. And at the next table the blonde waved her empty martini glass and said, "I think I've had too many drinks."

RESTAURANTS
WHERE THE ROMANTIC DECOR IS THE DRAW
by Ruth Reichl

....

THE LAST TIME The Times looked at the Box Tree it was a pretentious place serving fancy, not very good Continental food for $78 a person, prix fixe. That was six years ago. Since then there has been a lengthy strike, which ended last month in a victory for the workers. You might think that would have improved the restaurant.

No such luck. Today the Box Tree is a pretentious place serving fancy, not very good Continental food for $86 a person, prix fixe. But one thing has changed. The service used to be genial and attentive. Now it is as pretentious as the setting— when it is anything at all.

Consider, for example, a mid-week lunch. When I walk into the precious little entry, which looks as if it is trying out for a part in a Ralph Lauren ad, the hostess barely looks up. "Do you have a reservation?" she asks frostily. I do. "Your guest has not arrived," she says, pointing to a seat by the fireplace. "Wait there." She then graciously allows me to listen as she makes phone calls. Meanwhile, a waiter complains about what the cleaners have done to his jacket, and a manager loudly berates a busboy in the grill next door. I can't remember a less welcoming introduction.

My guest finally arrives. As we are led into the ornate dining room with its dark wood, stained glass and fancy fireplaces, I can't help wondering why I was forced to wait in the vestibule. But for the roses waiting patiently on each plate, the room is utterly empty. A few nights later I wonder, similarly, why the captain refuses to move us away from a large, loud party. "We have no other tables," he insists, but anyone with eyes can see that he is wrong.

He presses quickly on. "Do we have a host or hostess?" he asks, emphasizing the final syllable. This may be one of the last restaurants in America to give guests unpriced menus. Pity, for the person paying the bill would surely want his guests to know that the meal is as expensive as it is inept.

It is also very large. This is not necessarily a good thing. By the time you have slogged through an appetizer, soup, entrée and salad, you may dread the arrival of dessert. But should you somehow find yourself at the Box Tree (it is, after all, considered one of New York's most romantic restaurants), you will be happy to hear that it is not impossible to find a few acceptable dishes to go with the dreamy décor.

Appetizers are easiest. My favorite is the smooth terrine of duck liver served in a little crock with toast on the side. Snails are quite good, too, served in a ceramic dish and topped with Pernod sauce and grated cheese. Cold poached trout is moist and mannerly. But avoid the bizarre scallops with butternut squash and the horribly overcooked cumin-rubbed shrimp.

Soups are a problem. The lobster bisque is dreadful. The bisque of morels is even worse; once you get past the taste of sherry, it is absolutely impossible to tell what you are eating. The "consommé of whole cow" is fun for its title, but not much more. But the carrot and ginger velouté is perfectly fine, and the cool yogurt and cucumber soup is refreshing.

Main courses are the most difficult. Avoid, at all costs, anything made with lobster. The waiter described the lobster fricassee, served at lunch, as a two-pound lobster removed from the shell and served in a beurre blanc. If the shell decorating the dish was related to the lobster that once inhabited it, it was no two-pounder. And that "beurre blanc" was gritty with uncooked starch and seasoned primarily with dill. Lobster Mornay at dinner was tough. Tenderloin of beef with Armagnac sauce featured the most unpleasant piece of beef I have ever been served in a restaurant; it had neither taste nor texture. Veal medallions with wild mushrooms were only a marginal improvement. If you are in the mood for meat, choose the rack of lamb. Salmon is also unobjectionable: two fat fillets on a bed of lentils.

Each main course is served with an identical melange of vegetables and followed by a welcome salad of endive, watercress and Stilton.

You are almost at the end, and if you avoid the soggy apple tart and the runny crème brûlée, dessert holds no terrors. The vacherin, chocolate cake and raspberry brûlée are all perfectly pleasant.

Best of all, it is almost time to leave. Unlike other restaurants that charge these sorts of prices, the Box Tree does not shower you with little gifts to make you linger at the table. No petits fours, no chocolates. And although it can be nearly impossible to find someone willing to pour your wine, getting the check is never difficult. Just snap your fingers, and it is there in a flash.

THE BOX TREE

POOR

Ghosts

It was one of those brutally hot days, the air so still it seemed to snatch the breath from your mouth. Heat waves vibrated nauseatingly off the sidewalks, ghostly snakes waiting to strike. The tar on the streets was a sticky river that sucked at your shoes, threatening to devour them each time you crossed. "It's too hot," my friends all moaned when I asked them to join me for lunch.

Carol, however, was game. "Union Pacific?" she said. "Finally! Tell me who you're going to be."

"Oh God," I said, "it's too hot for a wig. I can't bear the idea of makeup, layers of clothing . . . Would it be terrible to come as myself? I'll make the reservation in your name, but I don't think I'll even eat. I just want to bask in the air conditioning and stare at the food."

But when we got to the restaurant, we found ourselves in a darkened vestibule so deliciously icy that the memory of the burning sidewalks was instantly erased. As the hostess led us around a small pool and past a serene curtain of water, Carol stuck out her hand, letting the falling drops splash onto her skin. "I have a good feeling about this," she said.

The restaurant was hushed and high-ceilinged, luminous with pale muted light. The hostess tucked us into a booth in the back. Golden sunshine streamed from a skylight, radiance stripped of heat. One waiter bustled about plumping pillows while another covered the table with bowls of lemons and glasses of iced water.

"I think you've been made," said Carol.

"Why would you think that?" I asked. "Just because we've got the biggest table in the place and—" I stopped, startled by the woman at the next table who had begun an audible moaning. "Mmmmm," she keened, her mouth full, her eyes wide, "mmmmm."

We both stared at her, but she was oblivious, hearing secret harmonies as she concentrated on what was in her mouth.

"I wonder what's she's eating," I said.

"Foie gras with wild strawberries," said our waiter, who had suddenly popped up. "It's divine. So rich and intense. Let me bring you some."

Carol sighed. "I love it when you're recognized," she said. "It's so much more fun than going out with poor Betty. But here's a question: Do you think that woman is a plant?"

"What?" I asked.

"A plant," she said. "You know, someone deliberately placed there to act out that little scene for you."

"I hadn't thought of that," I said.

"Sometimes," she said with a certain asperity, "I think you're too trusting. Hasn't it occurred to you that every time you're recognized the owners fill the tables all around you with their friends?"

"They do?" I asked.

"Oh please. Of course. They call everyone they know and invite them in for a free meal. They're supposed to rush right over, eat a lot, and rave loudly about the food. I hear those stories all the time."

"You never told me!" I said.

"How could you not know?"

I might have replied, but the foie gras had arrived and I was beginning to understand why the woman was moaning. It was a pale pink cylinder with deep red berries and tiny fava beans the color of new spring leaves skittering across the top. The first bite was a shock; the pâté had been soaked in Armagnac and spices, and they ignited the tongue. But with the second bite the intensity segued into something more muted as the strawberry-balsamic emulsion came forward to temper the taste. With the third bite the fava beans began to show themselves, their sleek smoothness shining against the velvet softness of the pâté. It was a dish that robbed you of conversation. For a long time neither of us said a word.

Carol broke the silence. "Tell me," she said, "about Rocco DiSpirito."

I had first tasted Rocco's cooking in 1995 at a restaurant called Dava, and it stunned me with its originality. But he was young then—not yet thirty—and unable to handle the crowds that came flocking to him. I heard so many rumors about food costs spiraling out of control that I was not surprised when the restaurant closed. A year or so later, when he turned up at the brand-new Union Pacific, the food was fabulous, but so slow coming out of the kitchen that I gave him only two stars. His fans howled in protest. "Rocco," they wrote in a campaign I suspected he might have orchestrated, "wuz robbed!" Even the food warrior, Mr. Shapiro, weighed in. "Go back," he wrote. "DiSpirito is a major talent. You've obviously made a mistake; this is a three-star chef."

And so here I was, undisguised, on the hottest day of the year, once again succumbing to his magic.

We ate a cool, bright summer salad—lengths of crimson watermelon interlaced with shiny strips of avocado. Pale lavender rings of calamari were woven across the top so that the slick avocado bumped up against the crunch of the watermelon and then collided with the slippery slices of squid. Encountering them in your mouth, you couldn't help focusing on the sensation of texture. After a while I tried letting go of the feelings on my tongue to simply concentrate on taste; that was when I discovered that the three had a startling similarity, a common tempered sweetness. The flavor was so seductive that it was a while before I realized that Carol had gone silent too.

"I'm listening to my mouth," she said. "Caramelized sweetbread with sorrel and muskmelon—it's the most amazing dish. Here, try it." She passed me a forkful, and my mouth closed over the surprising combination. Sweetbreads and melon were shiny, lustrous, and sweet against the faintly citric sourness of the sorrel. "I feel as if I've crawled into some magical food cocoon," said Carol, "where only good things could possibly happen."

"I know," I said. "That's exactly how I feel."

All afternoon we sat there, reveling in tastes and textures. A pristine white square of cod arrived, looking like an enormous marshmallow strewn with scattered cracklings. Biting in you expected ocean brine and got something altogether different, something rich and deep and mysterious. The fish, poached in goose fat, had absorbed the taste of the bird. It was a sensation both dizzying and exciting, as if you were flying and swimming at the same time. Chicken had also been transformed, slowly poached in a lemon-strewn bath until it lost its barnyard character. Torn into long strips, it was barely meat, just all soft tenderness, a vehicle for conveying spice and citrus and the plump flavor of the summer truffle puree upon which it perched.

The waiter set the plates down so lightly, he might have been tiptoeing through a room of sleeping people. Unwilling to break the spell, he didn't even ask what we wanted for dessert. I barely noticed when he removed the chicken, barely saw him replace it with passion fruit crème brûlée. All I knew was that the flavors had changed, that what was now in my mouth was sweet, soft, intense, and tropical, unlike anything I had experienced before. Without speaking Carol reached out and switched our plates, and now the taste in my mouth was raspberries and lavender, and I was in a wild garden with the wind blowing through my hair.

"Coffee?" asked the waiter. The sound was startlingly loud, the finger-snap of the hypnotist, bringing you back to yourself. Carol and I both looked up, surprised. "Yes," we both said, "coffee, yes, coffee." And then we just sat and stared at one another.

"That," said Carol, "was an out-of-body experience. I don't think I've ever had food that seemed so psychedelic. Do you think it's the chemo?"

"No," I replied, "because I'm not doing chemotherapy, and I had the same experience. It was amazing."

"How will you ever manage to write about it?" she asked. "How can that possibly be explained?"

"I won't," I said. "It can't." And even if I were capable of describing this meal, I thought, I'm not sure that I'd try. A critic has no business creating unreasonable expectations; setting your readers up for disappointment is the surest way to lose their trust. "Besides," I told Carol, "I don't think this can ever be repeated. It feels as if we're here at some magic moment."

"But you'll come back?"

"Oh sure. This is only the first visit. You know the drill: Never fewer than three visits, usually more. Always anonymously."

"But you're not anonymous now!" she said.

"I know," I said morosely. "That's the problem. I suppose I'll have to come back as Betty or Brenda or something."

"I thought you liked dressing up."

"I did," I said. "It used to be fun."

"What happened?"

I looked at her, unable to explain the impact of that meal with Marion. Thinking about what had happened, I saw that when I became Emily I had played with fire. If there was an Emily inside me—and now I knew there was—I needed to acknowledge her. Pretending she was someone else was no longer enough; it was time to stop playing games and be myself. It was time to think my own thoughts. But when I tried gathering the words to explain this to Carol, I found they were not there. So I just stared at her, silent.

Carol didn't press me. "So you're going to give up the disguises and go out as yourself?"

I shook my head. "That wouldn't be right. You know what it's like when I'm not in disguise: the steaks get bigger, the food comes faster, and the seats become more comfortable. No restaurant can change the food on the spur of the moment, but when the critic of the *New York Times* shows up, they can certainly show her a swell time. The kitchen selects its largest raspberries. The maître d' gives her the quiet table in the middle of the dining room with a dedicated waiter all her own. The sommelier makes sure that every wine she orders is a good one, and that her glass is never empty. The pastry chef makes an extra effort." I gestured to our large booth. "You *know* I can't let this happen every time I go out to eat."

"So what are you going to do?" she asked. "Do you hear what you're saying?"

I nodded. The words Marion had tossed so casually across the table at the Box Tree had been reverberating in my mind ever since, becoming louder every day. But how would I live if I couldn't be a restaurant critic? "I don't know what to do," I said. "There must be an answer. But I have yet to figure it out."

Carol offered no advice, and we sat there, drinking our coffee and eating the icy little chocolates that the waiter brought, reluctant to go back to the burning sidewalks waiting outside in the real world.

RESTAURANTS
A SHORT TRIP FROM PROMISING TO POLISHED
by Ruth Reichl

....

THE WOMAN at the next table is moaning. I try to discover what has caused this reaction, but she has just finished the final forkful and all I can see is her eyes, wide with the wonder of whatever is in her mouth.

Perhaps it is the bluefin tuna tartare. It is a small mound of cool, rosy fish that has bite (fresh wasabi), texture (crunchy pieces of Asian pear) and flavor (chocolate mint and the slight bitterness of linseeds). It is a surprise in the mouth and the best tuna tartare I've ever tasted. Or she could be reacting to the caramelized sweetbreads with sorrel and muskmelon. The combination of the rich organ with the sweet melon and the slight sourness of sorrel is absolutely fabulous. It might be the ragout of blue crab, too, an extraordinary combination of wild leeks, chanterelles and seafood that does a pirouette in the mouth. Or perhaps the eccentric salad of calamari, watermelon and avocado, layers of crunch, softness and crackle that taste delicious.

The woman has finished now, but she sits, very still, like someone who still hears a concert after the music has stopped. The waiter sees my look and says, "Foie gras with wild strawberries; it's divine, so rich and intense."

This is no exaggeration. The raw foie gras cru at Union Pacific is cured in brine, soaked in Armagnac and aromatic spices and topped with wild strawberries and tiny fava beans and served in a circle of strawberry juice and aged balsamic vinegar. The slightly bitter tang of apricot kernels is another note, a bell cutting through the richness. It is fabulous, and I would not be surprised to learn that I, too, was moaning as I ate.

When Union Pacific opened a year ago, it had enormous promise. The architect, Larry Bogdanow, had created one of the most beautiful, comfortable and soothing environments in Manhattan; with a curtain of falling water at the entrance it has the cool, calm look of Japan without a hint of austerity. And the chef, Rocco DiSpirito, had invented an exciting menu. Mr. DiSpirito has an interesting mind; he seems to think about flavor in ways that ordinary people don't. But in the early days, he had problems getting the food onto the tables, and the service had a nervous and slightly pretentious edge. As the restaurant has matured, Mr. DiSpirito has taken control of the timing and the staff has grown more confident. They are clearly excited about the food they serve.

With good reason. I have yet to taste anything on Mr. DiSpirito's menu that is not wonderful. If you choose to begin the meal with what he calls a "flight of little dishes," you are likely to encounter something very like the sort of inventive sashimi served at Nobu: slices of soft, sweet yellowtail wrapped around tuna tartare, muscular strips of fluke with yuzu (Japanese citrus), a few strawberries tossed with fava beans. They are little teases, and they make you very hungry.

There are Asian touches in the main part of the menu, too, but Mr. DiSpirito's influences seem largely French. His lobster, for instance, arrives looking like a Christmas tree ornament, a great ball of wonderfully tender lobster dripping with a foamy orange sauce that turns out to taste like the lobster bisque of your dreams. The pousse-pied, a succulent that grows near salt marshes, is the perfect counterpart; called salicorn on the menu, it is crisp and bracingly saline, so it cuts the richness of the lobster.

Chicken is transformed in Mr. DiSpirito's hands. His slowly poached bird arrives in tender strips atop a summer truffle puree. Halibut, that normally boring fish, is animated by its preparation, too: Mr. DiSpirito gently poaches it in goose fat and tops it with cracklings made of shallots.

"Do you like it?" the waiters are liable to ask about these dishes. It is hard to imagine anybody answering in the negative.

Wine adds another dimension to the meal; the unusual list emphasizes wines that are bright with enough acidity to make them friendly to this food. If you are unfamiliar with some of the German and Austrian selections, the sommelier, Urs Kaufmannis, is happy to be helpful. And should you decide to stick with bottled water, you have another nice surprise in store: The restaurant's policy is to charge $7 for the first large bottle of water and $3.50 for subsequent ones. It is just one of the thoughtful gestures that makes dining at Union Pacific such a pleasure.

All of this is a hard act to follow, but the desserts are as interesting as the main courses. The strawberry charlotte with pistachio ice cream is deeply flavored. Raspberries are set onto a tart with lavender and the crème brûlée is laced with passion fruit essence, topped with pineapple sorbet and served with a twist of sugar candy threaded with black sesame seeds.

Afterward, there are fruit pâtés

and wonderful chocolates that manage to be both cool and soft. Mr. DiSpirito keeps things at an intense pitch, right to the very last bite.

UNION PACIFIC
★ ★ ★

"Tell me I didn't dream that meal," Carol said in the fall. "It seems to have happened in another lifetime." It was true: that smoldering summer had been a turning point for both of us.

The restaurants that were opening that season all seemed to be downtown, and each time I traveled to Bond Street, Bop, or Blue Ribbon Bakery, I found myself passing my parents' old apartment, looking up at their window and wondering what they would make of my present life. They were so much with me that one night at Montrachet my mother marched right up to the table to remind me that she had been with me the first time I visited the restaurant. "That was ten years ago," she said caustically, "and here you are, *still* reviewing restaurants. Do you intend to spend your entire life practicing this ridiculous profession?"

"But Mom," I protested, "I thought you were proud of me now!" Did I say it out loud? I'm not sure; by then she had disappeared, floating right through the wall.

But Babbo was the one that really got to me. It was just a few blocks from my parents' place, and although no ghosts came to haunt my table, each time I visited the restaurant the air began to vibrate. The food was strange, too; no matter what I ate—ethereal ravioli filled with brains, spicy squid stew, cured anchovies with bagna cauda—I tasted black bean soup.

"I think the food was fabulous," I wrote after the first visit, "but it was hard to tell. What a weird experience! I wonder what is going on?"

On my second visit, when the air once more became electric, I looked around and suddenly understood. How had I missed this? Babbo occupied the small brick building that once had been the Coach House. It had been my parents' favorite restaurant, the place where we celebrated big birthdays, special events, and major anniversaries. Thirty years had passed since my last visit, and the new owners had gutted the room, but now the gracious contours of the long-gone restaurant began to shape themselves around me. No wonder I was tasting black bean soup! The Coach House had been famous for it.

Now when I went to Babbo I tried hard to concentrate on the present, but the past was there, igniting sparks all around me in the air. I had joyfully rediscovered the Dubonnet, but things had changed since then, and now the weight of my own history was sitting heavily on my shoulders. I tried different disguises, thinking they might help, but I had gone beyond them and each time I opened my closet my mother's blue silk dress rustled disapprovingly. "Move on, move on," it murmured as the hangers slid along the pole.

I threw up my arms and on my final visit to Babbo went as myself. That turned out to be danger of a different sort: when I was recognized the kitchen sent out so much food that I thought I might explode before escaping out the door.

"The food was great, but let's not do that again," said Michael as we staggered onto the street.

My own little drama, however, was insignificant compared to what Carol was enduring. Late that summer the doctors performed yet another of their horrible procedures, rewiring her as if she were a car to circumvent her digestive system. Carol began living on liquids, vehemently insisting that it was a temporary measure, a minor inconvenience that would soon be behind her. But when the leaves changed color Carol was still drinking liquids, and before our eyes she began to shrink in on herself, growing smaller and thinner every day.

During the first year Carol had been fiercely concentrated on her illness, convinced that sheer vigilance would make her better. In that phase we heard about every test, every twist, every nuance of the terrible disease that she was going to beat. We all mastered the language of cancer. But as victory began to slip away, Carol stopped talking about CA 125 levels. Then she stopped talking about sickness altogether, as if she could appease the cancer by keeping silent. She seemed reluctant to divulge her pain, afraid that admitting it would make it worse.

From what I could tell, the doctors were torturing her. One morning when I called, she told me that she had been to the hospital during the night for an emergency procedure that involved sticking tubes down her nose, and doing unspeakable things to her body. She said it casually, the way another woman might have mentioned that she had gone to see a play.

"But they released me," she said. "Why don't you come over?"

I was surprised. Carol and I didn't visit each other's homes; our friendship was conducted entirely in public places. This seemed somehow portentous.

She lived in a narrow Chelsea townhouse, purchased when the neighborhood was still unfashionable and painstakingly restored. When I opened the gate, her little dog came barking frantically to the door, sniffed me anxiously, and followed close on my heels as I climbed the stairs to the snug room at the top.

Carol was wrapped in blankets, looking drawn and drained. I wondered what horrors they had put her through at the hospital, wondered why she continued to fight so fiercely.

"I intend to live," she said, although I had not asked the question. Her voice was cracked and raw from whatever they had done, and I wanted to tell her not to talk—it sounded like such an effort. But she moved quickly onward, not giving me the chance. "Thanks for coming. Last night I realized that there was something that we needed to discuss."

"What?" I asked.

"You," she said, looking out into the garden she had created down below.

"Me?"

"Yeah. I know you're thinking about giving up your job. What are you going to do next?"

I was taken aback by her directness. I had been dancing around the subject, afraid to actually utter the words. But faced with her frankness, I said the first thing that came into my head: "I'm going to get out of the dining room and go back to the kitchen." And then I put my hand to my mouth, because what I had said seemed right and true, although I hadn't expected it.

"How?" asked Carol.

"I don't know," I said. "Maybe I'll write another cookbook. Maybe I'll open another restaurant. Or I could always go back to being a food editor."

"Listen to me," said Carol. She put her thin hand on my arm and her voice grew very serious. "If you're thinking of taking over the Dining section, don't."

"What are you talking about?" I asked.

"Do you think I don't know about your deal with the paper? Do you think I don't know that they want you to go back to editing when you get tired of being the restaurant critic?"

It was true, but I wondered how she could possibly know that. But then, not much happened on the fourth floor that Carol was not in on.

"Don't," she said. "You won't be happy."

"I can't believe you're thinking about that at a time like this," I said. "You have better things to worry about."

"Like what?" she asked. And then we both burst out laughing because the question was so absurd. "I had to tell you this," she said when it died down, "because no one else will. But please believe me; you're not cut out to be an editor at the *New York Times*. They're hell on editors. They'll second-guess your every move. You'll have to go to a million morning-after meetings about what you should have done, or what you shouldn't have. You'll hate it. I know you liked being an editor at the *Los Angeles Times,* but this *Times* is different. Believe me, it's not for you."

"You got any alternative suggestions?"

"Find something else. Write a book, become a consultant, get a job on the radio. But remember what happened to Bryan. Don't wait. Make your deal *before* you quit the job."

"I know," I said. "The power's the paper's, not mine."

"Exactly," she said. "As soon as you give up the job, nobody will give a damn what you think."

"Where do I start looking?" I asked.

"Don't ask me," she said. "See a job counselor or a psychologist or an astrologer. Do *something*. I just had to tell you before it was too late."

At the time I thought she meant before I ended my career. Later I understood that the ending Carol had in mind was her own.

It always gets cold in New York just before Thanksgiving, a mean, icy bitterness that serves as a terrible warning of the frozen months ahead. A wind comes sweeping through the city and the leaves, which have been clinging tenaciously to the trees, fall off in a single day, leaving nothing but bare shivering limbs in its wake. The sidewalks grow so cold that the chill seeps through the soles of your shoes and up into your bones. Your skin goes dry, your fingers crack open, your lips begin to peel. It is the most depressing time of the year.

But 1998 was the bleakest fall I can remember. All anybody was interested in was Monica Lewinsky, and Michael went around moaning about the way real news was being ignored. One night Michael came home jubilant; he'd been offered an interview with a man called Osama bin Laden and he was making plans to go to the Mideast. "He operates a shadowy network called Al Qaeda," he said, "and the F.B.I. has put him on their watch list. I think we're all going to be hearing a great deal about him."

But the more I heard about the group, the more frightened I became. It didn't sound safe over there, and I began to be afraid that Michael would fly off into the wilderness and never return. When he came home, deeply depressed because the trip was off, I was secretly relieved.

"My bosses just don't get it," he said bitterly. "They've killed the interview." For weeks he was so angry and upset that I began to think it would have been better worrying about his safety than enduring his pain.

But by then I had other worries. Carol was going into the hospital more and more frequently. Tests at first, when the things they were doing seemed increasingly horrid although she refused to tell us what they were. Then her room in the Klingenstein Pavilion began looking too lived in, filled with all the plants and books and little knickknacks hospital rooms acquire when they are no longer temporary. She knew the nurses too well. Soon I began to understand that although Carol was happy to see me each time I showed up, she was also waiting for me to leave so she could return to what had become her real life. Carol had entered the realm of the terminally ill.

When a person has lived generously and fought fiercely, she deserves more than sadness at the end. Carol's memorial was stubbornly joyful. Looking around at the people gathered to celebrate her life, I felt that each of us was thinking about what she had given us before she died, each vowing to do something to honor her wishes.

First I sent a check to Mother's Voices, the charity she had supported so passionately after her daughter died of AIDS. And then, because I didn't know what else to do, I dug out the little scrap of paper Marion had given me and dialed the number.

"I've been wondering whether you'd call," the astrologer said when I identified myself.

"It's been a while," I replied, a little embarrassed.

"It's okay," he said. "I know that you're reluctant." His voice was old and deep, which helped some. "Don't be uncomfortable," he continued. "You need not be a believer; for many people this is no more than a way to focus thought."

He asked me when I was born, and where. "What time?" he wanted to know.

"Two-fifteen," I said.

"Fine," he replied, giving me his address. It was in Greenwich Village. I wondered if that was significant.

I'd been expecting crystal balls and candles, perhaps a black cat or a bat or two. His apartment, it turned out, was quite ordinary. Small, bright, and cluttered with art and books, it lacked the slightest whiff of mysticism. We chatted for a bit, talking about food and painting and what a wonderful woman Marion was. After a while it occurred to me that the conversation was going on just a little too long, and I asked if something was the matter.

"Yes," he said with a sheepish look. "I've read your columns, and it just seemed to me that your horoscope was off. I was trying to draw you out to see if I was mistaken."

"Are you?"

"No. I've never come upon something like this. Your horoscope doesn't fit. It seems inaccurate—the horoscope of an entirely different person. I don't understand it. Are you sure you were born on January sixteenth?"

"Yes," I said.

"In Manhattan?"

"Yes."

"At two-fifteen in the afternoon?"

"No," I said, "two-fifteen in the morning. I mean the middle of the night."

The clouds rolled right off his face. "That's a relief!" he said. "This changes everything." He began recasting charts, humming happily to himself. After a few minutes he looked at me and said, "Would you mind going away for a while? I'm going to have to redo everything."

I went outside and wandered down the street, back in the Village I had grown up in. I passed Ottomanelli's, where my mother used to buy whole suckling pigs, and the Lafayette Bakery, where she bought the French bread my father loved. I went down Tenth Street and looked at the garden where the Women's House of Detention used to stand. And then, on an impulse, I crossed the street and walked to Jones Street, looking for my father's butcher shop, wishing that Jimmy would still be there.

He wasn't, of course, but the shop was unchanged, and when I went inside the familiar scent of sawdust, cold air, and minerals rose up to greet me. The new butcher was reaching across the counter to hand a slice of bologna to a little girl standing next to her mother, and when he saw me he folded another slice and handed it over. "I'm just cutting up this lamb," he said, picking up a saw. "Sonia's taking the right leg. I could trim up the left one for you. Rub it with olive oil, throw in some cloves of garlic, and set it on a heap of rosemary; you couldn't ask for a finer family meal."

"I'll take it," I said.

"Nothing like getting back into the kitchen, is there?" he asked.

"There's nothing like it," I replied, and I imagined that Carol was at my side, smiling.

It was late afternoon when I got back to Alex's apartment, and it was starting to get dark. "Come in, come in," he said. "I have many interesting things to tell you." This time he started talking before I had even settled into my chair.

I was skeptical, but I hoped that at least some of the things he said were true. At the very end, just as he was putting the charts away, he removed his glasses, rubbed his tired eyes, and said, "One last thing. I think you're going to be changing jobs very soon."

"Oh?" I said. "Do you know what the new one will be?"

"That," he replied, "I couldn't tell you. But I can tell you this: you will learn a great deal—and you will enjoy it."

I didn't really believe him, but I left feeling relaxed and happy. It was dark outside now, and the stars were beginning to come out. I swung the lamb, wrapped in pink butcher paper and twine, thinking that I would roast it with garlic and scallop some potatoes.

"Cooking tonight?" asked Gene when he saw me with my parcels.

"Yes," I said. "I'm going to make a special dinner just for the family. Do you like lamb?"

"Lamb," he said. "Lamb is lovely."

"I'll bring you a plate," I said as he parked the elevator. "Lamb and scalloped potatoes."

He smiled and slid the elevator door open. Somewhere a phone was ringing, deep and insistent. "Hurry," said Gene, grabbing my parcels as I fumbled for the key. "That's your phone." Behind the door we could hear the urgent bell, still tolling. I grabbed the key and fitted it into the lock. Pushing the door open, I dashed inside and ran down the hall. Behind me I could hear the rustle of paper as Gene settled the groceries onto the kitchen counter.

The phone was on its fifth ring when I reached it. "Hello?" I said, thinking it would be too late, that only the emptiness of space would answer me.

But a voice was there—male, with a decided English accent. "Is this Ruth Reichl?" it asked.

"Yes," I said, "this is she." Behind me Molly and Brenda, Chloe and Betty, Miriam and Emily gathered expectantly together.

"This is James Truman," said the voice, "calling from Condé Nast. I'm looking for a new editor for *Gourmet*. I wonder if you would be interested in meeting me for tea?"

"Yes," I said, "I would be interested." And from deep inside me six voices all echoed yes, yes, yes as we prepared to join forces and move on.

A SIMPLE CELEBRATION MEAL

Roast Leg of Lamb with Garlic and Rosemary

The butcher called this a family dinner, but I think leg of lamb is perfect for guests. It's the most forgiving meat you can cook. Unlike beef or pork, which is ruined when overcooked, lamb is good in every state: it's wonderful both rare and well done, so if your guests are late or you're forgetful, dinner will be just fine. (This recipe is for rare meat; if you like your meat well done, cook it longer.)

1 small leg of lamb, about 6 to 7 pounds, trimmed of all visible fat
4 cloves garlic, peeled and cut into 6 slivers each
1 bunch rosemary
2 tablespoons olive oil
Salt and pepper

Remove the lamb from the refrigerator 1 hour before starting. Preheat the oven to 350°F.

Make 8 small slits in the lamb on each side, and place a sliver of garlic and a leaf of rosemary in each slit. Massage the olive oil into the meat, and season with salt and pepper.

If you have a rack, place the lamb on the rack on top of the remaining rosemary and garlic. If you don't, simply put the meat on top of the rosemary and garlic in a roasting pan. Cook uncovered for about 1½ hours, or until an instant-read thermometer inserted away from the bone registers 125°F. Remove the lamb from the oven and let it rest for 20 minutes before carving.

Serves 6 to 8

Roasted Brussels Sprouts

These sprouts are roasted until they're almost incinerated, which gives the little nuggets an amazing, almost candy-like sweetness. Even people who think they don't like Brussels sprouts invariably like these. (Another possibility for this underused vegetable: Cut each sprout into a finely shredded julienne, sauté in butter just until wilted, about 7 minutes, add salt and pepper and a bit of cream, and serve. It's sort of like hot cole slaw, only richer and incredibly delicious.)

If you're making the leg of lamb, crank the oven up to 425°F as soon as it comes out of the oven. While the lamb is resting, you can cook the sprouts: the timing is perfect.

2 pounds small Brussels sprouts, trimmed
3 tablespoons olive oil
Salt and pepper
4 slices thickly cut bacon, diced

Preheat the oven to 400°F.

Put the Brussels sprouts on a baking sheet or cookie pan with sides, sprinkle with the olive oil, and toss so that each sprout is coated. Spread the sprouts out so they are in a single layer, and sprinkle with salt and pepper. Top with the diced bacon.

Cook, turning the sprouts once, for about 20 minutes or until they are are very dark and crisp.

Serve at once.

Serves 8 to 10

Scalloped Potatoes

Nobody doesn't like these.
If you're cooking the lamb, you can cook the potatoes at 350°F right alongside and remove them at the same time. If they start to get too brown on top, simply cover the pan with foil toward the end of the baking time.

1 clove garlic, cut in half
1 tablespoon unsalted butter
2 cups milk
3 cups heavy cream
Salt and pepper
4 pounds baking potatoes, peeled

Preheat the oven to 325°F.

Rub two roasting pans, each about 6 x 10 inches, or two 9-inch round cake pans with the garlic, and then coat them thickly with the butter.

Combine the milk and cream in a saucepan, and heat until just about to boil. Season with salt and pepper, and remove from the heat.

Cut the potatoes into ¼-inch-thick rounds and arrange them in layers in the pan. Pour the cream mixture over the potatoes (it should come just to the top but not cover them). Bake uncovered, pressing the potatoes into the milk every 30 minutes or so, for 1 to 1½ hours.

Remove the pans from the oven when the potatoes are golden and allow to sit for 10 to 20 minutes before serving.

Serves 8

Last-Minute Chocolate Cake

This cake just calls for a scoop of vanilla ice cream on each slice.

4 ounces fine-quality unsweetened chocolate
¾ stick (6 tablespoons) unsalted butter
¾ cup brewed strong black coffee
2 tablespoons Grand Marnier
¾ cup sugar
1 egg
1 teaspoon vanilla extract
1 cup all-purpose flour
½ teaspoon baking soda
¼ teaspoon salt

Preheat the oven to 300°F.

Butter and flour a 9-inch-by-5-inch loaf pan.

Combine the chocolate, butter, and coffee in the top of a double boiler or in a very heavy pot, and stir constantly over low heat until melted. Let the mixture cool for 15 minutes. Then add the Grand Marnier, sugar, egg, and vanilla. Stir well.

Stir the flour, baking soda, and salt together, and add this to the chocolate mixture. Pour the batter into the prepared loaf pan and bake for 30 to 40 minutes, or until a toothpick inserted in the center comes out clean.

Serves 6

RECIPE INDEX

★

ACKNOWLEDGMENTS

Rereading these pages I find that somehow Caz has been left out. That is not right. Don Caswell, copy editor, perfectionist and longtime bane of my existence, is the embodiment of everything that makes the *New York Times* a great paper.

Here's a typical Caz story. It's a few months into my tenure at the *Times,* and I'm pulling my chair up to his desk for the first time. He looks me over balefully, points to the review I've just written of a middling French restaurant and asks, "The chef's name is Jean Pierre?"

"Yes," I reply.

"You're missing the hyphen," he says. There is acid in his voice.

But I am ready for him. Waving a stolen menu under his nose I show him the chef's name printed there. It has no hyphen. Caz raises an eyebrow. Caz, I am to discover, always raises an eyebrow. "Meaningless," he says. "Menu-writers are so careless. You should have called and talked directly to the chef."

"For a hyphen?" I ask. Caz raises an eyebrow once again, silently giving me to understand that anyone who fails to grasp the importance of hyphens has no business at his paper.

Magazines employ fact checkers to follow behind the writers and tidy up their work; newspaper writers, however, are on their own. Those who are very lucky find a Caz to challenge every assumption. The man infuriated me on a weekly basis.

When our partnership began, sometime during my first year, I learned to dread his calls. He always had at least ten penetrating questions that had completely escaped my notice. Early on we spent hours arguing over the difference between *convince* and *persuade,* but over time the tenor of the questions changed. Caz would look down at some column that had just sailed safely past three top editors and raise an eyebrow. "Do you really like this lead?" he'd ask. No more than that, but by then I had come to trust him so completely that I'd be rewriting before he had finished speaking. I watched him read the review in which both my long-gone parents appeared with serious trepidation. Finally he looked up. "Fine," he said. "But bear in mind that you've used up your ghost quota for the next three years."

Caz moved on to work with more exalted writers about a year before I left the paper, and my new copy editors rarely questioned much of what I did. Life was easier . . . but the columns weren't as good. I started going over and over my work, trying to ferret out the faults Caz would have found. To keep myself honest I taped the first Caz column above my desk; the hyphen in Jean-Pierre was circled in red.

But I have to admit that with this book I have taken many liberties that do not follow journalistic principles and would surely horrify Caz. Some of the characters have been disguised. It was not my intention to make anybody sorry that I'd written this book, and I've often changed names and distinguishing characteristics to avoid embarrassing people (there is no Myron Rosen working at the *New York Times*). In some cases I've exaggerated, in others I've conflated a few meals into one, or combined events that took place over a space of time into a single afternoon or evening. And I'm sure there are details that I've gotten wrong: I have copious notes about every morsel I ate during my tenure at the *Times,* but I was so busy that I stopped keeping a diary and I've relied on memory for events and conversations that took place a fairly long time ago. I've tried to be accurate, but I'm sure I've occasionally erred.

One thing, however, I am certain of. There were many people who were important to me during my tenure at the *New York Times* who make only brief appearances here. I'd like to express my thanks to Suzanne Richie,

Elaine Louie and Trish Hall, who were there with me and Carol for so many meals; they were the very best eating companions a person could possibly want.

Also to my part-time assistants, Erin St. John Kelly, Maria Eder and Allyson Strafella, who made reservations, joined me for meals and always remembered where I was meant to be, when, and most important, which wig I was supposed to be wearing. And if Roisin O'Hare, Anisa Kamadoli and Gus Moraes had not been real friends to our family while they were sitting for Nick, it would have been impossible to go out to eat night after night.

Thanks are also due to my many intrepid dining companions. Pat Oleszko was the best; I could always count on her to gather a group at the last minute, and in a pinch to eat not only what was on her plate, but on mine as well. Janet Maslin and Ben Cheever were ready to eat anything I asked them to, at any time, in any place. My brother Bob, the world's greatest eater, was invaluable: endlessly inquisitive, wonderful company and prepared to try everything from sea slugs to fried grasshoppers in the line of duty. If Jonathan and Nathalie Half had not been willing to show up on a moment's notice, life would have been much more difficult. Paula Landesman and Jerry Berger were also everything a hired mouth could possibly want.

Thanks, once again, to the MacDowell Colony, the most wonderful place a writer could possibly be. Just knowing that the Colony exists is enough to make me smile. And, of course, to my extraordinarily indulgent colleagues at *Gourmet*, particularly Doc Willoughby, Larry Karol and Robin Pellicci, who always pinch-hit when I need them to. Thanks to Ian Knauer for testing the recipes, and to Richard Ferretti, Paul Grimes, Nanci Smith and especially Romulo Yanes for services way beyond the call of duty.

I have been blessed with a wonderful agent, Kathy Robbins, and a fabulous editor, Ann Godoff, and I am deeply grateful for their help and their encouragement.

One last thing. Throughout the writing of this book Michael and Nick have been amazingly supportive. They did not complain—at least not too much—when I spent every weekend working. I'll take a break now. Really, I will. I promise.